The
LE CORBUSIER Guide

THIRD EDITION

Deborah Gans

INTRODUCTION BY ALAN PLATTUS

PRINCETON ARCHITECTURAL PRESS • NEW YORK

To Elizabeth Gans

PUBLISHED BY
Princeton Architectural Press
37 East Seventh Street
New York, NY 10003

For a free catalog of books, call 1.800.722.6657.
Visit our web site at www.papress.com.

© 1987, 2000, 2006 Princeton Architectural Press
All rights reserved. First edition 1987
Second edition 2000
Third edition 2006
Printed and bound in the United States
10 09 08 07 06   5 4 3 2 1

Image credits: Kanu Agrawal 212, 245; Lynne Breslin 250; Caroline Hancock 178; Elizabeth Harris 195;
Harvard University 188, 189; Kiran Joshi 244; La Bibliothèque de la Chaux-de-Fonds 12, 29, 151, 152, 160;
La Fondation le Corbusier 19, 20, 22, 63, 74, 79, 88, 93, 95, 116, 138 bottom, 165, 193, 200, 248; Francesca
Pfister front cover, back cover (bottom row), 38, 40, 41, 44, 46, 47, 49, 50, 52–55, 62, 64, 68, 77; Alan
Plattus 180; Peter Serenyi 208; Swiss National Tourist Office 165. All other images courtesy of the author.

Editing of third edition: Linda Lee
Editorial assistance on third edition: Lauren Nelson
Editing of second edition and book design: Therese Kelly
Editing of first edition: Robert Wescher
Cover design: Jan Haux

LIBRARY OF CONGRESS CATALOGING-IN-PUBLICATION DATA
Gans, Deborah, 1955–
    The Le Corbusier guide / Deborah Gans ; introduction by Alan Plattus.
    —3rd ed.
      p. cm.
    Includes bibliographical references.
    ISBN 1-56898-539-8 (pbk. : alk. paper)
    1. Le Corbusier, 1887–1965—Catalogs. 2. Architecture, Modern—
    20th century—Catalogs.   I. Le Corbusier, 1887–1965. II. Title.
NA1053.J4A4 2006
720'.92—dc22
                                                    2005021277

CONTENTS

4   Preface to the Third Edition
6   Preface to the Revised Edition
8   Acknowledgments
10 How to Use This Guide
12 Le Corbusier: A Dialectical Itinerary   ALAN PLATTUS
29 Le Corbusier: A Biographical Note   DEBORAH GANS

SITE LISTINGS
36 Paris and Environs
87 France
141 Switzerland
169 Europe
187 North and South America
203 India
247 Tunisia, Russia, Iraq, Japan

REFERENCE PAGES
260 Glossary of Corbusian Terms
264 Selected Bibliography
270 Maps

DEBORAH GANS

Since the publication of the second edition, Le Corbusier has become form-giver to a previous century, an occasion for reassessment of his work and also of our own architecture through his eyes. While we might conclude that we have fulfilled his promise of the biomechanical in our romance with both prefabrication and organic algorithms and that we have achieved his technological ambitions with our digital prowess, we also need to attend to ways we have failed to heed his warnings. That his buildings are smaller in life than in photos seems not just proof of his masterly control of scale but also a reprimand of our lust after literal size. Several of his recently spiffed-up works wear their new detailing with discomfort, like an admonishment to our preciousness. In defiance of our tired late-twentieth-century separation of Le Corbusier "the good architect" from "the bad planner," Le Corbusier of the twenty-first century argues for the intrinsic connection between the production of architecture and urbanism and their shared politics.

As a New Yorker who watched Ground Zero from its literal fall to the still thwarted rise of the new, I cannot help but think that we have lost our moral high ground in our judgment of Le Corbusier as at worst a collaborator in the degraded sense of fascism, at best a messianic paternalist who would do anything to effect his sense of good, and at least a brilliant self-inventing self-promoter, whose "political" techniques are now more than ever relevant. Those of Ground Zero who struggle to get The Vision built might identify with how Le Corbusier failed before them in his ironically parallel tale of a tower, the Plan Obus/Directeur, begun as an idealistic affirmation of Islamic-European brotherhood in Algiers. Iteration after iteration, his design retreated from its first melding of landform and built form, of social and economic classes, and of indigenous and imported populations and became a contained bulwark for capitalist ventures as he sought to realize the scheme under the regime of Vichy. At Algiers, his classically rooted politics of shaping the collective body, which he termed "planisme" (the condensation of physical and social relationships together as a plan), was subsumed by the politics of affiliation, but it remained his ideal.

Challenges to the authority of the plan begin even prior to events like community board hearings because they are intrinsic to it, arising from the irresolvable tensions between form and function, between the law of art and the social reality that situates it. In contrast to his sublimation of tension at Vichy, Le Corbusier at his best saw the politics of the plan as an ongoing act of engagement with many opposing interests, and a reaction to the passivity of architects in the grip of business as usual despite a housing crisis and growing economic inequalities. "The long view from the airplane teaches us that we are no longer spectators, we are participants,"[1] he insisted.

Participation took many forms for Le Corbusier, including grassroots planning, as expressed in his admiration for the collective design process of the Van Nelle tobacco factory in Rotterdam,[2] though his master plans dominate our understanding of his approach. Even his early and still-cursed Contemporary City for Three Million of 1923 was less a definitive design than a critical speculation on the inevitable shape of things to come, namely the capitalist hub of air-conditioned towers of business. His plan warned of the waste of sprawl, the power of the automobile, the distorting physical consequences of "the money machine"[3] and even of the need for homeland security with an acumen matched only by the suburban omen of Wright's Broadacre City. Corb's subsequent Radiant City, which moved away from the high-handed abstraction of the Contemporary City to a series of actual case studies, ultimately coalesced as a continental organization of agrarianism, green factories, and nodes of international finance and regional/historical civilization linked by four routes of water, highway, rail, and air. The major cross axes of these linear settlement patterns from Paris to Algiers and Barcelona through Rome set out to recenter the continent at a geographic and cultural opening between the Islamic and European traditions and between north and south. Like a truth foretold, this imagined pan-European union depended on global flows of people, goods, and currency and exceeded the grip of any single political authority.

"Town planning concerned him from the moment our man rose from his chair," writes Le Corbusier in *Talks with Students*.[4] In that moment, he crossed from stasis to motion, satiety to dissatisfaction, authority to the desire to participate in shaping the world. Politics is the will to push oneself away from the table. And while this guide is ostensibly concerned with seated man, walking man is implicit in it. Even the "ideal villas" have a humbleness of material and detail that rejects conspicuous consumption and site plans that challenge private property's obstructions to the generosity of shared landscape. It seems valuable to revisit Le Corbusier's architecture at this moment with his political imagination in mind.

This edition brings the newest means of accessing Le Corbusier to the traveler's table, namely the World Wide Web, which could eliminate visits to closed buildings even after the half-life of the newly updated sidebar information. We have improved the maps and the resolution of many images. There is an expanded bibliography that embraces new speculation. Finally, there are new photographs taken by Francesca Pfister that reveal the buildings as they are now and so sustain them.

1. Le Corbusier, *Aircraft* (Milan: Editrice Arbitare Segesta, 1996), 33.

2. Le Corbusier wrote of his visit: "Participation! I can truly say that my visit to that factory was one of the most beautiful days of my life." *Plans* 13 (March 1932). Mary McCleod reports the visit in "Urbanism and Utopia: Le Corbusier From Regional Syndicalism to Vichy" (PhD diss., Princeton University, 1985), which remains an authoritative source on Le Corbusier's politics.

3. Le Corbusier, *Aircraft*, 75. Kenneth Frampton describes Le Corbusier's anti-capitalism in chapter 7 of *Le Corbusier* (London: Thames and Hudson, 2001).

4. Le Corbusier, *Talks with Students* (New York: Princeton Architectural Press, 2000), 32–33.

PREFACE TO THE REVISED EDITION

DEBORAH GANS

The first edition of *The Le Corbusier Guide* dates from over fourteen years ago when, at the height of a certain phase of Post Modernism, the Renaissance and Enlightenment were held up as the proper field of inquiry by a generation of architects and educators who had known the last phases of High Modernism intimately. Much as Walter Gropius forbade Michael Graves to study Letarouilly's illustrative guide to the architecture of Rome (not coincidentally the first publication of Princeton Architectural Press), our teachers admonished us against the culprit responsible for failed utopias, urban decay, leaking roofs, and the absence of ritual. The world seem divided among disciples who had received the word of the master Le Corbusier directly, those whose mission was to kill the father (while simultaneously pilfering the grave), and a first generation of the genuinely ignorant. The centennial of his birth, which was the year this guide was published, marked a kind of psychological watershed in which he passed from a presence to historical figure. He, the author, was finally dead (22 years after the fact). The archive was finally published, the Fondation Le Corbusier prepared for the feasting of scholars and other predators. This corpus of Le Corbusier came into formal existence at a ripe moment in an age of criticism. In the decade since the centennial, there has been an explosion in the bibliography. The literature on the subject of Le Corbusier extends far beyond the lengthy story he wrote himself. It frames his production from a myriad of standpoints—the feminist, alternatively psychoanalytic, soft Marxist, poststructurally phenomenological, techno-philosophical, etc. And Le Corbusier, as slippery as ever, lends himself to this co-option splendidly. After all, he hung with Josephine Baker, Georges Bataille, Jean Prouvé, Eileen Gray, the Vesnin brothers, the Rockefellers, William Zeckendorf, André

Breton, Jawaharlal Nehru, Charlotte Perriand, André Malraux, Marshal Pétain, Louise Bourgeois, Albert Einstein, and Benito Mussolini to name a few. Similarly, he has reentered the consciousness of architecture and the city in new guises, in the small villa and extra-large halls built by the Eurodollar, and the "new modernism" of stone-and-glass-country houses more carefully detailed and less ideological than any real Corb.

Which brings us to the reason behind this second edition. The febrile activity surrounding Corb in the past decade forced a rewrite that did more than update visiting hours and directions (although we really have tried to update them and to provide better maps). Thanks to the extreme patience and generosity of publisher Kevin Lippert, this is a book from which most words were deleted although many persisted in returning to the page (I'd like to credit myself with a new book—changing the title to *Chien Mechant*, Beware of the Dog, in honor of the private houses that need canine protection from accurate directions). The expansion of footnotes and bibliography in this revised edition is the vehicle of introduction to the literature. The text remains devoted to what must inevitably become the smallest output surrounding Le Corbusier: his buildings. The revision gratefully uses the newly available scholarship to describe the buildings more accurately and completely in terms of their materials, technology, clients, and the conditions of their conception. It tries to test new interpretations against the direct observation of the building *in situ*. In revisiting the buildings armed with the new research, I have seen new things, and also had experiences all the more astonishing because they happened for a second time. In the end, the conclusion remains that the secrets of the building belong to the traveler.

ACKNOWLEDGMENTS

I begin the acknowledgments to this third edition by thanking again everyone who contributed so significantly to the research of the others: Alan Plattus, Madame Frey of the La Bibliothèque de la Ville in La Chaux-de-Fonds, Madame Evelyne Tréhin of La Fondation Le Corbusier, Elizabeth Harris, Lynne Breslin, Mark Glen and James Wallace, who traveled to Chandigarh long before me, Diego Wainer, and Francesco Passanti. While I did not again burden Bill Considine, Carol Willis, Thomas Schumacher, Liz Moule, and Stefanos Polyzoides, or Matthew Jelacic with the re-reading of the text, their insights into the other editions remain intact. My travels over the years have been aided by two grants from Pratt Institute and the hospitality of Dean IJS Bakshi and Professor Kiran Joshi of the Chandigarh School of Architecture, Yatin Pandya of Sangath Ahmedabad, and Anand Sarabhai and Jean Jacques-Duval, who were gracious guides to their own buildings. Ann Pendleton-Jullian and Guillaume Jullian de la Fuente directed me and us all to a "lost" work of Le Corbusier with their scholarship on La Sainte-Baume. The guide still has the identity carefully defined by previous editors, Robert Wechsler and Therese Kelly, editorial assistants, Eugenia Bell, Mirjana Javornik, and Jane Sheinman of the press, and also Yasemen Omurtag and Deniz Célik.

In shaping the new edition, the ambition of current editor, Linda Lee, and editorial assistant, Lauren Nelson, to raise the production value is everywhere apparent, as is their zero tolerance for factual and stylistic error. In shaping new thoughts I have relied, as I often do, on the wisdom of Kenneth Frampton. Amy Herda and Mary-Jane Starcks have redrawn the maps with elegance and accuracy. Francsca Pfister's photographs of the Parisian buildings bring new life to the volume and the work. Behind all these changes stands publisher Kevin Lippert, who also supported the hefty extension of the second edition. His commitment to this small guide now spans twenty years. Finally, I would like to thank my darling daughter, Emma, who could rightfully lay claim to every moment taken to finish this book and yet has tolerated with charm and humor the pesky presence of Le Corbusier ("that man who ruins my summers").

Deborah Gans
New York City, 2005

HOW TO USE THIS GUIDE

Paris will be the focus of most itineraries devoted to the architecture of Le Corbusier. It is his adopted city and the place where he came of age. Within its environs is a representative sample of his built work. It contains most of his purist houses, and an early foray away from the crisp surfaces of Purism. It has his first buildings at a scale larger than the individual dwelling and an example of his post-World War II style. A traveler with limited time to spend might begin and end the journey here.

For those with more time or ambition, there is a logic and a pleasure in an itinerary that follows the outlines of Le Corbusier's life's work. Beginning at his birthplace in La Chaux-de-Fonds, Switzerland, the route continues to Paris, to the perimeter of France, and finally to the international scene. The one path not retraced is Le Corbusier's own youthful journeys, first to the monuments of Renaissance Italy, then to the capitals of Europe as an apprentice to architects of the Modern Age. Escaping from the machine of the present, he traveled through the folk cultures of Eastern Europe and was drawn inexorably to the Acropolis. Although we do not follow this map, Le Corbusier recapitulates it for us many times in his own architecture. If, after Paris, our itinerary must for practical reasons mix chronology, that has some parallel in Le Corbusier's thinking. Even as he completed his Parisian villas in "the new spirit," he began to question his own categories of history, culture, and technology and to call up others simultaneously: atavistic folklore, the utopian future, the modern and the antique.

The pleasures of this itinerary include not only the buildings (which are generally farther away than one expects and no longer in the pristine condition shown in the *Oeuvre Complète*) but also the process of getting from one to the next. On the "open road" it is a pleasure to remember Le Corbusier's own joy of self-propulsion in the automobile, efficiency and speed in the train, and the thrill of flight as he experienced it with the poet of flight, Antoine de Saint Exupéry.

Upon arrival at a building, the complex rendering of the particularities of the spot, the locale, and regional culture can surprise, all the more because of Le Corbusier's supposed indifference to these matters. Down the road a piece from the cavelike Maison le Weekend is a strikingly similar nineteenth-century water-storage facility whose presence sharpens the house's critique of the bourgeois neighborhood like a good joke. From the corner, the glass facade of the Parisian apartment at Nungesser et Coli disappears into the rhythm of bay windows along the block, suggesting a possible melding of the city of the future with that of the present. While Le Corbusier did state that he went in search of a site for his parents' cottage at Vevey with the plan in his pocket, the lakeside landscape he found and then shaped completes the architecture. As one journeys, the polarity between site-specific response and universal typology that is a truism of Corbusian rhetoric comes undone. The archetypal mounds, caves, and ziggurat that compose Ronchamp's larger site plan place this chapel, uniquely born of its hillside, in a floating mytho-poetic context as well. Despite the fixity of its component parts, the Unité is particularly transformed by each of the landscapes it rises above. Le Corbusier describes this phenomenon of mutual reflection between building and site:

> Effect of a work of art (architecture, statue, or painting) on its surroundings: waves, outcries, turmoil (the Parthenon on the Acropolis at Athens), lines spurting, radiating out as if produced by an explosion: the surroundings: both immediate and more distant, are stirred and shaken, dominated or caressed by it. Reaction of the surroundings: the walls of a room and its dimensions, the city square . . . yes even the bare horizons of the plain and the twisted outlines of the mountains, the whole environment brings its weight to bear upon the place where there is a work of art, the expression of the will of man.

The unraveling of the site's complexities belongs to the traveler.

In visiting the sites, there are a few simple guidelines. Many of the works are occupied houses where privacy should be respected. Where the buildings are public institutions, with listed phone numbers and web site addresses, it is advisable to contact them first to confirm visiting hours. Public transportation and its limitations are listed for each building, but always check local schedules. In the same township as the site, the residents (and tourist office) can generally supply directions to the "Le Corbusier" and are glad to do so.

LE CORBUSIER: A DIALECTICAL ITINERARY

ALAN PLATTUS

Le Corbusier is the name of a phenomenon: the deus ex machina of twentieth-century architecture, but of a peculiar kind. This machine both resolves and, just as frequently, provokes many of the crises in the extended plot of the drama of modern architecture. In the history and interpretation of that architecture it seems to be so often the case that all roads lead either to or from Le Corbusier—and occasionally both—that even at 35 years' remove one feels a certain sympathy with Alison Smithson's characterization of life in the shadow: "When you open a new volume of the *Oeuvre Complète* you find that he has had all your best ideas already, has done what you were about to do next."[1]

And while the 35 years in question are precisely those years since the death of the man, years of radical reconsideration of the architecture he produced and promoted, the phenomenon most certainly persists. It survives, and in fact continues to grow, not only through the ongoing work of archival excavation, the publication of which often provides an explicit reminder of what Smithson and her generation experienced, but also—and arguably most importantly—through our inevitable self-fashioning in terms of that phenomenon. That is to say, we construct ourselves as architects or, more generally and grandly, as modern, postmodern, or even antimodern individuals, partly by means of, or at least in relation to, the manifestations of the Corbusian phenomenon.

More than a few of the most significant works of architectural theory and criticism of the postwar years take as one of their central tasks (acknowledged or unacknowledged) the interpretation, analysis, and criticism of some aspect of Le Corbusier's performance.[2] It is not simply that Le Corbusier supplied

1. Allison Smithson, quoted in Reyner Banham, "The Last Form-giver," *The Architectural Review* (August 1966).
2. See Colin Rowe's seminal essay, "The Mathematics of the Ideal Villa," *The Architectural Review* (March 1947).

several of the ubiquitous iconic images of modernity, but that those images, far from exhausting their significance at the iconic level, like so many of their neighbors in the textbooks, turned out to support, indeed required a critical and historiographic sophistication and inventiveness that has permanently altered the rules of the game and raised the stakes for architectural theory and practice. Even for the most general surveys, Le Corbusier's work, with its virtuoso manipulation of multiple and often apparently contradictory themes, and its unpredictable and seemingly inexhaustible transformations, has provided the most challenging—if rarely the limiting or climactic—case.

All of which is to say that Le Corbusier is unavoidable. This is nowhere more clear than when it is the evaluation of his controversial performance that is at issue, whether in revisionist historiography, which pivots on what it would eventually repress, or in anti-Modern polemics, which use the polemical tactics, and even the graphics, originally deployed by the object of their attack.[3] Those who would bury him most thoroughly end up confirming his fundamental contribution, albeit transposed into a new key. Furthermore, until very recently, and still more often than not, to challenge, reevaluate, or reject modern architecture was to wrestle with its original Proteus in one or more of his many guises. This suggests that the effect of half a century of commentary, criticism, research, and design has not been so much to situate Le Corbusier as to dissolve him into the collective bloodstream of the century in a way done only to a few other characters-become-phenomena, such as Freud, Marx, and Picasso. Like them, Le Corbusier has become not so much an object for our discourse as part of the very ground upon which that discourse must be founded.

How impossible then, but how absolutely necessary, to pursue an unmediated encounter with the works that have inspired, provoked, and precipitated such a large part of our critical and monumental heritage. To undertake a Corbusian grand tour is simultaneously to reinforce and to discredit the mythology that the architect himself helped to construct. Going either as friend or foe, it is something of a pilgrimage and, like most pilgrimages, the quest for revelation, novelty, or experience will be a pretext for a more desperate mission: the confirmation of what we believe ourselves to have already found. And yet, the fundamental heterogeneity of the work seen *in situ* somehow never loses its capacity to surprise and to defy the various unifying fictions proposed and imposed willy-nilly by its critics.

In our age of single-issue architecture, when even the most faithful revivals of Le Corbusier's work engage one—or at most a very narrow band—of the issues that preoccupied the subject in question, his richly multivalent production may be somewhat difficult to digest, like some exotic dish or subtle wine which demands the attention of all our faculties and is an amalgam of an alarming range of flavors.[4] Indeed, most of the buildings, after an initial moment of recognition, tend to slip out of

3. In the revisionist category, see Alan Greenberg, "Lutyens' Architecture Restudied," *Perspecta* 12 (1969), which helped initiate the spectacular reconstruction of Lutyens, in part by comparing his work to that of Le Corbusier and Wright.

4. Some projects designed by practitioners of *le style Corbu* provide analytic demonstrations that have significantly increased the understanding and availability of the originals. See the texts and projects of *Five Architects* (New York, 1972).

5. The best comprehensive monographic treatment remains Stanislaus von Moos, *Le Corbusier: Elements of a Synthesis*.

6. The best recent dialectical treatments of Corbusian dialectics are two essays by Alan Colquhoun, "Architecture and Engineering: Le Corbusier and the Paradox of Reason," *Modulus* (1980–81), and "The Significance of Le Corbusier," *The Le Corbusier Archive* 1.

7. Clifford Geertz, "Deep Play: Notes on the Balinese Cockfight," in *The Interpretation of Cultures* (New York, 1973), 453.

8. For a treatment that allows Le Corbusier to function as the critic of his own urbanistic oversimplifications, see Manfredo Tafuri, "Machine et memoire: The City in the Work of Le Corbusier," *The Le Corbusier Archive* 10.

the focus provided by various versions of Corbusian orthodoxy: contrary to the neat classroom analyses, they are not really fully resolved compositions; contrary to the loudest criticism, they are not really disastrous in their contexts; and contrary to their author's polemics and touched-up photographic representations, they are not sleek, seamless, timeless *machines á habiter.* Insofar as all of these questions and many others ought to remain open and on the agenda, the role of an introduction is not to provide yet another definitive account, however clever or comprehensive. One should try, rather, to delineate the rudimentary outlines and mechanisms of the Corbusian discourse in its mediating role, not as an absolute structure or set of rules, as Le Corbusier himself unfortunately often suggested, but as a set of available interpretive strategies, as he actually deployed them.[5] These strategies may hold the specimen in focus long enough to allow one to begin to appreciate its spatial and thematic density, and then, like Wittgenstein's ladder, they may be thrown away.

To describe these strategies, as I will, in terms of the dialectical possibilities sponsored by apparently opposing, but complementary, categories, is to indulge in a habit of mind that is both Corbusian and structuralist. Many of the most powerful recent descriptions have exploited that convergence and have found in the ostensibly dualistic character of Le Corbusier's thought and work an interpretive principle of considerable utility.[6] We shall be tempted more than once to invoke an amended version of Clifford Geertz's observation that "societies, like lives [and, I would add, like architectural projects], contain their own interpretations. One has only to learn how to gain access to them."[7] In this instance it is, more often than not, the architect who indicates and even opens the door, supplying us with the means to decipher his code. And if that is increasingly the case with modern art in general, culminating perhaps with "conceptual art" in the sixties and its architectural correlatives, then Le Corbusier is exemplary and precocious in this respect. The promenade architecturale is only the most dramatic example of how, with didactic intent, he "teaches us to gain access" (here, quite literally) to the interpretive experience of architectural space. At the same time, this space is presented as the intersection—but not necessarily the resolution—of the extraordinarily complex, although provisionally binary, formal, and iconographic thematics of his projects. And so it is not simply that we have constructed a fair amount of our culture from the *disjecta membra* of the Corbusian phenomenon, but that Le Corbusier remains, in our metatheoretical elaborations of his characteristic strategies, his own best critical guide.[8] The hermeneutic circle has become a figure eight; our problem is less one of closure and more one of maintaining some degree of equilibrium as we execute the loops and turns.

The more we seek to classify Le Corbusier, the more the phenomenon seems to deconstruct itself in a potentially infinite number of variations on whatever theme we have chosen. Le Corbusier's sketches abound with illustrations of the sort of analogical thinking that supports this conceptual promiscuity.9 Seeing the buildings only intensifies their propensity to ramify, rather than stabilize, interpretation. Just as one cannot not know Le Corbusier, it is moderately difficult to know him. There is, after all, no *œuvre complète*, only the ongoing work of interpretation, to which Le Corbusier himself knowingly and brilliantly contributed and in which we are inextricably implicated.10

ROMANTIC AND CLASSICAL: CULTURAL DIALECTICS

Of all the possible dichotomies that might be useful for the characterization of Le Corbusier's attitude and his crucial position vis-à-vis the twentieth-century avant-gardes, the thoroughly slippery opposition of romantic and classical seems the most comprehensive. This is due not only to the ambiguities of those terms, but also to their emphasis on the extent to which Le Corbusier's work is embedded in, and cuts across, the principal strata of Western culture since the Renaissance. As a card-carrying member of the Parisian avant garde of the twenties and a corresponding member of any number of other European movements, he responded to, and exploited, a view of history, and of the role of the artist/intellectual in relation to history, that was grounded in the romantic challenge to the discourses of the Enlightenment. But as an unregenerate idealist and a believer in, if not always a practitioner of, the philosophical tradition of French rationalism that culminated in the Enlightenment, he balanced—or juggled—the relativism of that evolutionary view of history with the absolutist spirit of the classical tradition, especially in its French version.11

The specifically romantic roots of Le Corbusier's early reading and training in La Chaux-de-Fonds are now as well known as his alleged rejection—or, at least, suppression—of his juvenilia in later years.12 What remained, and continued to be of fundamental significance for Corbusian polemics as for modernism in general, was the essentially romantic search for a "style for the age" and the image of the modern artist as midwife to the birth of such a style.

9. On Le Corbusier's analogical thinking, see Alexander Tzonis and Liane Lefaivre, "Syncretism and the Critical Outlook in Le Corbusier's Work," *Architectural Design* 55 (1985).

10. An itinerary through the primary and secondary sources starts with a look through the 32 volumes of *The Le Corbusier Archive* and the 4 volumes of the *Le Corbusier Sketchbooks*. A visit to the Fondation Le Corbusier in Paris will provide some idea of the scope of the scholarly enterprise.

11. This is essentially the interpretation proposed by Colquhoun in "The Significance of Le Corbusier."

12. For Le Corbusier-Jeanneret in his larval stage, see Paul Turner, *The Education of Le Corbusier: A Study of the Development of Le Corbusier's Thought, 1900–1920* (New York: Garland, 1977), and Mary Patricia May Sekler, *The Early Drawings of Charles Edouard Jeanneret 1902–1908* (New York: Garland, 1977). Both authors also have important essays in Walden, *The Open Hand: Essays on Le Corbusier*, which contribute to the discussion of Le Corbusier's romanticism.

This was, after all, only a somewhat grander and internationalized version (in keeping with the universalizing tendencies romantically attributed to modern technology) of his youthful search for a Suisse-Romande regionalist style and his recurrent references to a Mediterranean style. All these formulations were predicated on the cultural relativism according to which romantic historiography assigned to each age, each country, or each climate its characteristic forms of expression.[13] For the often voluntarily (if artificially) deracinated intellectuals of the avant garde it was the spirit of the age, the zeitgeist, which tended to take precedence over other determinants. By the time Le Corbusier reached his intellectual maturity, evolutionary historicism had unequivocally identified the eitgeist with the progressive forces of modern science and technology.

The young Charles-Édouard Jeanneret had to adjust his evolutionary pace to that of the rapidly moving zeitgeist—to bring himself up to speed. His early travels, especially those between 1907, when he first ventured forth from La Chaux-de-Fonds, and 1911, on the eve of his "Journey to the East," were designed to do precisely that. Travel was a quintessentially romantic form of experience. His version of the Grand Tour, reconfigured to point toward a progressive future rather than a moribund past, took him through the capitals of European modernism—in a highly significant order: from Vienna to Paris to Berlin to Paris—and through the offices of several of the leading figures of what Henry-Russell Hitchcock so poignantly termed the New Tradition. The "constituent facts" of his life were, in effect, made to correspond to the constituent facts of the history of modern architecture and, in good Darwinian fashion, his ontogenesis as an architect could be seen to recapitulate the phylogenesis of modernism itself.[14]

These facts, however, encompass more than the name-brand monuments of emergent modernism. More importantly, they include the anonymous monuments and artifacts of industrial modernity. As Le Corbusier described it more than a decade later, it was as if he had already anticipated the limits of any critique based upon the Ruskinian romanticism of his youth as well as of any reform based solely in the decorative arts, with their romantic image of the artist/craftsman, such as he found persisting in the Wiener Werkstatte (already under prophetic attack by Adolf Loos).[15] His sense of the zeitgeist pointed to the need to inform himself of—and architecture with—the exigencies and possibilities of both industrial production and new techniques of construction, and in both cases he was able to find and appropriate formulations in which the new futurist romanticism of the machine was sublimated in the fundamental idealism shared both by the romantic tradition as descended from Hegel and by its apparent opposite, the classical tradition as descended from Renaissance aesthetic theory.[16]

In the case of industrial production, Jeanneret learned from the practical example set by the Deutsche Werkbund during his employment with Peter Behrens in Berlin in 1910, but ultimately he absorbed the rationalism of Werkbund practice through the idealism of Herman Muthesius's theory of types. In the same way, the significance of his employment with Auguste Perret in Paris in 1908, far

13. For the role of historicism in Le Corbusier's thought, see Alan Colquhoun, "Three Kinds of Historicism," *Oppositions* 26 (Spring 1984), the introduction to his *Essays in Architectural Criticism*, and the two essays cited above.
14. On Jeanneret's early travels, see the studies by Paul Turner cited above and Le Corbusier's own accounts in his first book, a study commisioned by his school in La Chaux-de-Fonds, "Étude sur le mouvement d'art décoratif en Allemagne," in Le Corbusier, *The Decorative Art of Today*; and in the Introduction to vol. 1 of the *Oeuvre Complète*.
15. See the Loosian arguments in *The Decorative Art of Today*.
16. For a more detailed discussion of the chronology and arguments relevant to Le Corbusier's development and use of the positions schematically outlined here, see Colquhoun, "Architecture and Engineering"; and Reyner Banham, *Theory and Design in the First Machine Age* (London, 1960), chaps. 15–17.

from being limited to his introduction to the practical discipline of reinforced concrete construction, was magnified through association with French structural rationalism and the French tradition of academic classicism.[17] The dialectical possibilities inherent in both lessons, but suppressed in the relatively stable compositions of both Behrens and Perret, adumbrate the creative tension implicit in the polemical juxtapositions that frame Le Corbusier's arguments in the twenties. The romantic search for a "style for the age" becomes identified with the classical transcendence of styles, just as the search for a "new architecture" turns out to have been a search for architecture *tout court*.

The operative term here remains "search," for in spite of what seems like an argument tending towards resolution, one continues to find the themes and figures associated with the romantic-classical polarity in a state of suspension. Apparently blended, or confused, at one moment, at the next they have separated into distinct strands to be recombined in some new, equally unstable substance. In the seminal years of the magazine *l'Esprit Nouveau*, which Le Corbusier edited with the painter Amédée Ozenfant and the poet Paul Dermé from 1920 to 1925, the critical potential of these recombinant themes is especially apparent. Just as romantic ideas of progress and of the immanence of the new had been employed throughout the nineteenth century as cudgels to bela-

17. On the interaction of these two traditions, see Robin Middleton, "The Abbé de Cordemoy and the Graeco Gothic Ideal," *Journal of the Warburg and Courtauld Institutes* XXV and XXVI (1962–1963).
18. See Banham, *Theory and Design*, chap. 15; and Christopher Green, *Léger and the Avant-Garde* (New Haven, 1976).
19. On the "Journey to the East," see Le Corbusier's account in *The Decorative Art of Today* (1925), and the posthumously published *Le Voyage d'Orient* (1966); Ivan Žaknič, "Of Le Corbusier's Eastern Journey," *Oppositions* 18 (Fall 1979); and Giuliano Gresleri and Italo Zannier, *Viaggio in Oriente, Gli Inediti di Charles Edouard Jeanneret* (Venice, 1983).

bor the forces of academic reaction, so now, at a crucial juncture, classical ideas of reason, natural law, and the timeless and transcendent autonomy of the work of art were invoked to redirect the energies of the avant garde. In the "age of mechanical reproduction," in the face of the socially and formally entropic forces unleashed by the modern metropolis, the classical could be genuinely radical. This is the point of the purist revision of cubism put forward by Ozenfant and Le Corbusier in 1918, with its emphasis on the classical invariance of the *objet-type* set against and stabilizing the dynamic decompositions of futurism and analytic cubism.[18]

In Le Corbusier's four books of the mid-twenties, based on articles published in *l'Esprit Nouveau*, this dialectic is transmitted through the medium of photographs providing a comprehensive iconography of modernity, in both its rational and romantic aspects, and sketches illustrating the "lesson of Rome" and universal classicism. The source of most of the sketches that depict architecture as the "pure creation of the mind"—and a continuing source throughout his literary and architectural career—was Le Corbusier's "Journey to the East."[19] And if the first part of young Jeanneret's Grand Tour may be identified with his recapitulation, and projected extrapolation, of the inexorable progressive emergence of the spirit of the age, then the 1911 trip should be understood as a voyage of discovery, of the collection of evidence for the countervailing values associated with classicism. The distinction is articulated by Le Corbusier's depiction of northern Europe as clusters of sites associated with culture and industry-with the historical emergence of modern

Western civilization—while eastern Europe and the Mediterranean are characterized by sites associated with culture and folklore, with the ahistorical continuity and universal "spirit of order" shared by both classicism and the vernacular.[20] Le Corbusier's own description of the significance of these travels is unequivocal:

> I saw the grand and eternal monuments, glories of the human spirit.
>
> Above all, I succumbed to the irresistible attraction of the Mediterranean . . . .
>
> The Turkey of Adrianople, Byzantium, of Santa Sophia or Salonica, the Persia of Bursa, the Parthenon, Pompeii, then the Colosseum. Architecture was revealed to me. Architecture is the magnificent play of forms under light. Architecture is the coherent construct of the mind. Architecture has nothing to do with decoration. Architecture is in the great buildings, the difficult and high-flown works bequeathed by time, but it is also in the smallest hovel, in an enclosure-wall, in everything sublime or modest which contains sufficient geometry to establish a mathematical relationship.[21]

20. Peter Serenyi has included Mediterranean and Northern in an interesting list of Corbusian polarities, in "Timeless But of Its Time: Le Corbusier's Architecture In India," *The Le Corbusier Archive* 26.

21. Le Corbusier, *The Decorative Art of Today*, 206–207.

22. On Le Corbusier and the academic tradition of classical composition, see Banham, *Theory and Design*, chaps. 1–3; and with particular reference to Rome, Kurt Forster, "Antiquity and Modernity in the La Roche-Jeanneret Houses of 1923," *Oppositions* 15/16.

23. See Richard A. Etlin, "A Paradoxical Avant Garde: Le Corbusier's Villas of the 1920s," *The Architectural Review* CLXXXI, no. 1079 (January 1987), and "Le Corbusier, Choisy, and French Hellenism: The Search for a New Architecture," *The Art Bulletin* LXIX, no. 2 (June 1987).

And yet for all the apparent decisiveness of this comfortably neo-Platonic theoretical position, once it is set in a context broader than the polemical moment in which it was posed, it, like the examples it cites, tends to blur around the edges. Even classicism, it turns out, is a plural and dialectically constructed phenomenon. One can find abundant evidence, in the Corbusian scripture and in projects from throughout his career, to suggest that the "lesson of Rome" included not only the purity of the Phileban solids, but also the sophisticated strategies of elemental analysis and composition, and the subtle equilibration of primary and secondary axes learned from Rome, but by way of the hated École des Beaux-Arts.[22] By the same token, the possibilities of Le Corbusier's ultimate architectural epiphany, his pilgrimage to the Acropolis, are hardly exhausted, or even limited, by his appreciation of the Parthenon as a classically static and absolute type. Rather, his comprehensive and highly romantic experience of the Acropolis from a moving point of view, as a dynamically balanced and even picturesque site plan, anticipates the way in which purist painting and architecture oscillate between the figurative identification of elemental forms and artifacts and the experience of those forms within a dynamic spatial matrix. The closure of a finite composition, and its status as a canonical type, is always balanced by the open-ended potential for addition, replication, or reinterpretation within the larger field of the landscape or the city.[23]

Thus, in spite of what has so often been claimed concerning modern architecture's relation to cultural traditions, one might argue that few critics before Le Corbusier had been capable or willing to find in a single monument the occasion for such a wide range of cultural and interpretive response. One thinks, per-

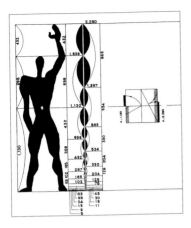

Modulor Man

haps, of Goethe, similarly suspended between classicism and romanticism, creating from the dialectical possibilities something that, in its context, can only be called modern. In any case, what seems certain is the sense that, since Le Corbusier, we cannot return to a simplistic view of any culture and its monuments, including our own.[24]

INDIVIDUAL AND COLLECTIVE: UTOPIAN DIALECTICS

For an architect who seemed, at least to an overanxious public, to transform himself and modern architecture with breathtaking flights of invention, Le Corbusier returned with stubborn regularity to monuments, images, and themes experienced and recorded during his early travels. The only rival to the Acropolis in terms of persistence and fecundity was the Carthusian Monastery at Ema, near Florence, which he visited in September 1907 and again in 1911 on the return leg of his "Journey to the East." While there was considerable romantic potential in the siting and character of Ema—Jeanneret's guide to medieval Tuscany was Ruskin—the most profound impression was derived, even at that early date, not from the particularity of the building but from the generic typology of the Carthusian monastic plan. This scheme—highly standardized and reproducible, the product of a strict "rule"—was identified by Le Corbusier as a diagram for an ideal communal structure, balancing" individual freedom and collective organization."[25] This was, of course, a fairly romantic conception of a possible social order. Indeed, a certain level of naïveté about social and political program would remain a characteristic feature—often a shortcoming—of even Le Corbusier's most architecturally ambitious and sophisticated projects.

The idea and image of the collective community represented by Ema was overlaid with other preoccupations, such as the utopian socialist speculations of Charles Fourier and the proposals of his followers, to which Jeanneret was probably first introduced in 1908 when, soon after his visit to Italy, he paid a call on

24. On Le Corbusier's revision of the canon with respect to the Acropolis, see Stanford Anderson, "Critical Conventionalism in Architecture," *Assemblage* 1 (October 1986): 21.
25. Le Corbusier, *The Modulor*, 28. See also Peter Serenyi, "Le Corbusier, Fourier, and the Monastery at Ema," *The Art Bulletin* XLIX (1967).

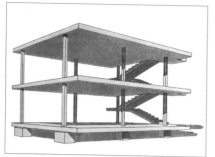
Maison Dom-ino

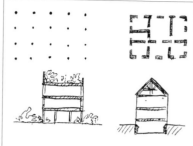
The Five Points

Tony Garnier in Lyon. Somewhat later, Le Corbusier's ongoing transformation of communal typology absorbed the modern image of the ocean liner, so powerfully evident in projects from the Cité de Refuge in Paris to the Marseille Unité. As for the individual cell of the Carthusian monk, he made this the ideal dwelling unit of the modern man. Transformed by way of the Maison Citrohan projects, with their appropriation of the vernacular Parisian studio-residence type in the interest of a prototype mass-production house, a thoroughly recognizable version of the monk's cell reemerges in the immeuble-villa unit. Both of these crucial prototypes were built only once as demonstration models, the Citrohan at the 1927 Weissenhof Exhibition in Stuttgart and the *immeuble-villa* as the Pavillon de l'Esprit Nouveau at the 1925 Exposition des Arts Décoratifs, but they served as the typological basis—or at least the kernel—not only for most of Le Corbusier's mass housing schemes, but for most of the major houses and villas of the twenties.[26] As such they usually carry with them the implication, and often the rules, of reproducibility in the service of an idea of the collective whole, as well as the explicit spatial image of the modern individual.

This individual turns out to be as complex as the spatial and typological transformations from which his image was constructed. Le Corbusier's "hero of modern life," the *homme-type* who will occupy the *maison-type* and ultimately be the citizen of the Contemporary or Radiant or whatever city, is an extraordinary composite: part monk, part steamship captain and airplane pilot; part worker, part intellectual captain of industry; part artist, part athlete. Le Corbusier has supplied us with many scenes from the life of this individual, and his brilliant typological and formal dialectics, for all that they tend to emphasize the opacity of the object and the autonomy of the language, are in the service of the explicit delineation of a modern lifestyle. As Colin Rowe has proposed, in discussing the formal logic of the free plan, "a building by Le Corbusier, whether successful or not, is always a statement about the world and never simply a statement about itself."[27] The fact that this individual turns out to be less like Everyman and more like Le Corbusier's carefully cultivated self-

26. For an analysis of the Villa Stein as "a set of of overlapping Maisons Citrohans," see Thomas Schumacher, "Deep Space, Shallow Space," *The Architectural Review* CLXXXI, no. 1079 (Jan 1987): 37.
27. Colin Rowe, "Neo-'Classicism' and Modern Architecture II," *Oppositions* 1 (1973): 25. For a critique of this position, see Peter Eisenman, "Aspects of Modernism: Maison Dom-ino and the Self-Referential Sign," *Oppositions* 15/16.

image, or like many of his clients in the twenties, no doubt has a great deal to do with the problems inherent in the collective entities he proposed.

Le Corbusier was, of course, devoted to the image of the modern man he created, replying, when asked to design a house for an architect: "Why an architect's house? My house is everyone's, anyone's house; it is the house of a gentleman living in our times."[28] Thus the double-height studio space, with its distinctive factory glazing expressing the principal volume, was asymmetrically central not only to houses actually built for artists, but to the house of the worker and the villa of the enlightened bourgeois. Le Corbusier proselytized at length for the virtues of this lifestyle. We still recognize that muscular gentleman of our times in the heroic figure of the Modulor Man, an updated version of the Renaissance Vitruvian Man through which, in characteristic Corbusian fashion, the universal validation of mathematics conspired with other arguments to guarantee his demonstration.

The Modulor Man, emblazoned on the side of projects such as the Marseille Unité, became the sign of the limits of Le Corbusier's utopian vision. For whatever the legitimacy of neo-Platonic anthropometrics, not everyone would find themselves comfortable on the rather spartan and procrustean bed made for the heroic artist-monk whose identity still provided the spatial theme, if no longer the poetics, of the Unité. Furthermore, the rule according to which these individuals were assembled to form a community was, more often than not, that of simple addition. Peter Serenyi's critique of the immeuble-villas project as "nothing but a collection of single figures put on top or next to one another by the architect," could be applied equally well to the bottle-rack principle of the Unité.[29] This is, in large measure, the disappointment of Le Corbusier's urban proposals as well: that the promised dialectics of individual and collective, public and private, city and landscape, chaos and order, which are identified as the proper concerns at the scale of urbanism, fail to rise above the level of mere additive or juxta-positional assertion. Indeed, diagrams that illustrate claims to "synthesize" individual liberty and collective forces "with the help of Ford" point to the roots, not to the solution, of the problem. Those occasions when the communal or urbanistic whole was more than the sum of its Corbusian parts—Cité de Refuge, La Tourette, Plan Obus—were those instances when Le Corbusier relied, for his modus operandi, not on the rhetoric associated with Fordism, Taylorism, or Syndicalism, but on transformational and architectonic strategies grounded in his own discipline, of which he was a master.[30] The genuinely critical possibilities of Le Corbusier's "utopia of forms" emerges when he was being most the architect, and least the ideologue, of modern life, when he was not offering architecture as a surrogate for revolution.

28. Quoted in von Moos, *Le Corbusier*, 53.
29. Serenyi, "Le Corbusier, Fourier," 278.
30. For these "isms" in Le Corbusier's thought and practice, and the general problem of his politics, see Mary McLeod, "Le Corbusier and Algiers," *Oppositions* 19/20.

STRUCTURE AND ENCLOSURE: SPATIAL DIALECTICS

As one places Le Corbusier "in context" and traces the historical genealogies of the themes and images he inherited, it is easy to lose sight of the fact that he,

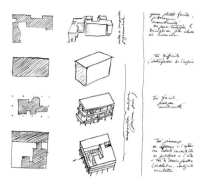

The Four Compositions

along with a handful of others, is responsible for the invention of a genuinely modern architectural space, within which those themes could be clearly and simultaneously articulated. That Le Corbusier could, as early as 1915, identify the generic conditions of modern construction, subject them to the typological analysis required by his classicizing predilections, and summarize the results in an icon so potent and concise that it would rival Laugier's primitive hut as a constructive emblem of its era, is remarkable enough.[31] He then proceeded, over the following decade, to extrapolate from the hypothesis of the Dom-ino not only a set of house types that challenged as they transformed the received domestic repertoire, but also and even more importantly, he formulated the basic rule structure of an architectural language predicated upon both modern construction and the revolutionary spatial experiments of cubist painting. The fact that, with respect to both space and technique, Le Corbusier's contribution turns out to have been fundamentally rhetorical, does not diminish the significance of the achievement announced in 1926 by the Five Points of a New Architecture.

Each of the Five Points, in their literal manifestations, can be traced in the history of the recent past. By the same token, each Point was connected with a particular, and sometimes idiosyncratic, polemic which might place it in apparent conflict with another Point considered in terms of its ancestry. For example, the free plan is derived in part from Auguste Perret's use of the concrete frame in his Rue Franklin building of 1903. However, the ribbon window, which was for Le Corbusier the index of a new mode of vision as well as the sign of his transgression of the expressive limits of trabeated construction, was a particular point of contention between him and Perret.[32] The argument is not simply one of anthropomorphism (the vertical window) versus abstraction, but also of a taste for finite resolution versus the dialectical possibilities opened up by the confrontation of free plan and free facade. These possibilities may all be inherent in the free plan, but it was Le Corbusier's pecu-

31. On the development of the Dom-ino, see Eleanor Gregh, "The Dom-ino Idea," *Oppositions* 15/16, and, in the same issue, Peter Eisenman, "Aspects of Modernism," and Barry Maitland, "The Grid." See also Paul Turner, "Romanticism, Rationalism."
32. This interesting debate is presented in Bruno Reichlin, "The Pros and Cons of the Horizontal Window: The Perret-Le Corbusier Controversy," *Daedalos* 13 (September 1984).

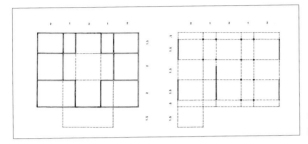

Villas Foscari (left) and Garches (right)

liar contribution, with a little help from his avant-garde contemporaries, to push all of them, simultaneously, to their logical limits.

From a logical point of view, the free plan has a certain priority among the Five Points, and it has, not surprisingly, been the principal target of recent attacks on the spatial characteristics of modern architecture and urbanism.[33] The positive critical value of the most perceptive of these attacks is their emphasis on the extent to which the free plan, like most of Le Corbusier's confrontations with architectural tradition, depends upon a conceptually symbiotic relationship with the spatial and representational systems constitutive of that tradition. Thus, the figural shaping, molding, or carving of space to create the particularized and defined "places" associated with traditional architecture and urbanism, is countered in the free plan by the displacement or interruption of continuous space by figural solids, the disposition of which serves to emphasize the freedom of modern architecture from the constraints of bearingwall construction. As an important corollary, the fusion of a system of structural and spatial modulation and a representational vocabulary that was fundamental to the logic and meaning of the classical language is dissolved in the free plan, which juxtaposes an abstract and rational grid of columns against freely disposed objects that are figural in the sense of both formal gestalt and rhetorical expression.

Those objects represent function. They often conspicuously contain the functional equipment that in traditional planning had been hidden in the poché of walls that both support and enclose. Thus the real significance of the separation between structure and enclosure does not lie simply in the formal and architectonic play of column and wall, but in the delineation of the relationships between what they stand for: the generic and mathematically regular order of structure and the particular and contingent order of the program as articulated by enclosure and circulation. To say this is not by any means to succumb to the simplistic pragmatic arguments often advanced by Le Corbusier for the Five Points. We have already seen that when push came to shove, he was more interested in the typological and poetic potential of any architectural problem

33. See, for example, Steven Peterson, "Space and Anti-Space," *The Harvard Architectural Review* 1 (Spring 1980).

than in its merely utilitarian accommodation. Nevertheless, the famous Four Compositions, which summarize Le Corbusier's domestic work of the twenties, must be understood as the refinement of a proposed solution to the pragmatic and theoretical problem posed since the eighteenth century by the need to assimilate increasingly complex and specific programs generated from outside architecture per se to the properly architectural discourse of form.

Le Corbusier's research into this problem must be understood in relation to two traditions. The first, the paradigm of which might be the French *hôtel*, particularly in its neoclassical phase, is articulated in a theoretical literature descended from Blondel, and treats the aforementioned problem as an exercise in hierarchical packing within the limits of a conventional, symmetrically massed and fenestrated building envelope.[34] The second is best represented by the picturesque English villa and is, at least with respect to the functional rationalization—as opposed to the earlier aesthetic formulation-of its massing, indebted to the arguments of Pugin, who ridiculed the absurdity of trying to stuff a modern program into the iconic container of a Greek temple. The first tradition was, of course, well known to Le Corbusier, who studied both the buildings and the texts in question, while the second passed to him via the German and Austrian appreciation of the free planning of English Arts and Crafts houses, which express rather than suppress the casual irregularities generated by the commodious distribution of the necessities of modern bourgeois life. Loos had already tried, in his *Raumplan*, to combine the two traditions, but it was Le Corbusier's development of the planning potential inherent in the Dom-ino that opened the way for a "transparently" modern—and dialectical—collage of the classically pure prism and the freely disposed functional "machinery" of programmatic rationality.[35] The Four Compositions illustrate the range of possible solutions, from the still *pittoresque* Maison La Roche to the literal wrapping of the L-shaped plan of La Roche in the taut skin of Villa Savoye.

Interestingly, the discretely revealing wrapper of the free facade that mediates the public presentation of Le Corbusier's domestic projects, holding the functional organs tightly if precariously in place, is generally absent in the large public projects of the twenties and thirties. In proposals such as the League of Nations and the Palace of the Soviets, and in buildings such as the Cité de Refuge, the Swiss Pavilion, and the Centrosoyus, Le Corbusier allowed the functionally expressive figural elements of the composition, representing, as they do, public functions such as assembly, to "appear" in public as part of a more or less monumental, classically grounded, and constructivist inspired ensemble. On closer inspection *in situ*, however, they too turn out to be carefully framed purist compositions, circumscribed by the limits of their actual or implied sites. As in the case of the villas, the formal interest is less in the possibility of a fully resolved synthesis than in those areas of enormous spatial energy generated by the confrontation of systems operating according to apparently independent logics. Thus the

34. See Michael Dennis, *Court & Garden: From the French Hotel to the City of Modern Architecture* (Cambridge, Mass., 1986), chap. 6.

35. The persistence of this dialectical theme in Le Corbusier's work is demonstrated in Alan Colquhoun, "Formal and Functional Interactions: A Study of Two Late Buildings by Le Corbusier," *Architectural Design 36* (May 1966).

autonomous centers of these systems compete with each other and with the abstract geometric center of the composition, as well as with the equally insistent perimeter of the entire field.

CENTER AND PERIPHERY: DIALECTICS OF PLACE

It is tempting to assert that the thematics of center and periphery are crucial not only to the formal analysis of Le Corbusier's work, but to his entire world view and to the trajectory of his life as well. He provisionally identified Paris as the center of activity, but only, as we have seen, after comparison shopping among the available European cultural capitals. Even as early as the late twenties, Le Corbusier, with his keen and opportunistic sense of cultural geography, was looking beyond what had become his polycentric Mediterranean cultural homeland to the new worlds at the periphery of Western civilization: the Soviet Union, North and South America. Ultimately and ironically, the ideological and architectural burdens of a world capital in search of a site were laid upon the plains of the Punjab— upon a provincial capital at the edge of the Indian subcontinent—where grand ambitions are dissipated in a field so vast that the familiar, lively dialogue of center and periphery is lost altogether.

Again, the loss of genuinely dialectical energy seems characteristic of the problems of Le Corbusier's urban proposals. If the later urban schemes, from St-Dié to Chandigarh, chart the gradual dissolution of the field within which public centers and edges might meaningfully interact, then the early projects are perhaps all too clear about the schematically distinct formal and political identities of center and periphery. This is, as has often been noted, in dramatic contrast to the dynamics of virtually all of his individual projects, as Colin Rowe has pointed out in his influential comparison of Villa Stein at Garches and Palladio's Villa Foscari:

> . . . at Garches central focus is consistently broken up, concentration at any one point is disintegrated, and the dismembered fragments of the center become a peripheral dispersion of incident, a serial installation of interest around the extremeties of the plan.[36]

It is at this point—trapped in the layering between shallow and deep space, between center and edge, when one is inclined to think that such an account of Corbusian dialectics is mainly a product of staring until one goes crosseyed at the two-dimensional images of plan and elevation as if they were cubist paintings— that Le Corbusier rescues us with an interpretive strategy based upon the actual experience of the space in which these suspicious events transpire. The promenade architecturale is more than a preferred route of circulation; it is a hermeneutics of modern space which provides a rigorously orchestrated tour through the themes, images, and ordering systems deployed in a given project.[37] Nor is it entirely farfetched to suggest that one's own itinerary among the various outposts of the Corbusian phenomenon extends the interpretive role of the promenade architecturale at the level of the individual project—as it describes the powerful relation-

36. Colin Rowe, "Mathematics of the Ideal Villa," 12.
37. On the romantic roots of the promenade and its development in nineteenth-century theory and historiography, see the two articles by Richard Etlin cited above.

ship between shifting centers and a periphery full of its own interest—while appealing to the model of experience preferred by Le Corbusier in his own heroically autodidactic quest for the elusive vantage point—whether at the center of things or outside, beyond the edge.

NATURE AND CULTURE: DIALECTICS OF MYTH

Vantage point, or point of view, is in fact a fundamental issue in all of Le Corbusier's work: built, drawn, painted, and written. In the case of the changing, but always crucial relationship proposed between an idea of nature and the constructed artifacts and monuments of human culture, point of view not only expresses but often determines the character of that relationship. Le Corbusier's projects frequently have as one of their principal purposes the provision of a specific view of nature as the means of establishing a dialog with it. Indeed, the "captive" nature, or artificial terrain, provided by the roof garden or the *jardin suspendu*, has as much to do with the establishment of a foreground and a horizon against which a more or less distant nature is viewed, as it does with literally bringing a piece of nature into the building. This sense of nature framed by an architecture that carefully establishes its distance from it, is the dominant mode of the relationship in question in most of the Corbusian work associated with the "machine aesthetic." Whether nature is seen as subject to and manifesting the same rational principles of order as those which govern the world of man-made form, or whether it is seen as a benignly "wild," romantic other, the point of view tends to fix the limits of the relationship.

It is, however, nothing more or less than a changing point of view that eventually threatens to dissolve the distance between nature and culture, recalling Le Corbusier to his organicist roots in the fin-de-siècle culture of Art Nouveau, but now, on the far side of the Modern Movement, at a very different scale of concern than that of the ornamental motif. One should not underestimate the role of Le Corbusier's painting in the reformulation of his vocabulary with respect to the natural world. From the mid-twenties on, the *nature morte* of machine-made, purist *objets-types* is joined, often within the same frame, by organic *objets à reaction poétique* with distinctly surrealist overtones. Eventually, both are subordinated to the ultimate organic form: the curve of the female body. But the fact remains that it was the neoclassical and Purist painter's framed view of a nature, against which the objets-types of classical or machine-age culture are set in sharp relief, that was challenged and opened up by what might be characterized as the aviator's view of nature. Le Corbusier's enthusiasm for flight privileged the aerial view as a supplement to earthbound modes of vision. From increasingly Olympian heights, he perceived the large-scale unity of nature and culture in which architecture can become a feature of the landscape and part of—rather than either master of or subject to—natural processes.

In the Contemporary City, nature, in the form of an English garden, is meant to be looked at as it flows continuously beneath the cruciform skyscrapers, which provide a rational and artificial modulation of, and counterpoint to, a tame landscape. Myth remains on the side of the machine, rushing through city and landscape, in its headlong flight into the future. In the Radiant City, however, the city has become another nature, designed to accord with natural processes and to allow for organic growth. In fact, the city has become quite literally a body, and the text that accompanies the project, while it still preserves the machine analogies of *l'Esprit Nouveau*, now abounds with biological analogies, in support of a plan with a head, heart, lungs, and guts. Unfortunately, it also articulates a rigid scheme of zoning which, oversimplified in the Athens Charter of 1933, was to have disastrous consequences for postwar urbanism.

Increasingly, however, the poetics of nature and culture tend to overwhelm rational, pragmatic argument; nature, still viewed "scientifically" in the Radiant City, usurps the mythic role of the machine as a metaphor for architecture. In the Plan Obus for Algiers (1930), the familiar themes of a road-based, linear city, continuous terrace housing, separation of traffic, and zoning of functions, are fused and transcended in a breathtaking image of the city as topography: a manmade nature that mediates and transforms the *objets trouvées* of the traditional urban culture of the Casbah and the existing landscape of the sea and mountains as it gathers into itself the functions of both.[38] After the epic failure of his plans for Algiers, Le Corbusier seems to have invested less mythic energy in urbanism, while the responsibility for the elaboration of such themes as the engagement and embodiment of the landscape fell to individual projects such as Ronchamp, which has so frequently been taken as the sign of the abandonment of the Apollonian dialectics of high Modernism.

38. The critical significance of Le Corbusier's projects for Algiers has been increasinlgy appreciated in recent years; see Manfredo Tafuri, *Architecture and Utopia* (Cambridge, Mass., 1976; original, Italian ed., 1973), chap. 6; Tafuri, "Machine et memoire"; and Mary McLeod, "Le Corbusier and Algiers."

39. See Kenneth Frampton, "Le Corbusier and the Monumentalization of the Vernacular, 1930–1960," in *Modern Architecture: A Critical History*.

40. This sort of critique of the ideology of the career is associated with recent post-structuralist criticism, but for an interesting and important architectural parallel, see Robert Venturi, "Diversity, Relevance and Representation in Historicism, or Plus ça change . . ." *Architectural Record* (June 1982).

41. See James Stirling, "Garches to Jaoul: Le Corbusier as Domestic Architect in 1927 and 1953," *The Architectural Review* CXVIII (September 1955).

ANCIENT AND MODERN: HISTORICAL DIALECTICS

There have been any number of descriptions, and almost as many explanations, of the dramatic sea-change that was increasingly manifest in Le Corbusier's work from around 1930 on.[39] While it is important to understand the significance of these apparently new developments, one should also recognize that their importance tends to be exaggerated, especially by historians fixated on a linear account of something called a career, which must preserve a semblance of unity.[40] The "rupture" that announced the second style is also, perhaps inevitably, overrated by a younger generation of architects, such as the British Brutalists, for whom the developments became the basis, rather than the ongoing exploratory expression, of their own careers.[41] From our point of view, it should be suggested, first of all, that the "new" themes and preoccupations had been present all along either in latent form or in the context of different dialectical relationships—as in the case of the relationship between nature and culture discussed above—and, secondly, that the "old" themes were hardly relegated to some scrap heap of youthful folly, but continued to be explored and elaborated, in some cases quite persistently, alongside later lines of investigation.

Kenneth Frampton's apt characterization of the post-1930 Corbusian project as "the monumentalization of the vernacular" should alert us right away. After all, Le Corbusier had already recognized, in the course of his "Journey to the East," that the vernacular, like classicism in its astylistic interpretation, was inherently monumental and, in its abstract typological refinement, not unlike the products of industrial civilization. Indeed, in going beyond the abstract appreciation of the vernacular to an interest in the tactile and expressive possibilities of its materials and techniques, Le Corbusier, rather than rejecting modernity, may have been opening up another area of *rapprochement* between the timelessness of the vernacular and the evolutionary perfection of the new. In projects like the Maison de Weekend and the Maisons Jaoul, vernacular materials and construction are used side-by-side with reinforced concrete and other industrial materials in a way that suggests they are not fundamentally incompatible, especially to Le Corbusier's *bricoleur* sensibility. Just as Le Corbusier brought a classicizing sensibility to the romantic experience of the zeitgeist, and a romantic sensiblity to the experience of the classical order of universal geometries and monuments, so he primitivized concrete and modernized the vernacular.

If anything is lost in this process, it is the sense of historical development. The more we are convinced by Le Corbusier's dialectics of primitivism and modernity, the more history tends to collapse in upon itself as the dialog between ancient and modern becomes desperately direct, dispensing with the intervening evolutionary steps. Those themes and images that tend to recur with the greatest frequency in the late projects are, in fact, those that emphasize the face-to-face confrontation of ancient and modern man. Such an image is that of the tent, which can emerge directly from the troglodytic vault, as in the garden pavilion of the Maison de Weekend, or from the heavy concrete shell of Ronchamp, or from the light metal parasol of the Maison de l'Homme (Heidi Weber Pavilion). It can be used serially and in utilitarian constructions, or it may float as an isolated sign atop larger, more complex structures.[42] The tent is clearly related to Le Corbusier's abiding interest in primitive huts and other *ur*-architectures, but in certain respects it is both more primitive and more modern. The "primitive temple" that Le Corbusier illustrates in *Vers une architecture*, as a study in regulating lines, is actually the movable tabernacle of the Exodus—a demountable architecture from before the first permanent settlement—but it is already monumental. As Le Corbusier comments: "There is no such thing as primitive man; there are primitive resources. The idea is constant, in full sway from the beginning."[43]

Like the biblical Hebrews, modern man, in his variegated tents, is nomadic, wandering from place to place in search of law—but also of experience.

42. On Le Corbusier's roof forms, see von Moos, *Le Corbusier*, 95-98.
43. *Towards a New Architecture*, 66.

LE CORBUSIER: A BIOGRAPHICAL NOTE

DEBORAH GANS

Le Corbusier with his mother and brother Albert Jeanneret

Le Corbusier was born Charles-Édouard Jeanneret on October 6, 1887, in La Chaux-de-Fonds Switzerland. He was the second son of Georges-Édouard Jeanneret, a watchmaker and mountain hiking enthusiast, and Madame Marie-Charlotte-Amélie Jeanneret-Perret, a musician and piano teacher. The family proudly traced their ancestry to the Cathars, who fled to the Jura Mountains during the Albigensian Wars of the twelfth century, and the French Huguenots, who migrated to Switzerland following the Edict of Nantes in 1598. They came to La Chaux-de-Fonds for the refuge it consistently offered to religious denominations, such as Calvinists, and to political figures, such as Rousseau and Bakhunin. All these strands figured in Le Corbusier's identity, from his ambivalence toward the patriarchal Juras to his interest in the mysticism of the Albigensian heresy.

Le Corbusier's education was dominated by the figure of Charles l'Eplattenier, a teacher at the local art school whom Le Corbusier called "My Master." L'Eplattenier combined into a national romanticism many strains of late nineteenth-century thought, from John Ruskin to Hermann Muthesius. He involved his students in his search for a new kind of ornament expressive of the Jura landscape that could sustain a local craft industry in the wake of the industrialization of watch manufacturing. Apprenticed at thirteen to an engraver, Le Corbusier abandoned watch making because of delicate eyesight, which continued to plague him to adulthood. He continued his studies in art and decoration with the intention of becoming a painter. L'Eplattenier insisted that the young man also study architecture and arranged for his first house commissions in addition to works of decoration executed collaboratively with other students.

After completing his first house, Villa Fallet, in 1907, and buoyed by such inspirational texts as Edouard Schuré's *Les Grands Initiés*, Nietzsche's *Zarathustra* and Ruskin's *Mornings In Florence*, Le Corbusier set out on a series of travels that lasted until 1912. These travels took him first to Italy, then Budapest and Vienna, Munich and Paris where he apprenticed himself to architects with philosophies at odds with L'Epplatenier, most significantly to Auguste Perret the rationalist father of concrete construction and to Peter Behrens leader of the Werkbund. He concluded with a *"Journey to the East"* heading to the Acropolis by way of the Carthusian Monastery of Ema, the Balkans and Turkey.

Le Corbusier's dutiful but ambivalent return to La Chaux-de-Fonds to teach beside L'Epplatenier and to begin his own practice as decorator and architect culminated in the constructed Villa Schwob and the propositional Maison Dom-ino, a pun on domus and playing pieces of the game. With the help of the engineer Max Dubois and Perret, he envisioned the Dom-ino reinforced concrete frame as an affordable, prefabricated system for the construction of new housing in the wake of World War I's destruction. The modular columns and slabs could be trucked to a site. The exterior cladding as well as interior walls were free from structural constraints. The Dom-ino differed from the then standard, poured-in-place Hennebique frame in both its prefabrication and its idealized form.[1] Its flat slabs without exposed beams and its straight columns without expressed capitols defied the current logic of reinforcing in search of pure geometry. The iconic patent illustration of the Dom-ino in perspective is a golden section in plan composed of two square open bays plus a stair. Variously interpreted as a statement of functional drive, technological aspirations, classical idealism, and "self-referential sign,"[2] the Dom-ino has come to be nothing less than the ideogram of modernity.

With the help of Dubois' patronage and Parisian engineering concerns, Le Corbusier's escape back to Paris in 1917 was permanent and complete. His hope was to fund his life as a painter through the financial success of a small brick manufacture but he eventually became resigned to the economic necessity of a life in architecture. Nonetheless, he dedicated most of his time until 1922 to painting and art criticism. First in the book *Après le cubisme* (1918) and subsequently in a related show at Galerie Thomas, he and the Amédée Ozenfant began a movement called Purism, which called for the restoration of the integrity of the object in art. As their style developed, it drew closer to Synthetic Cubism's structure of overlapping planes but retained a distinct attitude toward the mass produced tools of industrial culture, from laboratory flasks to café chairs, which they called type-objects (*objets-types*). While Purism shared its interest in the banal with other contemporary movements, it avoided questions of subjectivity, ostensibly rejecting the Dadaist and Surreal, although both found an eventual place in Le Corbusier's consciousness and work.

In order to distinguish their work as painters from that as critics, Le Corbusier and Ozenfant took

1. Paul Turner, "Romanticism, Rationalism, and the Dom-ino System," Walden, ed., *The Open Hand*, 14–42.
2. Peter Eisenman, "Aspects of Modernism: Maison Dom-ino and the Self-Referential Sign," *Oppositions* 15/16, 119–128.

pseudonyms. Ozenfant adopted his mother's name Saugnier. Jeanneret took the name of a cousin, Lecorbezier, because it sounded suitably like an *objet-type* and suggested the architect's crow-like (*corbeau*) profile. Until their acrimonious break-up in 1925, Le Corbusier's self-invention continued with the encouragement of the more assured Ozenfant. Adopting a costume of bow-tie, starched collar, and bowler hat, and a rhetorical style combining discipline, enthusiasm, ironic wit and moral outrage, he became what he considered to be the perfect standard for the times.

The post-war industrialized culture in all its aspects became the theme of the journal *l'Esprit Nouveau*, founded in 1919 and published until 1925 by Le Corbusier and Ozenfant with the poet Paul Dermée. *Vers une architecture*, arguably Le Corbusier's most profound book, is a collection and restructuring of essays from the journal. The book proposes an architecture that satisfies both changing technology and the timeless concerns of architectural form as defined in western antiquity. It also includes two housing types, the shoe box Citrohan and vaulted Monol which were to dominate his architecture throughout his life, and his first urban plan for the Contemporary City. The Citrohan took immediate inspiration from the balcony section and double height salon of the bistro Legendre, rue Godot-de-Mauroy where the architect lunched daily. It is a consequence of the Dom-ino frame and of the entire history of trabeation back to the Greek temple (especially as depicted in its ruined state). The Monol took inspiration from the docks in Casablanca by Le Corbusier's mentor Perret and the consonant history of vaulted architecture back to ancient Rome.

During the 1920's, Le Corbusier realized his first mature architecture in a series of villas for artists, their patrons, and a few industrialists. In 1922 he had formed an architectural partnership with his younger cousin, Pierre Jeanneret, located at 35 rue de Sèvres that lasted until the Second World War and revived on different terms with the commission of Chandigarh. Jeanneret played the quieter role, developing design documents and dealing with clients on a daily basis. The absence of a state program for housing in France contributed to the firm's inability to realize their ideas on a scale comparable to their German counterparts, for example. The one exception was a complex of workers' housing in Pessac (1925) built for a sugar cube industrialist. Photographs show Corb, accompanied by the other European luminaries like Mies van der Rohe and Sigfried Giedion, wandering among Pessac's newly planted fruit trees, petal colored buildings and sea of mud. For the 1927 Deutscher Werkbund exhibition in Stuttgart, Le Corbusier built a pure version of a Citrohan house and a related double-house. His booklet for the exhibit codified his principles of design as Five Points of Modern Architecture,[3] namely the pilotis or piles that raise the house above the ground, the roof garden atop the flat roof slab, the free plan unencumbered by structural partitions, the similarly free facade, and the strip window providing even horizontal illumination at eye level. These points derive an optical, spatial and psychological attitude toward architecture from the potentials of the concrete frame. Le Corbusier eventually categorized the potentials of this architecture as Four Compositions,

3. Le Corbusier with Alfred Roth, *Zwei Wohnhäuser von Le Corbusier und Pierre Jeanneret.*

illustrating each one with a house built during the twenties. They are the "easy" picturesque wandering of Villa La Roche; the "absolutely pure and difficult" disciplined box of Villa Stein; the simple, transparent "network" of Villa Baizeau; and the very "generous" Villa Savoye combining the purity of Stein and the amplitude of the other compositions.[4]

With writings and houses, Le Corbusier and Jeanneret achieved a status and skill that seemed about to secure them their first public commission, the League of Nations (1927). The elimination of their entry (ostensibly for the countermanded use of China ink) after winning numerous rounds of competition was widely understood as the triumph of academicism over the modern. It instigated the formation by Le Corbusier, Giedion and Gropius of the organization CIAM (Congrès International d'architecture Moderne) as a counter attack. Le Corbusier received the commission for the Swiss Pavilion as compensation but he remained bitter over the experience. His subsequent inability to obtain much public work in the 1930s fueled his prejudice. In France, the Cité de Refuge of the Salvation Army was to be his only other major built work until after the Second World War. Similarly in Russia, early support for his ideas lead to the commission for the extremely large Centrosoyus building (1928) but collapsed with the shift in political power in the face of his competition entry for the Palace of the Soviets (1935).

Despite his varying fortunes, Le Corbusier settled on a pattern of work and life. In 1930 he married Yvonne Gallis who had some involvement in the couturier world to which Le Corbusier was also tangentially connected. He subsequently adopted French citizenship. During the thirties until the disruption of the War, he would spend mornings painting in his home studio at Porte Molitor. His wife, a gourmet cook, would prepare lunch. Afternoons he would spend in his office on rue de Sèvres, working with Jeanneret, Charlotte Perriand and his young international staff. At least one evening a week, he and Jeanneret would join a game of basketball at the eurythmics studio/gym of his brother Albert. He vacationed on the Mediterranean, near Cap Martin, where he would take Olympian swims.

Even as Le Corbusier completed the ultimate purist house, Villa Savoye (1929), and implemented his first glass curtain walls at the Centrosoyus and Cité de Refuge, a renewed interest in nature tempered his attachment to the *machiniste*. From 1925 onward, the female figure and other natural forms had entered his painting as objects of poetic reaction (*objets à réaction poètique*) to be distinguished from the type objects of a now officially defunct Purism. Natural materials appeared in a rough state in his rural houses, such as the unbuilt Maison Errazuris for Chile (1930), and in tandem with sophisticated technique in his urban buildings, such as the Pavillon Suisse (1930). Some factors in this shift were his experience with the real limits of modern construction, the worsening economic situation of the thirties and the exposure to new landscapes. His travels to Algiers (1929) and flights over Brazil, first with Antoine de Saint Exupéry (1928) and later in a German zeppelin (1936) inspired, among other things, his sinuous viaduct city proposals for Rio and Algiers.

4. Le Corbusier, *Precisions*, 134.

With the worsening economic situation throughout Europe, and strenuous opposition to his ideas evident in some circles, Le Corbusier turned increasingly to urban planning. In his proposals and writings on the city, he developed a vision often summarized as utopian that mixed an ecstatic and largely intuitive humanism with critiques of the social wreckage left in the wake of industrialization.[5] His observation of the crisis in Swiss watchmaking, then the destruction of World War I, the slums of Paris, and the global poverty revealed in his travels led him to the conclusion that industrialization was an independent force with its own historical evolution that, due to Thorsten Veblen's "cultural lag," created urban pathology. The sickness of the great city could be healed by this same industrial economy brought into harmony with individual and collective need. The vehicle for harmony was "the plan". Plan referred to a socio-economic order implemented by undefined political leadership and also to the physical plan of the architect/visionary. The *Planisme* of Le Corbusier first envisioned a centralized Contemporary City for Three Million (1925) surrounded by workers' suburbs, but moved increasingly toward dispersed order. The linear Radiant City (1935) had separate worlds of egalitarian leisure and hierarchical work arranged along an expandable spine of circulation. The Three Human Establishments (1943) was really a continental vision of agrarian settlements, small concentrated cities of commerce and linear industrial cities connected across large landscapes by advanced infrastructure and automobiles. He produced a plan for virtually every city in which he lectured: Barcelona, Geneva and Paris in 1932, Geneva, Antwerp, Stockholm and Algiers in 1933, Hellocourt, Zlin, New York, and Paris in 1935. The 1933 CIAM meeting aboard a boat headed toward the Acropolis produced a bible of urban planning consonant in its values to the Radiant City which Le Corbusier published as *The Athens Charter* in 1943.

Le Corbusier's insistence that "urbanism is the key" to life and his determination to effect change demanded his engagement with power and politics.[6] He began his political life as an ally of captains of industry and global capitalism but by the thirties had joined the syndicalists, a French socialist group who advocated that independent groups of workers (*syndicats*) own and manage the means of production and minimize the organizational structure outside of their unions. His position was ambiguous enough that he could operate as a visionary planner in the emerging Soviet state and propose the public ownership of land in a publication of the Redressement français, an organization of capitalistic industrialists. He became an active contributor to the syndicalist journals *Plans* (1931) and *Préludes* (1932–5). Through their editorial boards he began a rapprochment with the extreme right wing whose version of syndicalism left political decision making to a council of guild masters. *Préludes* had a connection to the Fascist movement. Le Corbusier himself had a brief affair with Italian fascism trying to interest Mussolini in his ideas of the Radiant City. During World War II, Jeanneret joined the Resistance while Le Corbusier left his retreat in Ozon, Pyrenees to approach his syndicalist friends in power at Vichy. For eighteen months he attempted to make his way in Vichy circles, first as part of a commission

5. Anthony Sutcliffe, "A Vision of Utopia: Optimistic Foundations of Le Corbusier's Doctrine d'urbanisme," in Walden, ed., *The Open Hand*.
6. Robert Fishman, *Urban Utopias in the Twentieth Century*, 244–286 and Ermanno Ranzani, "Un incontro difficile," Domus 687: 30-45.

to study housing and then as an increasingly annoying advocate for his plan for Algiers. After a failed attempt to personally enlist Marshal Pétain in his cause and his denouncement by Algerian authorities as a Bolshevik, he left Vichy on 1943, finally subdued if not chastened in his passion for authority in any form.

After Liberation, Le Corbusier was able to take part in the Reconstruction of France, although not at the scale of another Vichy collaborator Auguste Perret, who received the commission of Le Havre. Le Corbusier paid a temporary political price for collaboration in that architects avoided employment in his office. He reorganized as a group venture first as ASCORAL (Association des Constructeurs pour une Rénovation Architecturale) a CIAM offshoot devoted to reconstruction in all its social and physical aspects. When that dissolved in 1946, he established the more limited ABTAT (Atelier des Bâtisseurs) concerned specifically with his commission of reconstruction, the Unité d'habitation at Marseilles. He prepared plans for St. Dié and La Rochelle. He was selected as French delegate to the architectural commission of the United Nations. For a moment it seemed that many years of somewhat self-imposed martyrdom had borne fruit. He told an interviewer in New York, "For thirty years I'd been a consultant talking in a desert. Since 1945 I've lead the architectural movement in France. I have arrived at a stage where things in my life flower, like a tree in season."[7]

By 1950, this moment had passed; no city had accepted his plans. The U.N. had disappointed him by making Wallace Harrison chief architect in the execution of a design he considered his own. The United States delegation to UNESCO refused to accept him on the design team. Despite this litany of official rejection and the bitterness it engendered, Le Corbusier entered on a productive period marked by the emergence of an aesthetic based on the plastic use of exposed concrete. Projects for several Unités, the chapel at Ronchamp (1953), the convent at La Tourette (1957) and the commission for the capitol of Chandigarh, India (1952) filled the decade. He also produced two defining written works in this period, the *Modulor 1 & 2* (1949/1955) and *Poème de l'angle droit* (1955).

Le Corbusier brought to bear on all his postwar architecture the research he conducted beginning in 1947 on the Modulor, a system of proportion and measure that applies the geometric properties of quadrature and the golden mean to the human body.[8] Through the ladder of golden means found in the Fibonnaci series, he created two interpolated scales, the red and blue series, that extend the measure of the body to infinitely large and small dimensions. He asserted the aesthetic value and utility of these series as standardized rules of few parts. Ultimately, he understood the Modulor as part of a great physical and metaphysical tradition extending from Renaissance anthropometrics, Vitruvius and Pythagoras.

Nothing made him happier than Albert Einstein's solicited response to the Modulor's virtue as "a scale of proportions that makes the good easy and the bad difficult."[9] The text of *Modulor 1 & 2* is a wandering paean to his dual ambition for rational certitude and communication with the immeasurable of "*l'espace indiscible.*"

7. Geoffrey Hellman, "From Within to Without," *The New Yorker*, April 26, 1947.
8. His earlier "regulating lines" used a similar geometry for proportionning but without reference to the body and without defined sequence.
9. Einstein, in *Modulor* 2, 131.

Poème de l'angle droit is an even more personal and cryptic exploration of man's relation to the cosmos rooted in the architect's attachment to nature and the various forms of spiritualism stemming from it. An *"iconostase"* of images and accompanying verse describe a dualistic structure of spirit and matter related to his Catharist heritage, populated by natural elements, archaic Greek figures and forces associated with alchemy and Surrealism. Specific images of the poem, such as the bull and the Open Hand appear as emblemata on his late architecture and painting, while its general themes permeate his dramatic use of light and water.

Toward the end of the 1950s, Le Corbusier withdrew from full practice despite the activity of his office to spend increasing periods of time at his cabin in Cap Martin. His wife died in 1957. His mother died in 1960 and he was not well. The figure he often chose to identify himself with in later life was Don Quixote, Jeanneret filling the role of Sancho Panza. To the generation in charge of the expansion of Paris and planning of La Défense in the early sixties, his was a view to be passed over, if not avoided, so that his love for Paris, that "magnificent city"[10] remained unconsummated at the scale he hoped for. His executed work from this period does not fall into a single category but much of it moves away the primitivism of his Indian architecture toward a refined handling of materials, including steel. He was at work on a project that promised to be of major significance in terms of his own development, the Venice Hospital (1965), when he died of a heart attack while swimming in the Mediterranean.

10. Le Corbusier interviewed by Hugues Desalle, 15 May 1965, in *The Final Testament of Père Corbu*, trans. Ivan Žaknič, 127.

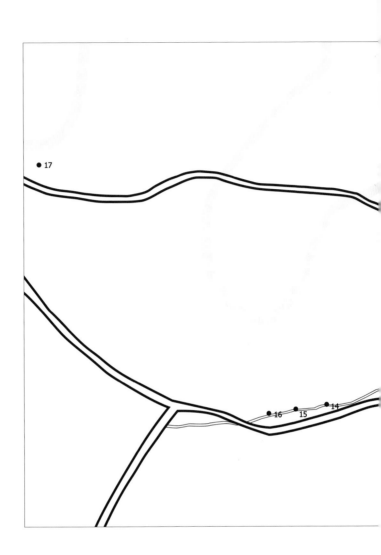

PARIS

1. Villa Planeix (Planex)
2. Annexe du Palais du Peuple
3. Asile Flottant
4. Cité de Refuge
   (L'armée du Salut)
5. Atelier Ozenfant
6. Pavillon Suisse
7. Pavillon du Brésil
8. Villas La Roche-Jeanneret
9. Immeuble et Appartement de
   Le Corbusier
10. Villas Lipchitz-Miestchaninoff
11. Villa Cook
12. Villa Ternisien
13. Maisons Jaoul
14. Villa Besnus (Ker-ka-ré)
15. Villa Stein (de Monzie)
16. La Petite Maison de Weekend
   (Villa Henfel, Villa Félix)
17. Villa Savoye
   (Savoie, les Heures Claires)

VILLA PLANEIX (PLANEX)

1924–1928

Le Corbusier and Pierre
Jeanneret

ADDRESS
24 bis, boulevard Masséna
Paris 75013

ACCESS
Private residence visible from
the boulevard and from rue
Regnault. Interior accessible by
appointment. Alterations have
been made in the studio door
and square studio window.
Subdivisions have been made
in the interior. By appointment
only. Tel 01.45.83.73.50.

DIRECTIONS
Walk east along boulevard
Masséna from the Porte d'Ivry
métro stop.

LOCALE
The boulevard leads east to a
zone of warehouses along the
Seine and west to a strip of
large, modern apartment com-
plexes. Slightly to the north is
Le Corbusier's Cité de Refuge.
See the Cité entry for a more
extended tour.

Planeix is perhaps the most urbane of the houses
that, in the 1920s, defined Le Corbusier's purist
phase. Choosing as a model the elite city dwelling of
the past, the architects made Planeix culturally contextual not as a good neighbor to the adjoining buildings, but as a patrician critique. The architects chose
a classical and particularly Palladian mode of urban
house and inverted many of its features according to
the Five Points.[1] Pilotis and a glass wall replace the
traditional solid and rusticated base. Roof terraces
assume the position of the attic story, the terrace
handrail delineating the lost cornice line. While
these transformations represent didactically the
capabilities of concrete construction, other displace-
ments have a nonconstructive logic. The Palladian
tripartite organization of the facade has been
extremely distorted in the balance of window and
wall. The placement of the private functions of
the bed and bath in the projecting loggia converts
this classical intersection of urban and private realm
into one telegraphing surveillance. Stanislaus von
Moos has suggested that this enclosed projection is
also a conscious reversal of the huge open loggia of

1. Colin Rowe makes this general
   argument regarding Palladio in
   Mathematics of the Ideal Villa,
   2–24.
2. Stanislaus von Moos, Le Corbusier,
   Elements of a Synthesis, 81.
3. For the history of the project see
   Gilles Ragot and Mathilde Dion, *Le
   Corbusier en France*, 34–5.

Adolf Loos' house for Tristan Tzara in Monmartre (1926–27).[2] In ironic comment on Corbusier's rhetoric of light and air, a building permit was denied the original plans because of the inadequate ventilation of the bath and bedroom. The cyclopean window and side lights were added in response. The main residence takes its traditional place on the piano nobile, but the artist studio above dominates the composition through the central figure of the papal balcony. The vertical windows at the periphery of the facade disengage the house from the street wall of its less distinguished neighbors. Even the glass wall and pilotis at street level send mixed signals. The four columns recall the court of a Roman house, but the glass wall divides the room in two, half inside, half out. There is no visible continuation from the central garage entrance to the main floor.

The physical and semiotic structure of the front facade of Villa Planeix serves as a foil to the flexibility and openness found within. The client, M. Planeix, was active in formulating the open plan. A sculptor and painter by avocation, Planeix had a business making funerary monuments which expanded in the aftermath of World War I. Of modest means, he consistently exhorted the architects to consider the future rearrangement and expansion of the house.[3] His shifting scenario for the eventual program was a real test of the potential fluidity of plan implied in the diagram of the Dom-ino. The house was finally built to include two duplex rental ateliers at street level as suggested by Jeanneret. The expansive glazing of the rear garden facade, the open plan of salon and studio, and the location of the entrance stair outside the house all fulfilled the need for flexibility. This planning also reinforced the connection of interior to the landscape: the main rooms of the house center not on the front loggia of the street facade, but on the two-story garden at the rear. Bordered by a railroad spur, the irregular, steeply sloped site features picturesque paths around a large tree. The house is a miniature palace entered from an elaborate backyard.

Le Corbusier's Cité de Refuge. See the Cité entry for a more extended tour.

1. Colin Rowe makes this general argument regarding Palladio in *Mathematics of the Ideal Villa*, 2–24.
2. Stanislaus von Moos, Le Corbusier, *Elements of a Synthesis*, 81.
3. For the history of the project see Gilles Ragot and Mathilde Dion, *Le Corbusier en France*, 34–5.

section

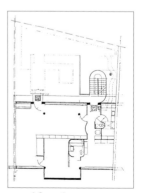

second floor plan

ANNEXE DU PALAIS DU PEUPLE

1926–1927

Le Corbusier and Pierre Jeanneret

ADDRESS
29, rue des Cordelières
Paris 75013

ACCESS
Le Corbusier's addition is
visible from the interior courtyard. Much has been altered
including the windows and roof
terrace, but the siting and
massing remain. Originally the
dormitory walls were faced in
white and cobalt blue tile.

DIRECTIONS
Métro Gobelins or Corvisart

LOCALE
The Salvation Army building is
on a side street. The annex is
in the rear, entered through an
archway and alley.

ASILE FLOTTANT

1929

Le Corbusier

ADDRESS
Quai d'Austerlitz
75013 Paris

ACCESS
Visible from quai outside
the railroad station Gare
d'Austerlitz

DIRECTIONS
Métro Gare d'Austerlitz

LOCALE
The barge is located north of
Pont de Bercy on the Seine.

CITÉ DE REFUGE (L'ARMÉE DU SALUT)
1929–1933

In the Salvation Army, Le Corbusier found a client in sympathy with his own social ideas, derived in part from such social utopian models as Fourierism and a direct encounter with Soviet socialist housing. At the time of these commissions, his politics, while ambiguous, tended toward the syndicalist, based on the value of labor organized and administered from above. As Brian Brace Taylor elucidates, Le Corbusier's faith in authority and order as key to social reform attracted him to the Army's paternalistic organization in the service of social engineering.[4] The Army's program to save the faltering by educating them in the fundamentals of human existence harmonized with his conviction that "to know how to dwell is to know how to live" (*savoir d'habiter, savoir vivre*). The Army's transient population even paralleled the propertyless nomadic resident of his utopian city plans. Recognizing a potentially fruitful client-architect relationship and the state's dependence on private institutions to supply social services, Le Corbusier recommended to Minister Locheur that the Army be appointed people's commissariat of housing. Out of the architect's and

Le Corbusier and Pierre Jeanneret with furnishings by Charlotte Perriand; dormitory wall with brise-soleil of 1958 largely by Jeanneret

ADDRESS
12, rue Cantagrel
75013 Paris

ACCESS
The interior of the building is renovated, but not restored. For now, the exterior remains as it has since 1975, with the brise-soleil addition of 1948 rendered in heretical shades of the chosen colors. The public rooms of the interior may be visited in the afternoon and evening. Salvation Army store building can be visited daily before 5 PM.
Tel 01.53.61.82.35.

DIRECTIONS
Métro Bibliothèque or Métro Porte-d'Ivry

The Cité borders the warehouse district along the Seine to the south of the bridge. An itinerary starts at Gare d'Austerlitz and its adjoining structures by E. Freyssinet, descends to the barge, and goes south along the water to the exhibition hall at Quai de la Gare, continuing past Dominique Perrault's new Bibliothèque de France on to the Cité. Behind the Cité de Refuge slab and connected to it is the Centre Espoir (1978) by G. Candilis and B. Verrye, 39–43, rue du Chevaleret. Le Corbusier's Maison Planeix is located several blocks away, on blvd. Masséna.

client's shared belief in the moral effects of salubrious living conditions came this series of projects.

Le Corbusier executed three built projects for the Salvation Army and planned an unrealized quartier of housing named Cité d'hébergement, which would have extended from the Cité de Refuge headquarters. All the commissions were obtained through the continuing patronage of Princess Edmond de Polignac, née Winaretta Singer (of the sewing machine dynasty), who had previously commissioned a villa in Neuilly which was never built. Like most of Le Corbusier's clients of the 1920s, she was attached to the Parisian artistic intelligentsia, in this case to a circle of composers which included Maurice Ravel and Le Corbusier's brother Albert Jeanneret. Through her continuing financial contributions to the building projects, the Princess was able to secure the jobs for Le Corbusier, as well as the sincere support of her friend Commissioner Albin Peyron. The original headquarters included a private suite for her use.

The first project of Le Corbusier, the Annex to the People's Palace, is a dormitory addition to an existing facility. A different architect, M. Préau had already established the programmatic parameters, such as the number of beds. Le Corbusier then rendered the dormitory as a collective Maison Citrohan, particularly reminiscent of his 1924 project for Beaulieu-sur-Mer on stilt-like pilotis. Three dormitory floors are framed by communal gardens on the roof and below. Here the Corbusian prototype for the individual family is enlarged and altered for the transient society of the Army residents.

The second project, the renovation of a concrete barge, provided a ready-made metaphor: the city of refuge as boat. Pointedly named the *Asile Flottant*, "floating asylum," it was conceived as shelter for vagrants and prostitutes during winter nights and a playground for the poor children of Paris during the summer. The architect designed a dormitory with bunks for 160, a dining room, kitchen, baths, separate apartments for the director and crew, and a roof terrace supported on concrete pilotis. Le Corbusier saw the ocean liner as a model of community in which individual freedom and collective pleasure are accommodated by a streamlined machine. In the asylum, he transferred this vision to the needs of an underclass and the reality of a barge left from World War I, creating a kind of primal ark for a heterotopia.

The final project, the Cité de Refuge, was a complex community on a grand scale. It contained separate dormitories and dining rooms for men and women, single rooms for mothers with children, a nursery, workshops, assembly rooms, library and counseling facilities. Except for the nursery, the program remains fairly intact. In the search for a building form resonant with the program, Le Corbusier in a sense turned the purist villa inside out, discarding the envelope and placing the geometric episodes of plan on a podium framed by the dormitory slab. In this it resembles contemporary Soviet projects and Le Corbusier's own contemporaneous compositions for the Swiss Pavilion, League of Nations, and Centrosoyus. Here each piece has a specific programmatic and material identity and also a role in a larger narrative of moral renewal.

The backdrop for the figural activity, but also the dominant piece by virtue of size and program, is the dormitory slab. Its primary characteristics, namely its size and its sheathing, both held great significance for the project. The first schemes for a reduced site called for a series of smaller slabs and courtyards perpendicular to the current axis, a strategy that allowed for incremental expansion within a more traditionally Parisian morphology.[5] The design for the expanded site produced the seemingly rationalized single slab. In fact, the linear repetitive structure allowed for great economy in construction. Employing Taylorized, assembly-line methods, separate crews moved sequentially along the slab completing the structure ahead of schedule. Although the original design called for a uniform monolith, zoning regulations eventually forced terracing on the north side, duplex penthouses on the roof, and slight setbacks on the south which generated a tilt backward (.04 m overall) in the huge glass wall.

4. The authoritative study is Brian Brace Taylor, *Le Corbusier: the City of Refuge*. See also Peter Serenyi, in Serenyi, *Le Corbusier in Perspective* and William Curtis, *Ideas and Forms*, 99–102.

5. Taylor, *The City of Refuge*, 43, 48-9.

6. *Le Temps*, 8 Dec. 1933, quoted in Taylor, *The City of Refuge*, 111.

7. Ibid.

dining hall, Cité de Refuge

The original glass sheathing, since altered, was the physical manifestation of a totalizing system of environmental control. The intended parts were an internal system of forced air, both temperature-controlled and humidified called "exact respiration" (*la respiration exacte*) and a hermetically sealed, double-glazed curtain wall (*mur neutralisant*) with a continuous cavity for the circulation of temperature controlled air. Similar to the life-supports proposed for the Centrosoyus, the mechanical and material system would maintain a constant temperature while providing maximum light and purified air. Like a bio-mechanical skin, the wall would mediate between the internal organs and external conditions.

At the building's inauguration, attended by the President of the Republic, the newspaper *Le Temps* reported, "This edifice, whose facade appears first of all like an immense glass window . . . has the appearance of a beautiful ship, where everything is clean, comfortable, useful, and gay."[6] To this layered imagery Le Corbusier added the metaphor of a "factory of good" (*usine de bien*), explicitly linking spiritual purification and mechanistic functioning. As *Le Temps* observed, the intended transformation of the individual occurs through the mechanism of the architectural promenade:

> The turntable at the entrance [is a] long counter where unhappy people will come to deposit their misery like the rich deposit their valuables at the windows in a bank. In small private offices like confessionals, they will confide in officers on duty at all hours, day or night. In this kind of 'central social station' or 'clearinghouse' one will direct them on their way.[7]

Despite this praise for the building's metaphoric intent, both the Army and the public criticized the wall for its functional flaws. Unforeseen expenses, primarily the thirty-five-meter-deep piles required by unstable soil, resulted in the elimination of both the double-glazing and the central cooling plant. In the executed design, fresh air was pumped directly into the building without pre-cooling so that the dormitories overheated in the summer. The lack of a return air system aggravated the problem with

view of approach from rue Cantagrel

insufficient circulation. Deaf to complaints by the residents, Le Corbusier remained committed to the technology and its aesthetic formulation in sealed glass. The Salvation Army and city building authorities overrode his protests, however, installing operable windows in 1935. In the renovation after the bombing of World War II, Le Corbusier and Jeanneret abandoned environmental control for a more adaptive composite wall of fixed panels and operable wood windows screened by a shallow, hence largely ineffective, sunbreak. The contested issue of this wall was the colors, which were executed to the dissatisfaction of the architects.

The original polemic has faded as the curtain-walled, climate-controlled, high-rise building has come to predominate; but the urban strategy retains its force. Viewed from the north, the slab at mid-block glides above the sea of urban fabric, dropping almost miraculously at its end to the scale of the infill site on rue de Chevralet. From the south, a collection of independent objects of disparate size composed through their spatial proximity appears part of the assemblage of the city framed by the slab behind. From the perspective of the podium, the city literally drops away, the entry sequence dominates and the journey begins.

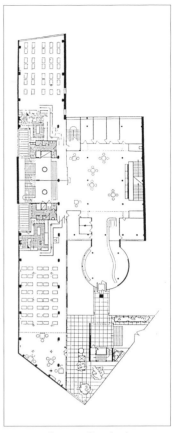

plan at podium level

entrance Cité de Refuge

Le Corbusier, Amédée Ozenfant

ADDRESS
53, avenue Reille
75014 Paris

ACCESS
Private residence visible from
the street. Interior visits by
appointment. The original
saw-tooth skylights and first-
floor cornice are missing; the
garage door has been filled in,
a new door added at the top of
the stair, and the second-story
door made a window.

DIRECTIONS
Métro stops Alésia or Cité
Universitaire, line RER B.

LOCALE
The neighborhood contains some
of the nineteenth-century studio-
workshops that influenced Le
Corbusier's early houses, as well
as buildings contemporaneous
with the Atelier Ozenfant. Of special interest are the private
houses of rue Villa Seurat,
including nos. 4 and 89 by A.
Lurçat (1926), no. 5 by Bertrand
(1926), and Maison Orloff
(1926) and Maison Muter
(1928) by A. Perret. Maison
Guggenbuhl by A. Lurçat (1926)
is at 14, rue Nansouty, and Maison Braque (1927) by A. Perret
is at 2, rue du Douanier.
    A possible itinerary continues
through Parc Montsouris to rue
de la Cité Universitaire (no. 3 is
by M. Roux-Spitz [1930]), then
down to boulevard Jourdan
and Cité Universitaire, to Le
Corbusier's Swiss and Brazil
Pavilions.

The client for this studio-residence was Amédée
Ozenfant, Le Corbusier's mentor in the development
of Purism. Ozenfant was a painter and a critic who
moved easily among arts and industries, designing
a streamlined automobile body called the Hispano-
Suiza (1912) and establishing an aesthetic journal *l'Élan*
(1915). He made several ventures into the world of
fashion with the designer Germaine Bongard, the
sister of Paul Poiret, and then with his Russian wife.
For Ozenfant, at least, these interests were never
contradictory.[8] Following their introduction through
Auguste Perret, Ozenfant encouraged Le Corbusier
to paint seriously and the two began painting
together in the evenings. Together they produced the
manifesto *Après le cubisme* (1918) to accompany an
exhibition of their purist paintings at the gallery of
Germaine Bongard. While clearly indebted to cubist
principles of simultaneity, the artists presented
Purism as a restoration of the primary forms of
nature to an art rendered abstract and non-system-
atic by Cubism. The aesthetic of order and geometry

represented by refined objects of daily use (*objet-types*) was timely in its relation to the socio-political calls to order which pervaded Paris after the Armistice.[9] With Paul Dermée, they founded the magazine *l'Esprit Nouveau* (1920–25) in which they published a more complex purist argument for modernity entwining notions of art, industry and marketplace. After a period of intellectual tension, the seven-year relationship came to an end, ostensibly in a dispute over the display of paintings, including their own, in the Villa La Roche.

In the pages of *l'Esprit Nouveau*, and at the Salon d'Automne (1922), Le Corbusier proposed several versions of a universal dwelling called the Maison Citrohan, based on the potentials and demands of the machine age. Conceived as a standardized object of mass production, it had a reinforced concrete structure, metal sash windows and prefabricated details, all designed according to a module. For the organization of this "architectural mechanism," Le Corbusier looked to various sources, including vernacular Mediterranean types and a small bistro he frequented in Paris which had a double-height salon and small kitchen tucked beneath a mezzanine. As Reyner Banham has observed, however, it was the nineteenth-century Parisian studio-workshop that provided Le Corbusier with the directness of the vernacular, the spatial formula of the café, and the forms of industry together in a single entity.[10] Atelier Ozenfant, as such a Parisian studio-workshop, was a particularly apt program with which to begin the exploration of yet untested ideas of dwelling. The house had service quarters and garage on the ground level; a piano nobile entered directly from the spiral stair with master apartment in the front and a gallery at the rear; and a top floor studio.

The generic aspects of the Citrohan dominate the expression of the building: concrete floor slabs and piers, glass facades with industrial metal sashes, non-bearing partitions freely disposed, a dominant double-height studio space with mezzanine and circulation along the edge. Elements particular to the house evoke related industrial sources, such as the

8. For a discussion of Ozenfant and fashion see Mark Wigley, *White Walls and Designer Dresses*, 182–84.

9. Christopher Green in Raeburn and Wilson, *Le Corbusier: Architect of the Century*, 119 and Charles Jencks, *Le Corbusier and the Tragic View of Architecture*, 50–52. Also see entry Pavilon de l'Esprit Nouveau.

10. Reyner Banham, *Theory and Design in the First Machine Age*, 217–18.

11. For urban context see "Casa Atelier Ozenfant," *Domus* 687: 39–42.

12. The idea of crystal is prominent in Purism. See Amédée Ozenfant and Charles-Édouard Jeanneret, "Vers La Cristalle," *La Peinture Moderne*, 137–38.

13. Tim Benton, *The Villas of Le Corbusier*, 31–43 and Curtis, *Ideas and Forms*, 104–109.

Corner view

original skylights now gone, or the metal ship's ladder leading to the library "cockpit." This vocabulary sets it apart from its neighboring arts and craft houses, although its relation to the street is similar.[11] Unlike the architect's contemporaneous Villa Besnus, no underlying neo-classical model tempers the whole, although pieces of plan are rendered as evocative fragments of classical figures—such as the half-apse entry.

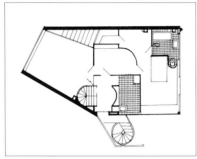

First floor plan

The idiosyncratic character of the house arises from this use of halves as a means of adapting the rectangular and frontal Citrohan to the irregular corner site. The facades have an underlined symmetry about the corner structure, despite the lack of internal symmetry in plan or program. The two doors, two strip windows, and two square windows are mirror images, reflected and folded across a center line. As halves of a symmetrical whole, each facade is like one of the fragmented half-figures in plan. The paradoxical consequence of this doubling of the surface is the reading of the studio as a transparent, cubic volume, or purist "crystal,"[12] set with in the block of the building.

The other feature which most distinguishes Ozenfant from the typical Parisian studio and its contemporary versions by Perret and Lurçat is its tortuous procession, the direct forerunner of the expanded architectural promenade of Villa La Roche.[13] It ascends from the spiral stair barely touching the ground, through the compressed foyer to the expansive studio inundated with light overlooking the greenery of avenue Reille and the reservoir. The final, "reserved view" is obtained by climbing through the trap door at the top of the studio ladder to a small roof garden. The occupant who follows this vertical trail is the cerebral artist, as much Le Corbusier as Ozenfant.

PAVILLON SUISSE

1930–1933

Le Corbusier and Pierre
Jeanneret

ADDRESS
7, boulevard Jourdan
Cité Universitaire Internationale
de Paris
75014 Paris

ACCESS
The building has undergone a
major restoration as of 2005,
with yet another renovation of
the window wall. One of the
student rooms is visitable, as
are the ground-floor public
rooms. Tel 01.44.16.10.10.
www.fondationsuisse.ciup.fr.
Entrance fee: 10 francs.

DIRECTIONS
Métro stop Cité Universitaire,
line RER B. The Swiss Pavilion
is at the eastern end of a row
of international dormitories
facing onto an athletic field.
Le Corbusier intended visitors
to arrive by car on the north
side, in front of the stone wall.

LOCALE
The architects' Swiss and
Brazil pavilions are both
located in the Cité Internationale
of the Cité Universitaire. The
campus has other buildings of
note, including the Netherlands
College of W. M. Dudok
(1930). From the curved wall
of the Swiss Pavilion continue
along the driveway about 200
meters to reach the Brazil
Pavilion. For an extended
itinerary see Atelier Ozenfant.

Under the guidance of Professor Füter of Zurich and the influence of Raoul La Roche, Sigfried Giedion, and Karl Moser, a federation of Swiss universities awarded Le Corbusier and Jeanneret the commission for a dormitory for Swiss students on a newly formed campus of international hostels. The award was intended as compensation for the disappointment of the League of Nations Competition, where the architects were initially granted but finally denied the prize. Despite its small size and limited budget, the Swiss Pavilion emerged as a major work, influential to the Modern Movement.

Together with the contemporaneous Cité de Refuge and related works by international architects such as Walter Gropius and Mosei Ginzberg, the building introduced an organization based on the expression of program elements as independent volumes. No single building envelope subsumes the parts. Here the particular format of the parts— slab on pilotis with a free-formed public zone beneath—became the model for a multitude of postwar buildings. For Le Corbusier, these parts and their assembly had social agendas. Together they described the intended housing of linear apartments in Le Corbusier's utopian Radiant City (*Ville Radieuse*) of 1931. In both utopian city and dormitory, single-story apartments are raised above a continuous landscape on pilotis and organized along a corridor in relation to light and view. Collective facilities for housekeeping and recreation as well as workshops and meeting rooms liberate and ameliorate daily life. The collective facilities for the pavilion as built were reduced to the modest refectory.

The three material systems of the building reinforce the logic of the plan.[14] The dormitory floors are of steel frame, "dry" assembly, meaning that the parts and connections were factory produced. A radical departure from the idea of free plan, the structural bay is the module of the dormitory room, 2.7 x 4.0 m. Le Corbusier thought of the rooms as packaged cells inserted into the frame and wrapped in lead plates for sound proofing (to little effect). The exterior sheathing of the frame is a glass skin (*pan de verre*) facing south, conceived as a bio-technical machine for providing maximum light, air, and view. In contrast to the architects' other experimental curtain walls, this one had operable sliding panels from the beginning, defined as square openings of 2.5 meters within horizontal fenestration. Overheating still remained a problem and the building has been reglazed twice with modifications to the surface and blinds. Reinforcing the logic of the south wall, the northern wall along the corridor has punched windows in a stone facing. The side walls are blank, suggesting that the slab is but a fragment of a possible utopian environment.

This steel cage sits on top of a poured concrete table of slab and pilotis. The rendering of the concrete as a sensual support to the floating glass is fundamental to the expression; yet, these pilotis were originally conceived as

14. Edward Ford, *The Details of Modern Architecture* 1: 250–51 and Le Corbusier, *Oeuvre Complète* 2: 87–89.

15. Le Corbusier, *New World of Space*, 50.

16. For column placement see Barry Maitland, "The Grid" in *Oppositions* 15/16: 111–12 and Le Corbusier, *Oeuvre Complète* 2: 79.

17. For structural analysis see Santiago Calatrava, "The Open Hands—Architecture Engineering," in Palazzolo and Vio, *In the Footsteps of Le Corbusier*, 190–91.

18. *Gazette de Lausanne* in Le Corbusier, *Oeuvre Complète* 2: 76.

19. Richard Moore, "Alchemical Symbolism in the Poem of the Right Angle," *Oppositions* 19/20: 117–19.

northern facade

slender steel posts extending the frame system. The Swiss engineer Ritter questioned the ability of the steel pilotis to take wind loads and called for their elimination. Le Corbusier persisted but changed their form to curved concrete of dimension generous enough to also contain the vertical drainage. The soil conditions required that the foundation piers be sunk sixty meters, justifying in Le Corbusier's mind the choice of pilotis.

As a third material system, a load-bearing wall of rough rubble in combination with interior columns, supports the single-story roof. While the monumentalized pilotis have a visceral presence, only the wall physically engages the landscape. Sinuous curves had recently appeared in Le Corbusier's viaduct cities for Brazil and in his paintings of women, but they had never so obviously appeared in his architecture. He cryptically described them as "acoustic" as if to suggest the synesthetic connections of sound and space made by the Symbolists. He explained that given the small site, "the slight curve in the wall gives the suggestion of tremendous extent and seems to pick up by its concave surface, the whole surrounding landscape."[15]

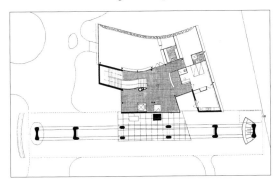

On the ground floor interior, the curved lines of columns and partitions extend the logic of the acoustic. Le Corbusier described them as "deliberately deformed," creating a space that is at once layered and fluid.[16] The columns, like the pilotis, are irregular in shape and varied in placement and color. Between the light and dark gray columns along the refectory is a perceptible shear line. The cause of the

ground floor plan

deformations seems to be the coming together of stair tower, slab, and bridge structures from the floors above.[17] The result suggests that this confluence of volumes has warped space itself.

On the opening of the pavilion, critics attacked Le Corbusier for his materialism. He fueled the attack himself with a rhetoric stressing the mechanistic functioning of the material systems in the production of a hygienic environment. The published images of the monk-like cells of the dormitory and the vigorous male students lounging under the shade of muscular pilotis suggested a complex set of values, but the mechanistic overtones of the glass wall, the concrete, and the lobby photomural of microscopic nature, convinced some that this was a soulless vision that could pervert young minds.[18] In retrospect, the biomorphic forms, composite structure, and natural materials embrace the primitive and even the mystical. The refectory mural painted by Le Corbusier as part of a postwar restoration in 1948 provides a lens through which to view the building's more naturalistic aspects. Typical of his late art, it is loaded with natural and mythological imagery derived from his *Poème de l'angle droit*, a personal cosmology. On the right side of the mural, an open hand holds a winged female creature, perhaps Capricorn. To the left is Medusa and a crescent figure, perhaps a moon or the head of a bull or Minotaur. One reading of the mural suggests a kind of alchemical transmutation of matter.[19] The inscription by the symbolist poet Stéphane Mallarmé helps link this mysticism with the earlier acoustic shapes of the building. The complete stanza of the inscription reads:

Stairwell looking to lobby

> *O rêveuse, pour que je plonge*
> *Au pur delice sans chemin,*
> *Sache par un subtil mensonge,*
> *Garder mon aile dans ta main.*

> My dreamer, that I could plunge
> Into sheer, errant delight,
> Know how by a subtle lie
> To keep my wing in your hand.

PAVILLON DU BRÉSIL

1957–1959

The Brazil Pavilion was a joint commission of the Brazilian architect Lúcio Costa, who provided the initial proposal, and Le Corbusier, who oversaw design development and construction. Twenty years previously, Le Corbusier had joined Costa and a group of young native architects in search of a modern Brazilian expression. The initial result was an energetic interpretation of a Corbusian vocabulary as seen in the Ministry of Education Building in Rio (1936), for which the paternal master took rather excessive credit. In this case, Costa maintained his authorship and the pavilion as built subscribes closely to his proposal, although shifted in its orientation from west to east. Costa's design intentions focused particularly on the lobby sequence which he was able to execute on a site visit to Paris in 1956. The mélange of national styles still in evidence at the campus underlines the challenge of bringing a modern national expression to Paris and the anxiety it caused the architects, in particular Le Corbusier, who tended to the formulation of universals.[20]

The utopian universals of Le Corbusier's Radiant City prevailed at the Brazil Pavilion, in that it is

Le Corbusier and Lúcio Costa with André Wogenscky, Jacques Michel, and Fernand Gardien; furnishings by Charlotte Perriand

ADDRESS
4, avenue de la Porte Gentilly
Cité Universitaire
75014 Paris

ACCESS
Public rooms are visitable with permission of lobby attendant. For an extensive tour, direct requests to the director of the pavilion. Tel 01.58.10.23.00, fax 01.45.81.36.60. www.maisondubresil.org. The building has undergone major restoration as of 2005.

DIRECTIONS
Métro stop Cité Universitaire on line RER B. The closest gate is at l'avenue de la Porte-de-Gentilly at the east end of the campus. It is also 200 m from the Swiss Pavilion.

20. For correspondence between
architects see Ragot and Dion, *Le
Corbusier en France*, 76–8.

the direct descendant of the Swiss Pavilion. In both, a dormitory slab on pilotis straddles the freely expressed volumes of communal rooms. The pilotis simultaneously grant the slab a monumental identity and relieve the ground from that presence, allowing for continuous view and passage through the campus greenery. At the Brazil Pavilion, the program also included a series of individual music rooms furnished by Charlotte Perriand.

The differences between the two pavilions reflect Le Corbusier's own gradual shift away from the machine aesthetic still embodied in the Swiss Pavilion's glass wall. Implied in this shift toward the primitive is a certain loss of faith in modern techno-

view on approach

logical culture and a renewed interest in the individual's direct connection to a spiritually charged nature. Economics also figured. Le Corbusier first conceived the structure as steel frame as at the Swiss Pavilion, but the postwar price of steel caused the change to a rough concrete. In the form of balconies, the concrete sun-breaks define the individual cell on the exterior and grant each student a framed connection to the landscape. This occupiable wall was developed concurrently for the Unité d'habitation of 1952, in which Le Corbusier's late utopian goals are most clearly stated.

The regionalist aspect of the pavilion can be distinguished from these characteristics of the late Unité. The colors, chosen by Costa, were described by Le Corbusier as "of Brazil." The intense contrasts in form and quality of light of the entry sequence

entrance lobby

and lobby seem a conscious evocation of the sensual aspects of the culture and its indigenous landscape. A dark, walled court with a ritualistic stele fills the space beneath the pilotis. One looks from a dark stone path into a curved glass cage bathed in a pool of light. An almost surreal quality figures in the entry sequence where every volume tilts; every curve induces a countercurve. Even the dormitory slab is not rectangular but rather tapered at either end and seemingly bent on the western side across the hinge of the central balconies. Costa and Le Corbusier intended to avoid simultaneously the failures of an International Style and its obverse, nationalistic expression. In so doing they raised the more elusive issue of the culture of utopia.

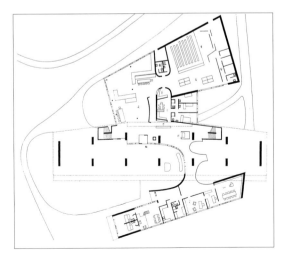

ground floor plan

Le Corbusier and Pierre
Jeanneret; 1928 renovation
with Charlotte Perriand

ADDRESS
8–10, square du Docteur-
Blanche
75016 Paris

ACCESS
The Fondation Le Corbusier and
Le Corbusier Archive are located
in the houses.[21] For visiting
hours and contact information,
go to www.fondationlecor-
busier.asso.fr. Both buildings
are closed Sundays, Monday
mornings, a part of August,
and public holidays.
Tel 01.42.88.41.53.

DIRECTIONS
The Villa is a five-minute walk
from Métro stop Jasmin, line
#9 or Michel-Ange, Auteuil.

The history of the adjoining villas' design and construction is long, complicated, and well documented.[22] Le Corbusier acted as the developer, finding the site and clients and negotiating acquisition of the property from the Banque Immobilière de Paris, a large land holder in the area. The development of the entire neighborhood of Auteuil at this period made the site attractive to the architect—who always saw his work in as large a context as possible—but also complicated issues of site lines and privacy as the area was developed. Le Corbusier could not obtain his desired south-facing lot, and the final, north-facing site came with height and depth limitations and an acacia tree that both Le Corbusier and the neighbors wanted to preserve. The early U-shaped schemes for three or more clients eventually became the L-shaped villa for the bachelor banker Raoul La Roche and the adjoining house for Le Corbusier's brother, Albert Jeanneret, his new Swedish wife, Lotti Raaf, and her three daughters.

The two clients fit Le Corbusier's initial conception, as outlined in his proposal to the bank, of an enlightened clientele for whom he would build an experimental housing estate. Albert was a composer and musician trained in Geneva and at the Dalcroze Institute in Hellerau, Lotti a journalist. Le Corbusier met La Roche through his friend and financial backer, Max Dubois, at a party of Swiss émigrés, after which La Roche became a benefactor of the journal *l'Esprit Nouveau* and a collector of purist paintings. Le Corbusier and his partner in the journal, Amédée Ozenfant, acted as bidders for La Roche at the Kahnweiler auctions of the early 1920s, acquiring for La Roche a group of paintings by Braque, Picasso, Léger, and Gris that now hang in the Museum of Contemporary Art in Basel. After visiting the Villa Schwob, La Roche commissioned the architects to build him a villa with a gallery to hold his new collection. While Le Corbusier's client relations were often strained, that with La Roche was uniquely positive, culminating in the bequest of his house. He rewarded the architects for the almost timely completion of the house with a Citroën car. Le Corbusier reciprocated with the gift of an album of original drawings.[23]

The differing household requirements of the clients did not dissuade Le Corbusier from his intent to treat the estate as a unity rather than as a conventional row of houses. This coherence can be described in sum as the purist villa, a complex of form and program. In both houses, very small rooms of specific function—bed, bath and kitchen—are set off against living spaces whose expansiveness is manufactured through architectural device and color as much as through square footage. Also in both, the experience of the top level and roof is privileged, in keeping with the traditional position of the piano nobile but with additional emphasis on the essential joys of light and the private domain. In the Villa Jeanneret, the reversed layout (*plan renversé*), as Le Corbusier dubbed it, places the bedrooms on the floor below the living area, which in turn connects to a roof garden protected from view so that Lotti could sunbathe in the nude. At La Roche, to the

LOCALE

This neighborhood in the sixteenth arrondissement was developed during the first third of the century as an affluent and stylish residential quarter. It consequently contains many buildings of interest in relation to Le Corbusier. Works by Hector Guimard include Hôtel Guimard (1910), at 122 ave Mozart; Villa Flore at no. 120 (1924); no. 3 (1922), on Square Jasmin; and 18, rue Heinrich Heine. Down the street from the Foundation is rue Mallet-Stevens (1927), with houses designed by that architect at nos. 7, 10, 11, and 12. No. 65, rue La Fontaine is by Henri Sauvage (1927). More Guimard houses are located to the east on rue La Fontaine: nos. 17–16, nos. 17–21 (1912), and no. 60. Avenue de Versailles boasts no. 25 by J. Ginsberg and B. Lubetkin (1932), no. 29 by Boesse (1929), and no. 142 by Guimard (1905). To the north of La Roche is 25 bis, rue Franklin by Auguste Perret (1903). Le Corbusier worked for Perret there. A possible itinerary continues south to Le Corbusier's apartment house at 24, rue Nungesser-et-Coli.

ground (bottom) and first floor (top) plans

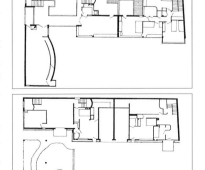

gallery ramp

roof terrace

atrium

east of the entrance hall were small, private quarters with a so-called purist bedroom. To the west side were spaces considered public enough to open to visitors twice a week, recorded for history in a guest book. A sequence of spaces beginning at the gate to the cul-de-sac moves through the central hall and gallery, culminating in the skylit library.

The term *promenade architecturale* used to describe the path through La Roche refers to this sequence of spaces and also to the multiplicity of views. Carefully placed wall openings, stairs and balconies divide the space and surfaces of the hall into layers with implied axes in a kind of three-dimensional plaid. Le Corbusier's purist paintings explored in two dimensions a similar gridding and asymmetrical balance. The overlapping of squares in plan and section generates related centerlines and symmetries. For example, the interior atrium balcony and the exterior gallery balcony are symmetrical about a centerline that is also the edge of the dining room. The exterior stepping profile of the villa can be understood as the shifting backward of cubic forms. The promenade orchestrates movement across these layers in relation to fixed moments such as balconies.

Related to the divisions of surface is the effect of cubist *coulisse*, in reference to the moments of great depth that occur through the gaps in the overlapping planes of cubist paintings.[24] The cuts in the wall surfaces of the atrium create such an effect, as for example, where space rushes through the open railing to the darkly painted library. Standing on the stair looking diagonally across the hall to the exterior, it seems the entire house and its surroundings impinge on the foyer.

In the gallery, in addition to the surface strategies of the cut and the layer, paint is applied according to Le Corbusier's principle of "architectural camouflage" in which color is used to allow "the affirmation of certain volumes or, on the contrary their effacement."[25] The walls and furnishings together create configurations reminiscent of purist still-life contours. Framing these events in a new spatial expression is the ramp, which appears here for the first time in his domestic work.[26]

The current furnishings of the room include the fixed table and shelving executed in collaboration with Charlotte Perriand as part of the 1928 overhaul of the gallery which had suffered from inadequate heat and light. Some pieces like the *casier standard* cabinet, *grand confort* seating and *chaise longue* were designed with

gallery

Perriand, while others were selected objects of mass production such as the Thonet chairs and department store curtains. As a montage of objects all valued for their extension of human needs into pure form, the original decor presents the animating spirit of Purism.[27]

The forms and strategies of the villas have a number of possible sources both historical and contemporary. Le Corbusier described the house in his Four Compositions as "picturesque and full of movement but requiring classical hierarchy to discipline it."[28] He used his terms precisely, for the siting of the villa on the cul-de-sac recalls the picturesque urbanism of Camillo Sitte, while the controlled activity of view suggests the *picturesque grèc* described by Auguste Choisy.[29] The entrance hall evokes references from the Pompeian House of the Tragic Poet to the multilevel entrance halls advocated by Hermann Muthesius.[30] The gallery facade recalls even Le Corbusier's own Villa Schwob. The house adopts also contemporary images from factories, trains and ships. However, all these sources are evident not as quotations but in sublimated form as part of a search for an authentic architecture whose expression exceeds its technique. As Sigfried Giedion, an early visitor to the house remarked, "a new statics which had been thought possible only through overhanging slabs of concrete [is] here realized through spatial vision alone."[31]

21. Beatriz Colomina describes the archive in *Privacy and Publicity*, 1-15.
22. Benton, *Les Villas*, 43–76 and Jacques Sbriglio, *Le Corbusier. Les Villas La Roche-Jeanneret*.
23. Le Corbusier, *Album La Roche*.
24. On the idea of *coulisse* see Colin Rowe and Robert Slutzky, "Transparency: Literal and Phenomenal" in Rowe, *Ideal Villa*, 168.
25. Le Corbusier *Oeuvre Complète* 1: 60.
26. The ramp first appears as a required functional element in a slaughterhouse Le Corbusier designed in Saint Nicolas d'Aliermont (1917).
27. For discussion of type objects see entry Pavilon de l'Esprit Nouveau.
28. Le Corbusier, *Precisions on the Present State of Architecture and City Planning*.
29. Jacques Lucan, "Acropole," in Lucan, *Le Corbusier: Une Encyclopédie*, 22; also Richard Etlin, "Le Corbusier, Choisy, and French Hellenism: The Search for a New Architecture," *The Art Bulletin* 59 no. 2: 265–277.
30. Kurt Foster, "Antiquity and Modernity in the La Roche-Jeanneret Houses," *Oppositions* 15/16, 131.
31. Sigfried Giedion, "The New House" in Serenyi, *Perspectives*, 34.

IMMEUBLE ET APPARTEMENT DE LE CORBUSIER

1931–1934

Le Corbusier and Pierre
Jeanneret; Furnishings in
Le Corbusier's apartment with
Charlotte Perriand

ADDRESS

24, rue Nungesser-et-Coli
75016 Paris

ACCESS

Private apartment house, lobby
accessible. Le Corbusier's
residence, later the home of
his long-time associate André
Wogenscky, can be seen on
Weds. by appointment with
the Fondation Le Corbusier.
www.fondationlecorbusier.asso.
fr. Tel 01.42.88.41.53.

DIRECTIONS

From métro Exelmans, walk to
avenue Porte Molitor or rue
Claude Farrère and along the
side of Stade Jean Bouin. It is
on the far side of stadium.

LOCALE

The locale was developed con-
temporaneously with the neigh-
boring buildings, by M. Roux-
Spitz (1931) to the left, and
Schneider (1931) to the right.
To the west is 18 bis, avenue
Robert Schuman (1930) by
Faurré-Dujaric. To the south in
Boulogne are 52, avenue de la
Tourelle (1927), by U. Cassan,
and several houses on rue de
Belvédère including no. 9 by
André Lurçat (1927) and nos.
6, 8, 8 bis, 10, and 12 by
P. Hillard (1930–33). The Parc
des Princes was completed by
P. Taillibert in 1970. A half-
hour walk from Porte Molitor
will take you to near Villas La
Roche-Jeanneret. Villas Lip-
chitz-Miestchaninoff, Ternisien
and Cook are even closer.

According to Le Corbusier's own statements, the
apartment house at Porte Molitor is as much a fragment of his Radiant City as a building within the fabric of Paris can be. It is an attempt to present the
elements of a new urbanism, "sky, green, glass,
cement, in that order of importance."[32] At the time of
its construction, the street was an undeveloped edge to
the city, with the gardens of Boulogne to the west and
an athletic park on the site of ancient fortifications to
the east. Intending to construct an entire villa-apartment (*immeuble-villa*), the duplex housing typology
from his earlier Contemporary City, Le Corbusier tried
to interest Edward Wanner, the builder of the Immeuble Clarté. Ultimately developed by the Société Immobilière Paris Parc de Princes (SIPPP) on a smaller site,
the constructed building of flats incorporated features
that Le Corbusier and the clients both touted as ideal

and revolutionary.[33] Le Corbusier hoped to challenge the existing Parisian building industry with a structure of metal supplied by Wanner, although in the end only the window framing and balcony details were executed in iron. Built of concrete, the columnar frame still allowed for an open and flexible plan "adaptable to the needs of the buyer."[34] Interior partitions could be rearranged and apartment units combined. In the manner of the Maison Dom-ino, pure horizontal slabs were achieved by placing hollow tile between the ceiling beams. The block infill was also a means of sound insulation. Sheathing of glass and glass block allowed for "the penetration of light and air deep into the building."[35] Taking advantage of the through-block site, each of the two apartments per floor has such a facade, as well as two interior courts to bring natural light to the foyer, baths and kitchen. The building was to provide the buyer with the social amenity of communal domestic services. It advertised central heating, a laundry and drying room, and an underground garage. Even the servants were to benefit from quarters located not in the proverbial attic but in ground floor and basement chambers opening onto a two-tiered garden. The adjoining public athletic facilities and gardens were understood as part of the building's total environment and marketing vision. According to the architect, the first residents "proclaimed the building granted them a new life."[36]

Despite the ambitious premise, the apartment facade is probably the most traditionally contextual of Le Corbusier's mature work. Strict zoning codes specified parapet heights, conformance to the established street wall, size and placement of balconies and bay windows. As a result, the design uses the new material of glass bricks in a composition that seems rather neo-Palladian in contrast to Le Corbusier's own first sketches and to the Maison de Verre (1932) by Pierre Chareau, which is most likely a source for the design. The balanced symmetry of the facade is not at odds with Le Corbusier's classical tendencies, but it represents only one voice in his typical dialogue which is here completed by the placement of the single column on center.

32. Le Corbusier, *Oeuvre Complète* 2: 144.
33. For history of the building process see Jacques Sbriglio, *Apartment Block 24 N. C. and Le Corbusier's Home.*
34. Le Corbusier in Ibid., 24–26.
35. Le Corbusier in Ibid., 28.
36. Le Corbusier *Oeuvre Complète* 2: 144.
37. Peter Carl, "Le Corbusier's Penthouse," *Daidalos* 28: 65–75.
38. Sbriglio, *Apartment,* 46.

entrance

lobby

The placement of structure on center is a strategy Le Corbusier had first developed in his four-square plans, in particular at Maison Cook. But whereas at Cook the circulation adapts to the column location, at Porte Molitor the demands of the architectural promenade appear to warp the column line. The entrance is shifted in relation to the center column; but on the interior, the lobby columns appear staggered along the path. On a typical floor, a column shift accommodates the entrance to the larger apartment and in turn bows the exterior wall. These apparent deformations are not, in fact, the structural order. The plan of the basement, where all columns are present, reveals a central bay framed by pairs of columns whose selective display creates the winding effect. Deep in the lobby, a mirror doubles the single column and so reveals by illusion the total order.

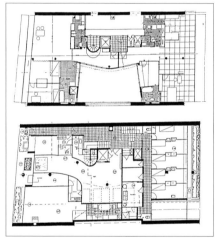

ground floor (bottom) and typical (top) floor plans

The controlled rationality of the structural pattern and imaginary centerline is countered by the lobby's curved walls, tilted floor plane, and diffuse skylight, all of which convey a sensual force. Installed in 1966, the mural in the lobby, Le Corbusier's *Poème de l'Angle Droit* (1941), complements this sensuality in its mythic description of natural forces. A related architectural vocabulary also had an important place in the design of the architect's own home and studio built on top of the apartment flats.

From the beginning, Le Corbusier and the developers planned that the architect would be a shareholder and would construct a *maisonette* duplex and roof garden upon completion of the units below. Financial difficulties beset the project, however, and Le Corbusier's residency was threatened by the absence of buyers and insolvency of the development corporation. He solicited prospective occupants from among his acquaintances, including James Joyce and André Honneger, and eventually secured two residents, the syndicalists Dr. Pierre Winter and François de Pierrefeu. Despite the eventual bankruptcy of the developer during the Depression, and his own flight from Paris during the Occupation, Le Corbusier retained this as his home from its construction in 1934 until his death.

The maisonette displays a more ambiguous and complex mix of forms and technologies than the building it sits upon. Its architecture includes the *de rigeur* machine-age "fourth wall" of glass, the streamlined cabin on the roof deck, floating doors, bare bulb fixtures and screen-like partitions; but there is also a party wall of rubble stone in the studio. Massive v-shaped struts support vaults derived from the Mediterranean vernacular. A curvaceous stair connects the levels. On the terrace of this fragment of the Radiant City realized, Le Corbusier used the masonry of an earthly and earthbound architecture.

Le Corbusier's studio

Over time, the curtain wall of the apartment itself took on some of this ambiguous quality. Originally detailed in painted iron, decay and neglect during bankruptcy and war forced its repair. In 1948, Le Corbusier replaced the metal with wood sashes similar to those in the Unité in Marseilles and inserted panels of stained glass and painted wood as well as double glazing. A second renovation in 1962 incorporated anodized aluminum sliding sash and neoprene.

In his wife Yvonne, Le Corbusier found a live subject of the "new life of Porte-Molitor" whose reactions could be noted intimately. She preferred the society of the street, cafes and bars to the monkish isolation of the roof dwelling. Nevertheless, Le Corbusier designed the flat with his wife in mind, speaking of her as the "guardian angel of the foyer"[37] and arranging the interior according to her idea of a "feminine touch."[38] The idiosyncratic bed at table height and the bathing appurtenances are suggestive images of the feminine as well. Yvonne's response to the bidet frankly placed at the bedside was to cover it with a tea cosy. In this maisonette, the careful contrasts among the materials and values of the Radiant City and those of the vernacular intimately illustrated the principles Le Corbusier chose to live by and hoped others, including his wife, would accept.

VILLAS LIPCHITZ-MIESTCHANINOFF

1923–1924

Le Corbusier and Pierre
Jeanneret

ADDRESS
9, allée des Pins
7, rue des Arts
92100 Boulogne

ACCESS
Private houses in a gated
complex, partially visible from
the surrounding main streets.
The buildings are in fairly
good condition. There have
been some interior and balcony
modifications to the original
design at Miestchaninoff.

DIRECTIONS
Métro Stop Jean-Jaurès line
#10, walk down rue du
Château to Denfert-Rochereau.
Alternately Métro stop Marcel
Sembat line #9 or bus #52
stop Denfert-Rochereau.

Originally conceived as an artist colony of three studio-residences about a communal garden, one of the clients, M. Canale of 3 rue des Arts, did not build his house according to the architects' plan. The building with *passarelle*, or bridge, was owned by Oscar Miestchaninoff, the other by Jacques Lipchitz, who executed sculptures for several of Le Corbusier's projects including Villa de Mandrot.

As combination studio-residences, the buildings are variations on the house executed for Ozenfant, which in turn has precedent in the nineteenth-century Parisian workshop and in Le Corbusier's Maison Citrohan, with its complex of sources. The functional requirements of large sculpture necessitated that the studios be returned to their traditional placement on ground level with dwellings above, the inverse of Atelier Ozenfant. Dignified prismatic volumes, these three studio-residences are distinct from the fluid vision of the column grid with cantilever slabs set forth in the Maison Dom-ino.

The extended context of a colony allowed for play among sculptural forms and with symmetries across the axes of the site. For example, two cubic volumes each with a cylindrical stair are mutual, reversed reflections. This mirroring continues in the relation of the windows to the corner tower. Paradoxically, this modulation of volume creates a reading of the buildings as surface rather than mass, as if the building skin is a folded plane. This illusionistic "limpid effect of suspension"[39] as Henry Russell Hitchcock has referred to it, was one of the most remarked on qualities of the purist architecture at the time. At Lipchitz-Miestchaninoff, Le Corbusier tried to insure this suspended effect by burying columns in the rubble fill of the walls to avoid surface cracks, even though this placement of structure ran counter to the free facade.[40] In Le Corbusier's development, the houses are a bolder imagistic use of form in relation to the still central figure of the seamlessly wrapped box.

LOCALE
Very near Maisons Cook and Ternisien.

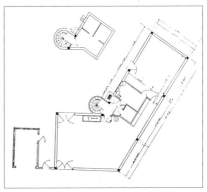

floor plan, Lipchitz

39. Henry Russell Hitchcock, *The Arts* 16: 24 quoted in Wigley, *White Walls*, 351.
40. H. Allen Brooks, ed. *The Le Corbusier Archive*: FLC 8049, 8058, 8018 and Ragot and Dion, *Le Corbusier en France*, 83–6.

VILLA COOK
1926

Le Corbusier and Pierre
Jeanneret

ADDRESS
6, rue Denfert-Rochereau
92100 Boulogne-sur-Seine

ACCESS
Private house visible from
street. Ground floor has been
altered.

DIRECTIONS
From the métro stop Boulogne-
Jean-Jaurès, walk along rue du
Chateau with numbers decreasing until a small traffic circle.
Take rue Denfert-Rochereau to
the left, with the numbers
decreasing. You will first come
to Ternisien at the intersection
of rue Denfert-Rochereau
and allé des Pins. Lipchitz-
Miestchaninoff is just within
the gated street of allée des
Pins. Villa Cook is several hundred feet beyond on the left.

LOCALE
The house is flanked by no. 8,
Villa Collinet of Rob Mallet-
Stevens (1926) and no. 4 by
Raymond Fischer (1927). No.
7 is by P. Patout (1928). Some
of the brief for the Cook house
regarding heights and terrace
exposures came from restric-
tions imposed by the owners of
Villa Collinet. As the neighboring pedigrees indicate, this
locale was developed during
the twenties. Placards on the
street in front of Cook describe
a brief architectural tour. Yours
might begin with Le Corbusier's
houses for Lipchitz-Miestchaninoff and Ternisien on allée des
Pins and finish in the neighborhood of his own apartment
building at Porte Molitor.

The clients for this house, the expatriate American
journalist William Cook and his French wife, Jeanne,
belonged to the intellectual and artistic circle that
included many of Le Corbusier's clients, the Steins
among them. In fact, the Cooks commissioned their
house within weeks of the Steins, but moved into it
long before their friends could inhabit the palace at
Garches. The speed with which the house was
designed reflects, in part, the extent to which it
expressed a set of thoroughly formulated ideas concerning art and industry. As Le Corbusier stated,
"here are applied very clearly the certitudes acquired
to this point."[41]

The certitudes took the form of what Le Corbusier called "the true cubic house" (*le vrai maison
cubique*). Plan, section, and elevation all derive from
the same square and in reference to one another.
The canon of the Five Points: the continuous strip
window, round pilotis, free plan, free facade and roof
garden is deployed in service to this cubic organization, but without the axial extension implicit in the
Maison Dom-ino. The four-square plan constitutes a
distinct type in Le Corbusier's oeuvre originating

with an early project for an artisan's house, in which a free-standing cube focused on a single center column is divided by a diagonal balcony. Associated by Le Corbusier with the economy of the worker's dwelling, Cook's *en suite* arrangement also has resonance with the neoclassical French *hôtel-particulier*.[42] The Jeanneret residence adjacent to La Roche has a four-square plan as well as the inverted placement of salon above the bedroom level found here. At Cook, the placement of columns along the centerline of the house divides the square into quadrants which are in turn composed of a square module. There is a diagonal path of movement throughout the house induced by the placement of the stair on one side of the centerline and the major spaces on the other. The wall along the centerline thus becomes a "second facade" through which one moves across the site.

section

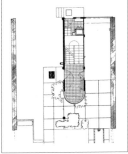

ground floor plan

The logic of the cubic house is a reflexive one, in which every square surface, no matter what its orientation, somehow reflects and transfers every other. Peter Eisenman has proposed that this self-referential logic is radical, distinguishing Le Corbusier's architecture from all that precedes it.[43] The central "second facade" can be understood as the perpendicular rotation of the street facade. Accordingly, the street facade is like the plan, a four-square composition with implicit diagonals. One diagonal connects the upper protruding balcony down and back in depth to the ground-level stair. The other joins the voids of terrace and entrance. This logic extends beyond the object to the organization of the site and the larger urban context. In his book *Urbanisme*, Le Corbusier makes a large dialectical distinction between the straight path of the car and the curved way of the donkey or pedestrian,[44] here represented by the driveway leading to the garage and the curved path extending to the rear garden, respectively. The facade then is the inscription of plan, section, street and garden onto a surface that presents them all simultaneously.

first floor plan

Behind the apparent lucidity of the cubic symmetry and self-referential structure, however, some aspects of design and construction are not so easily

41. Le Corbusier *Oeuvre Complète* 1: 130.
42. Richard Etlin, "Paradoxical Avante-Garde," *Architectural Review* 1079: 20–6.
43. Peter Eisenman, "Aspects of Modernism: Maison Dom-ino and the Self-Referential Sign," *Oppositions* 15/16, 118–28.
44. Le Corbusier, *The City of Tomorrow*, 11, 28–9.

assimilated to this cohesive truth. The idiosyncrasies result in part from the divergence of Cook from the canon of the purist villas. The standard module for windows and structure employed at most villas and Pessac was five meters. The module at Cook is 4.65 meters, most simply explained by the contingencies of the narrow site, which might also have generated the two-bay plan.[45] Less obvious is the use of a pre-cast deck system of I-sections with lightweight infill, in lieu of Le Corbusier's typical "lost-tile" method in which concrete is poured over spaced, hollow blocks. In both systems, the ultimate aesthetic effect of uninterrupted slabs is the same.

balcony close up

The most intriguing particularity of the house is the elaborate fenestration which incorporates sliders, casements, hoppers and fixed panels within the strip window. No decipherable geometric pattern determines their placement; rather an elaborate logic based on function seems the case. The large, fixed panel flanked by narrow casements at the salon is a canonical picture window. The clarity of view and reflectivity of surface were important enough to Le Corbusier that during construction he made the contractor replace all the installed glazing with plate glass at considerable expense to the client. In the rear kitchen, a fixed panel above the sink is another picture frame. The adjoining slider provides ventilation when the curtains have been put in their designated places in front of the narrow casements at either end. The maid's room is distinguished from all others by a hopper.[46] One photograph in the *Oeuvre Complète* shows all curtains completely drawn such that the bands of wall and bands of window take on a similar appearance, and the pattern of mullions across the facade is left as a hieroglyphic of the complexity of daily life.

45. Benton, *Les Villas*, 155–57.
46. Ford, *Details Vol. 1*, 239–41.

VILLA TERNISIEN

1926–1927

Le Corbusier and Pierre
Jeanneret

ADDRESS
5 allée des Pins
92100 Boulogne

ACCESS
Private residence visible from
street. Virtually nothing
remains of the original design.
The house appears much as it
did in 1936, after Georges-
Henri Pingusson's addition.

DIRECTIONS
Métro stop Jean Jaurès line
#10 or Marcel Semblat line #9.

LOCALE
Very near Villa Cook and Villas
Lipchitz-Miestchaninoff, it is
located at the corner of the
allée des Pins and rue Denfert-
Rochereau.

47. Le Corbusier, Oeuvre Complète
1: 122.

Le Corbusier described the house as a *"jeu d'esprit"*[47] referring to its witty adaptation of his studio type to a peculiar site. The Ternisiens engaged Le Corbusier after hearing him lecture at the Sorbonne in 1923. Originally, Madame Ternisien's painting studio stood at the rear, an unmodulated double-height box with industrial sash windows, the pure studio type. Paul Ternisien's music room engaged the corner with a curved wall evocative of the instruments depicted in purist paintings. A small, glazed dining room and entrance connected the two studios and framed the site's small tree. One can imagine the neighborhood of 1926 as an extended site unified by the nautical theme of Le Corbusier's purist shapes: the "smokestack" stair and ship's bridge of Miestchaninoff down the street, complemented by Ternisien's "pointed bow."

From the first, the Ternisiens planned to extend their house, and the original design provided for an eventual expansion above the piano room. Their dissatisfaction with Le Corbusier's services led them to engage Georges-Henri Pingusson for the 1936 addition which virtually obliterated the original house except for the ground-floor street wall at the distinctive corner.

original ground floor plan

MAISONS JAOUL

1952–1955

Le Corbusier, German Samper,
André Wogenscky, Jacques
Michel

ADDRESS
81 bis, rue de Longchamp
92200 Neuilly-sur-Seine

ACCESS
The house has been restored
with the help of the original
mason, Bertocchi. Jacques
Michel who drew the original
plans in Le Corbusier's office
supervised the work.

DIRECTIONS
Métro Sablons or bus #43
(stop Rue du Centre). Also, the
Métro stop Pont-de-Neuilly,
line #1 is several blocks from
the house along rue de
Longchamp.

LOCALE
Neuilly is a fine residential district in greater Paris bordering
the Bois de Boulogne. Not far
from the house, at 34, avenue
de Madrid, is the eighteenth-
century Folie Sainte-James of
F. J. Belanger, which Le Corbusier depicted in sketches of
Villa Church.[47] One possible
itinerary continues out to Tête
de la Defense, and from there
to the suburban villas.

With the construction of Maisons Jaoul and the chapel at Ronchamp, the architectural world first took notice of Le Corbusier's expressive use of rough masonry, in contrast to the machine aesthetic and rational principles proposed in his early architecture as the basis of Modernism. James Stirling questioned whether the Maisons Jaoul was a retreat from "participation in the progress of twentieth-century emancipation" into the realm of "art for art's sake."[48] The primitive and vernacular did take on increasing importance for Le Corbusier, but they had had a place in his thinking from the start. In particular, the vaulted Maisons Monol appeared in a project of 1919, in *Vers une architecture* (1923), and in the Maison de Weekend (1935). Simultaneously with Jaoul, he designed a vaulted masonry residence in India, Maison Sarabhai (1952).

Of the Monol projects, Jaoul is the first authentically vernacular in that it employs the Catalan vault, in which the concrete is poured over brick arches. The tile finish acts as a permanent shuttering so that no real form work is required. The vaults rest on load-bearing brick walls at the groin and perimeter. Steel tie-rods at fifteen-foot intervals, added to the structure by the consultant engineer during construction, take the diagonal thrust.

interior, with brick vault and fireplace

The roof covering is of sod, a traditional means of resisting thermal expansion. Set into the edge beams are boxes for bird nesting and rainwater heads. Stirling caught the building's aura in his statement, "built by Algerian workmen equipped with ladders, hammers and nails, [the house is] technologically no advance over medieval building."[49] He associated the pyramidal massing with traditional Indian architecture. As Benton observes, Le Corbusier's travels to India as well as Africa and South America exposed him to cultures where the combination of primitive and contemporary means had a social as well as technological basis.[50]

In fact, there is at least one significant revision of the vernacular structure in the use of the concrete edge beams. Their deep sections capable of spanning large openings allow for the spatial flow between the interior vaults. In an unbuilt extension to the house (1960) Le Corbusier proposed a steel truss super-

48. James Stirling, "From Garches to Jaoul: Le Corbusier as Domestic Architect in 1927 and 1953," Sereyni, *Perspective*, 55.
49. Ibid.
50. Tim Benton, "Six Houses" in Raeburn and Wilson, *Architect of the Century*, 67.
51. Kenneth Frampton coins the term "monumentalization of the vernacular" in a chapter by that title in *Modern Architecture*.
52. Le Corbusier, *Towards a New Architecture*, 191.
53. Ibid.,159.

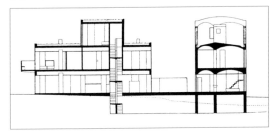

section

structure that would have stood above the vaults as yet another socio-technological critique.

Jaoul is also the first of the Monol projects to assimilate the undifferentiated vernacular of the vault and rough masonry to a monumental design.[51] Rather than low and linear, here the houses are multi-story

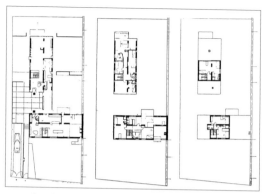

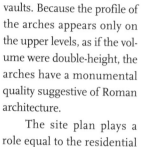

ground and upper floor plans

garden

blocks of superimposed vaults. Because the profile of the arches appears only on the upper levels, as if the volume were double-height, the arches have a monumental quality suggestive of Roman architecture.

The site plan plays a role equal to the residential blocks in the architecture of the enclave. As Le Corbusier expressed in his description of the Roman house, "every exterior is an interior."[52] The enclave has two residences in a perpendicular arrangement, the front house of the elder Jaouls constructed on a plinth above a sunken garage, and the rear block for their son and his family. From the street, the front house is an imposing presence which, together with the graded hillside, protects and defines the complex within. At terrace level, the houses appear as two-story volumes scaled to the size of their adjoining gardens. The terrace and gardens define a series of three interconnected exterior rooms. The passage defined among these architectural enclosures—from the edge of the ramp, to the center of the entrance court, and then to the long garden with its focal balcony—recalls the grading and shifting axes of Pompeii.

Along the exterior promenade, the views of the houses are often episodic and oblique. The corners of the houses thus become prominent features elaborately articulated with inset wood panels. Le Corbusier discovered the power of the three-quarter view in the architecture of the ancient Greeks, who angled their temples off the axis of movement. Here the compression of the sequence of exterior space achieves similar effect.

In his first mature statement, *Vers une architecture*, Le Corbusier frames modernity in relation to two distinct antiquities: Acropolitan Greece and domestic Rome. The shift "from Garches to Jaoul" is a reassessment of the dominant white temple of the machine-age, reread through the "lessons of Rome."[53]

VILLA BESNUS (KER-KA-RÉ)

1922

M. and Mme George Besnus commissioned Le Corbusier after reading his articles in *l'Esprit Nouveau* and seeing his exhibit at the Salon d'Automne in Paris (1922). Although the clients requested that their house resemble the display model of Maison Citrohan, Le Corbusier chose instead to develop a purist architecture, reinterpreting cubist design principles in the light of the French neoclassical tradition. The facades of the house presented the different sides of Le Corbusier's aesthetic argument.

As early as 1911, Le Corbusier had begun to express a commitment to French neoclassicism, which he saw as a necessary cultural component of industrialized production.[54] He related neoclassical proportions to his own device of *tracés regulateurs* (lines related by their angles to the ratios of the golden section), and employed this system at Villa Besnus. The garden side of the original house was a two-story, symmetrical block with a clearly separated stair tower. In its tripartite division, its proportions, and in some of the mannered details such as the wall brackets, the main block resembled le Petit Trianon, designed by Gabriel for Louis XV at nearby Versailles. The symmetry of the

Le Corbusier and Pierre Jeanneret

ADDRESS
85, boulevard de la République
94400 Vaucresson
Paris 19 km, Versailles 5 km

ACCESS
In 1935, shops were built along the front of the house and a tile roof added. The rear facade has retained more of the original detail.

DIRECTIONS
Villa Besnus is at the center of the village of Vaucresson, on the main street just beyond the train station at the intersection with rue Garrel. Commuter trains leave frequently from Gare St. Lazare in Paris. By métro, take RER B to La Défense, and then the local SNCF stopping at Vaucresson. By car, take A13, exit Vaucresson-Versailles. By train or car, the trip is under an hour

from downtown Paris.

LOCALE
The suburbs of Paris where Le
Corbusier's early villas are
located are older villages that
still have town halls and some
vintage buildings. Such sites as
Versailles are close and could be
included on a day trip.

original front facade

*first (bottom) and second floor
(top) plans*

54. Nancy Troy, *Modernism in the
Decorative Arts*, 112-15.
55. Le Corbusier, "A Coat of White-
wash," *The Decorative Art of Today*,
186–192.
56. Wigley, *White Walls*, 195–198.
57. Benton, "Six Houses," Raeburn
and Wilson, *Architect of the Century*, 50.

rear facade concealed an asymmetrical plan however,
resulting in a blind kitchen and unevenly lit living
room. While similar compositional devices appear in
the earlier Villa Schwob (1916), here they are rendered
abstractly and set within a white prismatic cube.

Le Corbusier pointedly relegated the symmetrical
front of le Petit Trianon to the backyard of Besnus. On
the street facade, asymmetry, decentralization, and
peripheral incidents held the original building in tense
equilibrium. Le Corbusier aligned the stair tower with
the front facade of the main body of the house, making
the entire composition asymmetrical. Within this
perimeter, an overlapping set of symmetries created competing centers. For example, the center
of the main block was a projecting box, but the
true pivot of the composition was a small vertical window. Tension existed among the elements in depth as well, the windows and
balconies shifting in relation to the datum of the
white wall. This wall was both a neutral back-
ground and a rhetorically loaded element
described by the architect as the simultaneous
"absence of decoration and presence of space."[55]
Besnus seems, in fact, to be his only all-white
building.[56]

As soon as the house was built, cracking
problems became apparent. Concrete slab was
a relatively new element in French domestic
building at the time, and its technical detailing
here was invented jointly with the builder
George Summer, a specialist in reinforced
concrete construction. Summer and Le Corbusier went on to build several houses
together using Summer's patented floor slab
system.[57] In this first case, however, the house
leaked and the clients complained. Within a decade
of its completion, it was transformed into a seemingly vernacular building with a pitched tile roof. The
bungalow with sun porch that exists now easily obliterated Le Corbusier's abstract manipulation of the
French neoclassical tradition.

VILLA STEIN (DE MONZIE)

1927–1928

In his architecture of the 1920s, Le Corbusier conducted a simultaneous exploration of contemporary technological culture and architectural systems of the past through the subject of the house. In part, his clientele determined his practice and his subject. Like other European architects of the time, his projects considered typologies and techniques for mass housing, but his built work consisted primarily of private houses for an increasingly monied intelligentsia. For Le Corbusier, this contradiction in economy was overcome by the pervasiveness of the problem of dwelling for all classes. To focus on the dwelling as the object of architectural discourse was, he felt, to bestow dignity on modern life. The dwelling was the problem of modern architecture; every building was in essence a house. He expressed all these ideas in the rubric *une maison—un palais* ("a house—a palace").[58]

While intending to monumentalize all dwelling, with the commission of a weekend house by Gabrielle de Monzie, the former wife of Minister of Construction Anatole de Monzie, he found patrons with the status, culture and wealth to support the

Le Corbusier and Pierre Jeanneret

ADDRESS
17, rue du Prof. Victor Pauchet
Vaucresson
Paris 19 km

ACCESS
The villa has been divided into condominiums but the exterior is mostly intact. The rear stair has been filled in and the front service door altered to align with the window above.

DIRECTIONS
From the train station, walk uphill bearing left along avenue Foch to rue du Prof. Victor Pauchet, continuing left with the golf course on the right and housing on the left. There is a sign indicating the limits of Vaucresson. The house is slightly beyond the sign on the left, opposite the golf course. If you reach the end of the

course and the beginning of the woods of Malmaison, you have gone too far.

LOCALE

Although known as the Villa Stein at Garches, or simply as Garches, the house is actually just across the town line in the slightly less tony suburb of Vaucresson. Both of the adjoining towns have center villages surrounded first by pleasant hilly neighborhoods with nineteenth-century houses and then by the more verdant setting in which the villa is located. Le Corbusier's Villa Besnus and la Petite Maison de Weekend are in villages nearby. The town of Malmaison begins five hundred meters west of the villa.

grandeur of a palace. The other clients in the venture were Michael Stein, brother of Gertrude, who had earned his fortune from the San Francisco street-car system, and his wife Sarah, a painter and early collector of Matisse. While the first schemes maintained a separation between the two families' apartments, eventually their lives became difficult to distinguish in plan. Having oftened vacationed together at various country estates, including the Stein's Italian Renaissance villa, the clients requested that Le Corbusier create for them a personal and modern equivalent. Colin Rowe has demonstrated Villa Stein's specific correspondence with the villas of Palladio, in particular Villa Foscari, from the identical 5 x 2.5 proportions of their volumes and the *a-b-a-b-a* rhythm of the structural bays, to the underlying though transformed disposition of stairways, doors and porches.[59] For example, the pyramidal composition of Foscari can be traced in the triangle of doors and loggias on the front of Stein. The porch of the Renaissance villa is echoed on the garden side of the modern one. Le Corbusier's mission to aggrandize the house is in essence parallel to Palladio's daring domestication of the temple front.

Despite the freedom inherent in the program and budget, the architects fashioned the strictest of their villas in terms of its obeyance to sets of formal and constructive principles that ruled all their houses of the 1920s.[60] Most of the idiosyncrasies of the other villas—the column grid at Savoye, the window openings at Cook—are absent here. The column grid is pure. The slabs are flat, poured according to the lost tile method in which hollow blocks are cast into the concrete to fill in between the beams. The cantilevers extend the length of the slabs. The windows are fixed metal sash with horizontal mullions at ground level and Corbusian-patented, wood frame, sliding strip windows above. The walls are an uninsulated, single-thickness of hollow pumice concrete block, finished on the outside with Kalk Cement and on the inside with plaster. The interior finishes also subscribe to the orthodoxy of the purist house: black

58. Le Corbusier, *Une Maison—Un Palais.*
59. Rowe, *Ideal Villa*, 2–24.
60. For Stein as canonical construction see Ford, *Details*:1, 241–45.
61. Benton, "Six Houses," in Raeburn and Wilson, *Architect of the Century*, 61.
62. Giedion quoted in Benton, "Six Houses," 62.

linoleum tile or average quality parquet flooring, painted surfaces. Where possible, furnishings are built-in as extensions of the concrete shell. For example, sills are extended as *tablettes*. Recesses are cast into window heads to hold the shades. Photographs suggest that the antiques installed by the Steins were awkward in part because their heavy luxury was in conflict with the insistent modesty of architectural finish. The office's stable of usual contractors executed the work according to their usual standards: George Summer, an expert in concrete, built the frame; A. Celio was the painter and glazier; Raphael Louis provided the window frames. The only indulged contractor was Lucien Crépin, the gardener whom Le Corbusier often insisted on using despite his expense. Here Crépin started his work before construction and by the end spent almost five per cent of the total budget.[61]

corner

If there is a Spartan quality to the appointments of this purist villa, there is also the luxury of space in sheer quantity and in its manipulation. Nervously guarding the moral flame of the Modern Movement but nonetheless seduced, Sigfried Giedion described "a luxury of space, which by its harmony achieves the new conceptions."[62] The visitor to the exterior of the villa today can still observe the richness of cubist layering within the facades, the overlapping planes real and implied that recede and emerge in relation to the reference of the white wall. The strip windows wrapping the corner of the house suggest layers which are both horizontal and vertical. On the rear, the proportions of the stripes are reversed, but their ambiguity and power to dissolve the surface are the same. While the space of the house seems collapsed onto a taut front facade, on the garden side it explodes into surfaces distant from one another. The composition moves diagonally back from garden to roof garden. Overlaid on this peripheral and centripetal composition are the

Rear facade

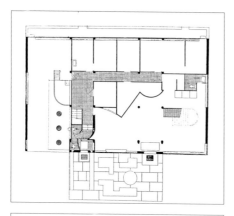

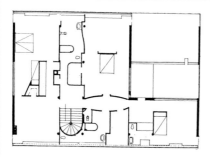

*Ground (top) and second
floor (bottom)plans*

63. Rowe and Slutzky, "Transparency," and Rowe, *Ideal Villa*,
167.
64. For Citrohan see Maitland,
"The Grid," *Oppositions* 15/16:
104.
65. Etlin, "Paradoxical Avant-
Garde," *Arch. Review* 1079: 36.
66. Le Corbusier, *Precisions*, 134.

Palladian figures of hierarchy and center such as the loggias.[63]

There is a luxury in this excess of relationships and of readings. The front elevation, while a cubist composition, also bears a striking resemblance to an ocean-liner deck. The interior grid can be read as Palladio's Foscari but also as a set of parallel Citrohan plans.[64] The particular curves and slants that once filled the interior and are still seen on the roof have the same sensibility as Le Corbusier's still-lifes but they evoke an eclectic array of sources.[65] The dining room suggests an episode from a Turkish bath; the roof structure a Roman apse or steamship funnel, the toilets a figure from a Parisian *hôtel*. In his categorization of the villas into Four Compositions, Le Corbusier depicted Stein as the "most difficult,"[66] austere, and unremitting envelope of walls, which he called the "mask of simplicity" around the Dom-ino frame. Behind the mask of simplicity and demeanor of Palladian restraint, the Corbusian imagination ran free.

LA PETITE MAISON DE WEEKEND
(VILLA HENFEL, VILLA FÉLIX)

1935

In his 1929 design for the protoype Maisons Locheur, Le Corbusier outlined a "second machine age" by combining vernacular and contemporary technologies in search of a relevant beauty and utility. This assimilation of primitive and sophisticated means is again profoundly apparent in the Petite Maison's vaults and their siting. The vaults reference such sources as August Perret's thin-shell concrete docks at Casablanca, Antoni Gaudí's suspended forms, Persian antiquities from the books of Dieulafoy, and Le Corbusier's own Maisons Monol prototype (1919), which consists of attatched units (*en serie*).

The client, M. Félix, the bachelor director of the bank Société Henfel, commissioned the house under dubious circumstances as a company retreat for his private use.[67] Discretion and relaxation combined as the primary requirements. Le Corbusier's other explorations of "peasant means" for leisure in Villa le Sextant and Villa de Mandrot were rural commissions in which the combination of local materials with prefabricated imports had an economic and regional logic. Here, as a weekend retreat within the environs of Paris, the vaulted house seems an ideological critique of its immediate cultural context. Its associations with peasant barns and industrial warehouses suggest an alternative to the bourgeois idea

Le Corbusier and Pierre Jeanneret

ADDRESS
49, avenue du Chesnay
78170 La Celle-St-Cloud

ACCESS
The skeleton of this house remains intact, but there have been major alterations to the exterior walls. This residence is barely visible from street due to fences and hedges that exceed its low-laying profile.

DIRECTIONS
Trains stopping at La Celle-St-Cloud leave Paris (Gare St. Lazare) frequently and take a half hour. From the station, walk uphill along avenue du Chesnay (5 min.) until it meets avenue de Verdun. The house is easy to miss because it is so low to the ground and stands behind a tall, overgrown fence.

LOCALE
La Celle-Saint-Cloud is one of a chain of small towns to the west of Paris with verdant residential neighborhoods and a

village center. From La Celle-
St-Cloud to neighboring Vau-
cresson and Le Corbusier's Villa
Besnus, it is a 20-min. walk, or
a 5-min. local bus ride east
along avenue de Verdun. From
Vaucresson continue east
toward the adjacent town of
Garches and Villa Stein/de
Monzie.

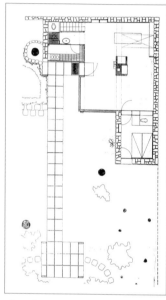

floor plan

67. Benton, "Six Houses," in Raeburn and Wilson, *Architect of the
Century*, 65–66.
68. The term of Stanislaus von
Moos, *Elements*, 95.
69. Alan Colquhoun, *Essays in
Architectural Criticism*, 75.
70. Le Corbusier, *Oeuvre Complète*
4: 125.

of dwelling represented in the neighboring houses. The 2.6-meter-high vaults of shuttered, poured concrete are covered with sod and placed against a soil embankment. From the adjacent higher ground, they form a cave-like shelter appropriate to a modern-day, ornamental hermit. Early photos of the house show a finely finished interior of plywood and Nevada glass blocks filled with light and open to the garden. From the inside, the house had an intimate relation with an intensely private landscape that evoked "*ur*-shelter,"[68] a primal dwelling in an Edenic setting.

This critique of dwelling occurs at the level of architectural language as well. As Alan Colquhoun has described, "it is not so much the case that vernacular elements are added to high architecture as that the tradition itself is modified to include them."[69]The modification induced by the Monol "*en serie*" is an architecture of continuous growth which undermines classical precepts of a finite, complete whole, hierarchical composition, and dominant frontal facade. The vaults are part of a continuous, conceivably endless extrusion cut at three varied lengths. The paved garden path describes the axis of growth. Le Corbusier exaggerated the condition of lost front by placing the entrance on the side of the vault and setting the regular perimeter into the embankment. In some late projects, such as the Venice Hospital (1964–65), these ideas occur in the extreme, creating buildings like cellular fabrics. Here, the classical tradition is present in what Le Corbusier called an architecture of "precise relations."[70] The ambiguous L-shape of the vaults is resolved on the interior as a dominant square room flanked by two small wings. The four-square plan is in itself a collapsed version of the classical nine-square plan, with the hearth at the center bay. A single module of the vault is placed as a garden kiosk or classical canopy, exactly twice as far from the kitchen as from the middle of the bedroom, to fix the geometric boundary of the vault ends. This canopy in the garden suggests the need of even a truly modern man to escape to a sheltered position in nature from the world he financed.

VILLA SAVOYE (SAVOIE, LES HEURES CLAIRES)
1929–1931

The last of the so-called purist villas, Savoye freely and confidently expresses a decade of Corbusian ideals. In distinction from other contemporary materialist and functionalist arguments, Le Corbusier described his ideals as "poetry, lyricism brought by techniques."[71] It is precisely its lyricism—the inexhaustible quality of the concise—that has made the villa a major icon of the twentieth century.

The creation of such a house required specific contingencies in site, client and program. The site was unencumbered and large, a verdant field literally and imaginatively. The couple's stated requirements were for a weekend home well-equipped with servants' quarters where they could enjoy the rustic landscape in style. M. and Mme Savoye were wealthy and cultured clients who belonged tangentially to Le Corbusier's crowd of artists and patrons. Monsieur was an important administrator whom Le Corbusier considered in league with the captains of industry capable of implementing his vision of the modern capitalist city. Madame Savoye, the active client, had clear requests—such as for a salon "not strictly rectangular but with [sic] comfortable corners"[72]—most

Le Corbusier, Pierre Jeanneret

ADDRESS
82 rue de Villiers
78300 Poissy
Paris 38km

ACCESS
Surviving World War II as a hayloft, saved from subsequent destruction by Minister André Malraux in 1959, and restored periodically according to changes in Corbusian scholarship, the villa is now a historic monument. Visiting hours are 10–5, except Mons. Open until 6 PM, 2 May–31 Aug. Closed 23 Dec.–1 Jan., 1 May, 11 Nov. If the gate is locked, ring the intercom for the concierge. Tel 01.39.65.01.06, fax 01. 39.65.19.33, www.monum.fr.

DIRECTIONS
Commuter trains run from Gare St. Lazare in Paris to Poissy about twice an hour and take

20 minutes. Similarly, RER A5 destination Poissy runs from La Defense frequently and takes under half an hour. From the train station at Poissy, the house is a ten-minute cab or bus ride (#50 La Coudraie) or an uphill walk.

LOCALE

Once a rural village, Poissy is now part of the greater Paris megalopolis. The open fields which originally surrounded the site have since been developed. The house is located on a hill above the shopping district, next to a high school and athletic complex.

71. Le Corbusier, *Precisions*, 139.
72. Correspondence from Mme. Savoye in Tim Benton, "Villa Savoye and the Architect's Practice," in Brooks, *Le Corbusier*, ff 27, 95.
73. Le Corbusier, *Oeuvre Complète* 2: 24.
74. Benton, "Architect's Practice," Brooks, *Le Corbusier*, also Benton, *The Villas*, 191–218 and Benton, "Six Houses," Raeburn and Wilson, *Architect of the Century*, 63–5.
75. Le Corbusier, *Towards*, 133. Banham is the first to make this observation in *Theory and Design*. See also Rowe, *The Architecture of Good Intentions*, 53.
76. Le Corbusier, *Towards*, 70.
77. Le Corbusier, *Precisions*, 139.
78. Rowe, *Ideal Villa*, 2–3.
79. Le Corbusier *Oeuvre Complète* 2: 24.

of which she was willing to abandon. As for the style of their house, the clients were, according to their architect, "totally without preconception either ancient or modern."[73]

The only sticking point of the program was the budget, which lead to a temporary radical departure from the initial scheme but then to its reinstatement in a dimensionally reduced form. Le Corbusier and Jeanneret reduced the bay size of 5 meters standard to most of their houses to 4.75 m, although some sliding windows remained as 2.5 meter units. Despite this planned shrinkage, the final cost was about double the contractual amount because of changes made during construction such as an increase to the ground floor height which required the refabrication of completed glazing. Even with these vicissitudes, it was only after construction—as the roof drains failed, the glass walls and skylight leaked, the damp infiltrated and the brittle walls cracked during the installation of additional wiring— that the client-architect relation became strained to the point that Le Corbusier actually paid to rectify the problems under threat of litigation.[74]

Villa Savoye is a statement of Le Corbusier's belief in the continuity between ancient and modern. In *Vers une architecture*, he had placed side by side pictures of a Bugatti automobile and the Parthenon, commenting "the Parthenon is a product of selection applied to an established standard."[75] It is in this spirit that Savoye was conceived as the natural consequence of machine-age standardization applied to classical architectural principles. Only the tools change; "the idea is in full sway from the beginning."[76] The Dom-ino is rendered here as a metaphoric transposition of classical trabeation: the pilotis are columns spanned by the simple lintel of the horizontal slabs; the entablature is defined through the extended metope-void of the strip window; the glass enclosure seems the shadow of a cella now housed within the lintel.

The analogy to the temple extends also to the understanding of the house's originality, reproducibility, site and type. Le Corbusier viewed the classical temple—and hence his rereading of it in this villa—as a standardized and international object, an *objet-type*. He harbored the dream of Savoye as the ultimately refined standardized dwelling for the elite.  While lecturing in Buenos Aires in 1929, Le Corbusier proposed Le Vingtième, a grouping of twenty Villa Savoye clones, each with its own curved driveway. In the small gatehouse at Poissy, as in the prototypical Maisons Locheur (1929), many of the villa's standardized themes—the strip window, the floating white box—appear in combination with a vernacular stone wall.

Even though Le Corbusier advocated the universal application of this pure type, the siting of the house is specific, but to a mytho-poetic rather than geographic location. Le Corbusier described how "the inhabitants, who came here because the countryside with its rural life was beautiful, will contemplate [the landscape] maintained intact, from the height of their suspended garden or through the four sides of the long windows. Their domestic life will be inserted into a Virgilian dream."[77] This allusion to a Roman poet's lyric reinvention of the harsh Greek landscape describes the siting of the house precisely.  Colin Rowe has demonstrated eloquently that for Le Corbusier, the architectural equivalent to Virgil's *Georgics* is Palladio's Villa Rotunda, also a Roman hybrid of a Greek legacy.[78] It is significant that the villa is not the norm of Palladio, the most typological and systematic of architects, but the exception that simultaneously exceeds and sets the standard. Like the Villa Rotunda, Savoye is a cubic pleasure home, physically disengaged from but optically surveying suburban farm land, and so transforming these surroundings into a pastoral dream.

Le Corbusier also sought to exceed the standard, to create art with his architecture by engaging emotion through experiential aspects—namely the "architectural promenade" described at Savoye as *"l'espace Arabe"*[79] in reference to the unfolding spaces and shifting view points

typical of the architecture of North Africa. As in many of his villas, the envelope of the house is a prismatic solid through which the promenade unfolds, paradoxically undermining its Platonic stability. Column placement, bay structure, color, even window mullions orchestrate the promenade. For example, the coloration of the house, like that of the landscape, shifts from dark green to pale green and blue as one rises to the roof. In unique exception to the flat slab structure used in his other purist villas, here the major girders running parallel to the ramp are dropped below the slab, creating a series of frames for the shifting view.

At Savoye, the promenade reaches an ultimate extension in length and significance, using plastic effect to convey the qualities of modern life in a narrative form that no one story line can summarize. Le Corbusier's imagined narrative began with the Savoyes' departure from their apartment in Paris, 105, rue de Courcelles, for the chauffeured thirty-kilometer drive to the countryside of Poissy, and culminated at the roof. The arrival sequence was designed for the car: the glass enclosure for its turning radius, the vertical mullions to emphasize its speed, the placement of the column opposite the door with regard to the disembarkment of the Savoyes. Once inside, the interior promenade appeals to the human scale, designed for the initiate, who is described in the original photographs of the foyer through clue-like artifacts: a bowler hat and trench coat, a glass flask with a cut flower on the *tablette*, golf clubs. The props are provided by the architecture as well: the foyer phone attached to a column for business connections, the sink for ablutions.

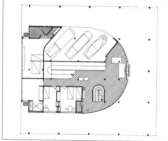

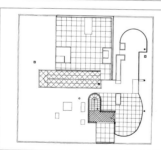

Plans of ground floor (top) and roof (bottom)

Thematically, beginning with the foyer sink and continuing throughout the house, the mystery and sensual fulfillment suggested by *l'espace Arabe* is overlaid with values of cleanliness and health and robust exposure. The hanging garden at the center of the house is a cloistered version of Le Corbusier's *immeuble-villa* terrace, a vehicle of light and air. The rooms are oriented for sun and view: salon to the northwest, terrace to the south, accommodations to the west, kitchen to the east. In the public room, the continuity of the strip window almost disintegrates distinctions between inside and out. The bedrooms, on the other hand, are arranged in a protective maze of privacy. Deep inside the house, in the master bathroom, a skylight and tiled chaise evocative of an undulating landscape reframe the value of the outdoors.

master bathroom

The ramp, composed in relation to the spiral stair, is the centerpiece of the promenade and the house, straddling interior and exterior, simultaneously unifying the ascent and slashing the space apart. The ramp is perhaps the most recurrent and important Corbusian motif. Le Corbusier valued it for its rational and poetic attributes, as a device of uninterrupted circulation that makes physical the imagined continuity of plan and section. Contemporaneously with Savoye, he proposed a public architecture of circulation based on multiple ramps at the Centrosoyus in Moscow (1928). Although the ramp first appeared in its purist form at Villa La Roche (1923), its origins can be traced to Le Corbusier's designs for slaughterhouses in which the ramp for the cattle was a programmatic given and a rational exigency of the Taylorized processing of meat. As tilted ground planes, Le Corbusier's ramps mimic the logic of landscape as well as of production and, in specific contexts, take on the attributes of a symbolic Acropolitan ascent. Its monumental rendering at Savoye inspired Sigfried Giedion to declare the ramp a space-time continuum, the artistic equivalent of particle theory.[80] Its destination at Savoye is the somewhat surreal window in the solarium wall, perhaps a reference to the Savoye's car window[81] or to Madame Savoye's bedroom[82] originally intended on this level. The aedicule which remains frames equally the Virgilian landscape constructed on one side of the wall, the ramped villa on the other.

80. Sigfried Giedion, *Space, Time and Architecture*, 529, 436.
81. Richard Etlin reports that Le Corbusier's draftsmen dubbed the reference to the car, *Frank Lloyd Wright and Le Corbusier*, ff 128, 217.
82. Benton, "Architect's Practice," in Brooks, *Le Corbusier*, 92.

ramp to solarium

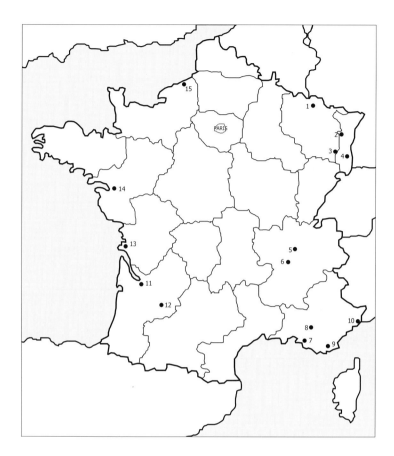

FRANCE

1. Unité d'habitation de Briey-en-
   Forêt (Cité Radieuse Le Corbusier)
2. Usine Duval
3. Chapelle Nôtre-Dame-du-Haut
4. Écluse de Kembs-Niffer
5. Couvent Sainte-Marie-de-La
   Tourette
6. Firminy-Vert
7. Unité d'habitation Marseille
8. Ateliers La Sainte-Baume
9. Villa de Mandrot
10. Le Petit Cabanon
    Grave of Le Corbusier and his
    wife, Yvonne Gallis

11. Quartier Moderne Frugès
12. Château d'Eau
13. Villa le Sextant
14. Unité d'habitation de Rezé
    (La Maison Familiale)
15. Cité Ouvrière

Le Corbusier, André Wogen-scky; engineers MM. Séchaud and Metz

ADDRESS
Cité Radieuse
Résidence Le Corbusier
Route D. 137
1 Avenue du Docteur P. Giry
Briey-en-Forêt 54150
Meurthe-et-Moselle

ACCESS
The building is now partially occupied by La Première Rue and Centre International de Pratiques et Recherches Archi-tecturales (CIPRA), a center for architecture hosting interna-tional groups of students and courses from the architecture school in Nancy as well as con-ferences and exhibits. Tel/fax 03.82.20.28.55. Tel 03.82.47.16.70, fax 03.82.47.16.79 for the residence of Le Corbusier. Email IFSI.s@Briey-cable.com.

In 1949, the mayor of Briey, Pierre Giry, conceived of a new township in the midst of greenery to pro-vide the laborers of the region with an antidote to their working environment. Had it been completed, this setting would have approximated the context Le Corbusier imagined but never realized for the Unité. The designated architect for the new town, Georges-Henri Pingusson,[2] oversaw the area plan for a Unité with separate communal and commercial facilities; he also designed adjacent housing of 49 terrace dwellings and 200 smaller units.

The third built Unité, Briey more closely resem-bles its immediate predecessor at Nantes-Rezé than the first Unité at Marseille. Those of both Nantes and Briey intended to house a working class, although at Briey the government sponsored the con-struction of rental units whereas at Nantes a worker's cooperative commissioned and owned the building. The stringent application of the national housing standards, HLM, forced Le Corbusier to reduce the apartment size even further from that at Nantes, where he thought them already too small. Neither building has the interior commercial street that Le Corbusier thought essential to the social program. Furnishings at Briey are correspondingly economical, such as the single swivel tap that fills a kitchen sink on one side and a small tub on the other.[3] Briey contains 321 apartments within precisely the same volume (110 m length by 20 m width by 50 m height) that at Nantes houses 294. In fact, some design drawings from Nantes were used for Briey, after the initial proposal for a steel-frame building at Briey was rejected.[4] Here, in modification of the experimental structure at Nantes, the "bottle-rack" frame for the apartments sits upon a horizontal table as at Marseille, which in turn rests on plate-like pilotis.

A gross mismatch of residents and setting, of regional economic dream and hard-time economic reality has made Briey the least successful of the Unités. The absence of the internal social equipment and architectural amenities seem merely details in the failure of its alternative urbanism. For a long period, the population of the building shifted continuously as the demographic of the working class changed from local laborers to immigrant workers whose cultural mores found little accommodation at Briey-en-Forêt. The decline of the local industrial base then reduced the overall population, eventually resulting in the abandonment of the building in the early 1980s. Recently, the building has found a new life as the setting for La Première Rue which hosts an international program in architecture and art.

DIRECTIONS
By car from Metz, take N.43 to Briey. In Briey, take D.906 toward Longwy, and then turn onto D.146 toward Mance. Follow signs to the Cité Radieuse.

LOCALE
The airport of Doncourt-les-Conflans, about 30 km west of Metz, has a gliding club designed by Jean Prouvé and Jacques Ogé with the help of Le Corbusier. Le Corbusier published a sketch of the building as "evidence" in *Modulor* 2.[1] He described how all three parties could work separately and yet produce an organic plan because of the unifying system of the Modulor. The roof was chosen from Prouvé's catalog and the plans drawn in Ogé's office. The documents remain in the Prouvé archive.

site plan

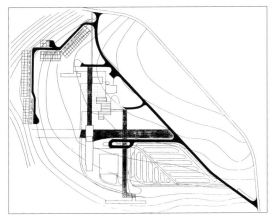

1. Le Corbusier, *Modulor* 2: 113.
2. Pingusson was the architect hired by the Ternisien's to add to the house originally designed for them by Le Corbusier.
3. *Architectural Design* 34: 163.
4. Gilles Ragot and Mathilde Dion, *Le Corbusier en France*, 181.

Le Corbusier and André Wogenscky, ATBAT with the associated firm of Boillat

ADDRESS
1, Avenue de Robache
88100 St-Dié, Vosges
Paris 388 km, Belfort 128 km,
Colmar 56 km, Mulhouse 100
km, Strasbourg 90 km

ACCESS
Private factory visible from
the street. Tours of the
factory can be arranged
by writing in advance.
www.usine.duval.free.fr.

DIRECTIONS
St-Dié is not on a major rail
line. Trains depart Nancy,
Epinal, and Strasbourg for St-
Dié about twice daily. Most
buses from these surrounding
cities require a transfer at Séle-
stat. From the St-Dié train station, the factory is about a
half-hour walk along the main

At Usine Duval, the factory that served as a model
for much of Le Corbusier's thinking became the subject of the architecture.[5] In *Vers une architecture*, Le
Corbusier had displayed factories as true forms
shaped by construction and economy but distinguished them from "architecture" per se, which ultimately moved the spirit. In his rhetoric of the
twenties, the factory became a metaphor for the production of value; for example, the Salvation Army
was a "factory of good." In the linear industrial city
and specifically in Le Corbusier's plans for the postwar reconstruction of St-Dié, the factory itself
received the metaphoric epithet "green" (*l'usine-verte*)
describing its situation in landscape and also its
plant-like function.

The commission for the Manufacture had its
ironic edge in that the owner of the factory, M. Jean-
Jacques Duval, had been an instrumental supporter
of Le Corbusier's unrealized plan for the town after
the destruction of World War II. Counter to Le Corbusier's urban plans for green factories in St-Dié,
this commission called for the reconstruction of the
family hosiery mill destroyed by fire on its original

site, at the center of town within view of the cathedral. The new building is framed within the memory of the old building and the destroyed city of St-Dié by end walls built of local stone from the ruins (as at Ronchamp). The green and utopian qualities of the project were thus muted, and the building became instead a study in "subtleties almost musical in nature" derived from the Modulor and applied to industry.[6]

The building section describes the manufacturing process as a vertical loop. (Certain changes in the process have occurred since the building's completion). The raw material of fabric and thread arrives on the ground floor where it is stored. From there, it goes to the third floor for cutting, then descends by toboggan or lift to the studio. A double-height space with balcony facing a continuous glazed wall, the studio is the centerpiece of the process and of the building. In front of its window, everyone has a place according to his/her role: ironers on a small balcony, seamstresses on the main floor, finishers underneath the balcony, and supervisors in a glass-encased lookout post on the upper level. The fabric makes a smaller vertical loop within this space, from sewing on the main floor to ironing on the balcony. The finished item returns to the ground floor to be packed, then exits via chute to the storage and loading dock. The Duvals have their offices on the roof.[7] The building systems serving the work appear along side it. Green for air-conditioning, yellow for electricity and blue for water, the exposed and color-coded pipes connect the building even more graphically than the abstract procession of goods.

The spatial structure accommodating these diagrams of process is a hybrid of Le Corbusier's early

street toward the cathedral. It is on the left, just past the cemetery.

LOCALE
St-Dié is located in the picturesque mountains of Alsace. Although much of it was destroyed during World War II, portions of the cathedral and a chapel survive. A possible itinerary moves south from St-Dié to the canal station designed by Le Corbusier outside of Mulhouse and then to Ronchamp.

typical floor plan

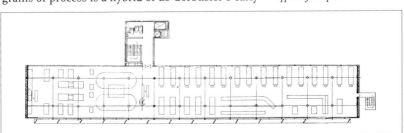

5. For displacement concepts see Alan Colquhoun, *Essays in Architectural Criticism*, 51–67.

6. Le Corbusier, *Modulor* 2: 161.

7. Conversation with M. Jean-Jacques Duval.

free plan and the emerging systems of his Unité. The studio is a Unité (or Citrohan) living room, located correctly above pilotis, below the roof garden and behind the brise-soleil, but extended along the entire length of the building. In place of the parallel walls of the Citrohan and Unité, there are columns that allow for the free flow of goods and activities through the space.

An image shared with the Unité is that of a great ship, which Le Corbusier considered metaphorically as an industrially produced floating utopia. At Manufacture Duval, the particular nautical references are found in the pipe rails at deck levels, the funnel-shaped conference room and the smokestack stair. If the Unité is an ocean liner for dwelling and recreation, the factory is a freighter for work, with a communal interior rather than cabins and a deck that belongs to the captain.

The identity of the building as a "green-factory" pertains then not to its site but to the social utopian goals of the internal workings. These internal workings are themselves understood as natural, in that they mimic the order of the living body. The circulation of the life-supporting substances of goods, people and services suggests animal functioning. First explored in Le Corbusier's buildings of the thirties through curtain walls and air conditionning, this biomechanical metaphor takes on a new character in the "green" architecture of wood windows and brise-soleil. The pre-fabricated wood frames with pre-drilled screw holes are installed in a continuous trough in a concrete sill. A small array of standard sized frames are paired and reversed to create a varied fenestration. The independent rhythms of concrete columns (625 cm spacing), window trellis (366 cm width), and brise-soleil alveoli (592 cm) overlap so that no bay repeats but all relate to the Modulor. To Le Corbusier, this modulation embodied an organic pattern and the integrated construction of building and society befitting a postwar world.

CHAPELLE NÔTRE-DAME-DU-HAUT

1950–1955

Le Corbusier at first rebuffed the invitation to design the chapel at Ronchamp, which came soon after Church authorities had rejected his project for the shrine of Saint Mary Magdalene at La Sainte-Baume. But believing that modern art could rejuvenate the Church, Canon Lucien Ledeur of Besançon and Father Alain Couturier, who would also be instrumental in the commission for La Tourette, prevailed on him to accept the job by promising him design freedom.

Dissent from within the Church was to be expected, but the completed chapel shocked the architectural world as well. Those who revered Le Corbusier as champion of reason saw the "freedom" of the chapel as an expressionist, irrational aberration.[8] The chapel is unique if not anti-typological within the work of an architect known for his typologies. Others saw its organic form as a humanistic enrichment of modern architecture and its Modulor proportions as evidence of its underlying rationality. From a current perspective, it appears an exploration of reason's limits and excesses. Supporting this are Le Corbusier's own impassioned equivocations in

Le Corbusier with André Maisonnier, benches by Joseph Savina

ADDRESS
70250 Ronchamp
Haut-Saône
Belfort 21 km, Besançon 91 km, Lure 12 km, Vesoul 43 km

ACCESS
Open to the public 9:30–6:30 April through September, 10–5 October and March, 10–4 November through February. For more visitor information go to www.chapellederonchamp.com. Tel 03.84.20.65.13, fax 03.84.20.67.51. It remains an important pilgrimage site. For the full intended effect, walk up the hill of Bourlémont to the chapel rather than drive.

By car, take the road from
Belfort to Lure, N.19 which
passes through Ronchamp. Turn
north off the main road at the
stone arch and proceed 2 km up
hill to the café and chapel. Once
in town, there are signs to the
chapel.
    Ronchamp is difficult to
reach by public transportation.
There is one early morning train
from Belfort or Lure to Ronchamp and one early evening
train in the opposite direction.
Service to Belfort and Lure
from major towns is frequent.
There are taxis from Belfort and
Lure train stations to Ronchamp. The ride from Lure is
less than 20 min.

LOCALE
Ronchamp is a tiny village. If
you intend to stay overnight in
the vicinity you might stay in
Belfort. From Ronchamp, possible itineraries include
Besançon, the region of Alsace,
and Geneva.

site plan

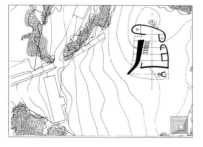

The Modulor: "It was a pleasure here [at Ronchamp] to allow free play to the resources of the Modulor, keeping a corner of one's eye on the game to avoid blunders. For blunders lie in wait for you, beckon you on, tug at your sleeve, drag you down into the abyss."[9] He challenged: "The Modulor everywhere. I defy the visitor to give the dimensions of the different parts of the building."[10] Taking the challenge in a brilliant analysis, Robin Evans has found Modulor measurements alternately displayed as ornamental lines on the floor and furnishings or buried as the structural armature within canted walls, whose curved surfaces exceed the Modulor's logic.[11]

The great source of inspiration for Ronchamp other than the Modulor was the landscape. The generalized terms Le Corbusier used to describe his work often overshadow the complexity of its site-specific response; in this case, he acknowledged the dominant role of the hillside from the first. The plan is four curved lines, an "acoustical" response to the four horizons viewed from the hilltop: the valley of the Saône to the west, the chain of the Vosges to the east, a small valley to the south, and a northern valley beyond which rise the Jura mountains and the landscape of Le Corbusier's youth. By "acoustic"—a term he had employed in the earlier Swiss Pavilion—he meant to describe "how the curved walls simultaneously gather and open to the landscape. . . to give a suggestion of the great extent of the landscape, far beyond the building's boundary"[12] and beyond the boundary of optical experience.

The site's history as a sacred place also entered into the design. The chapel stands on the foundation of a church dating from the twelfth century, which had been rebuilt several times before its total destruction in World War II. Worship on the hilltop dates back to a megalithic cult of the sun, continuing through Roman times until it became associated with an effigy of the Virgin with mystical powers. The coupling of sun and Virgin resonated with Le Corbusier's personal cosmology of masculine and feminine powers. Whereas his male principle is "strong objectivity of form against the light of the Mediterranean sun," the feminine is "limitless subjectivity rising against a clouded sky."[13] The site's associations with the Virgin led Le Corbusier to use the sensual forms of the rolling landscape and the female body found in his paintings. The feminine is explicitly named in the three light canons of Ronchamp, two white and one red, which Le Corbusier dedicated to the Virgin, his mother and, his wife Yvonne. Embodied in the singular site of Ronchamp, the uncontrolled subjectivity of the feminine is kept safely distinct from the rational program of modern architecture.

The inscription on a stained glass window, *mer* recalls the connection of mother and sea imbedded in the French language.[14] At Ronchamp, the absent sea and missing well spring are made present in the exterior water basin. Le Corbusier likened the roof form to a crab shell found on a Long Island beach. In the dim chapel, the roof swells up, the floor dips down, and the western wall ripples as if the space were somehow fluid.

Le Corbusier saw mountain and sea as opposite but complimentary poles of the natural world. The reference to water and sea is an effort to imaginatively complete the landscape of Ronchamp through architecture. Such an ideal landscape in its complete form existed for Le Corbusier at the Acropolis which extends "from the Pentelicus to the Piraeus, the mountains to the sea."[15] Based on the qualities of the site and his own sense of the sacred, Le Corbusier fashioned a personal acropolis at Ronchamp with a Panathenaic procession and an ontogeny of religious forms. The sequence starts at the bottom of the hill and the beginning of time with an artificial hillock like a dolmen or burial mound, before reaching the propylaeum of the youth hostel and parish house. The chapel rises out of the hill like a Greek temple in three-quarter view. To the east is a ziggurat, officially a monument to the dead of

8. James Stirling, "Ronchamp and the Crisis of Rationalism," *Architectural Review* 119: 155–61.

9. Le Corbusier, *Modulor* 2: 254.

10. Le Corbusier, *Texts and Sketches from Ronchamp*, unpaginated.

11. Robin Evans, *The Projective Cast*, 272–320.

12. Le Corbusier, *The Chapel at Ronchamp*, 110. Also, Jean Petit, *Le Livre de Ronchamp*, 35.

13. Le Corbusier *Modulor* 1: 224.

14. The words "mère" (mother) and "mer" (sea), are homonyms. For iconography at Ronchamp see the authoritative work of Danièle Pauly, *Lecture d'une architecture*, 347. Also see Danièle Pauly, "The Chapel of Ronchamp as an example of Le Corbusier's Creative Process," Brooks ed., *Le Corbusier*. For a discussion of the feminine see also Evans, *Projective Cast*, 287.

15. Le Corbusier, *Towards*, 187.

16. Le Corbusier, *Ronchamp*, unpaginated.
17. Ibid. Also, for the procession see, Stuart Cohen and Steven Hurtt, "The Pilgrimage Chapel at Ronchamp," *Oppositions* 19/20: 142–57.
18. For iconographic interpretation see Richard Moore, "Alchemical Symbolism in the Poem of the Right Angle," *Oppositions* 19/20; also Richard Moore, *Le Corbusier Myth and Meta Architecture: The Late Period.*
19. Le Corbusier, *Modulor* 2: 253.
20. Kenneth Frampton, *Modern Architecture*, 228–9.
21. For airplane technology see Ford, *Details* 2: 189–95.
22. Manfredo Tafuri, *Modern Architecture*:2, 319.

World War II but also an ancient altar, a sacred mountain, a necropolis. In Le Corbusier's own work it had appeared in the Mundaneum project (1929) as a museum of complete knowledge. To the west is a bell tower, the essential fragment of the Gothic cathedral that once stood here. Le Corbusier intended that the bells be electronically programmed to play modern music by Edgar Varèse so that the site would have a "structural link between time and sound" and a "limitless voice coming from the most distant ages and reaching the most modern hours of the day."[16]

A sequence of axial perspectives defined but not enclosed by these built outcroppings draws the pilgrim around the chapel counterclockwise and past the available entrances in a procession most critics describe as magnetic. The path comes to rest at the open-air altar in nature, the primary place of worship according to the architect: "Inside a little talk with oneself. Outside, 10,000 pilgrims before the altar."[17]

The iconography of Ronchamp exceeds a cohesive summation. Part of the mystique of the chapel is the process by which its roving array of inspirations culled from Le Corbusier's memory joined with his immediate responses to produce its form. Some have used the text of Le Corbusier's *Poème de l'angle droit*, which is steeped in mythology and alchemy, to unlock an allegory based on the figure of the bull-minotaur, whose profile might appear on the western wall.[18] Le Corbusier gives an array of disparate architectural sources: the stone storage chambers of the Serapeum of Hadrian's villa for the light canons, industrial dams for the battered walls, the mosques of M'zàb. He remarked that Ronchamp "was not a matter of pillars but of plastic event. . . ruled not by scholarly or academic formulae but free and innumerable."[19]

Underlying the sacred space is a tectonic argument between the pillar and plastic

Chapel, interior view

event. Ironically, after a lifetime asserting the primacy of the column and its pedigree in the Greek temple, the chapel appears constructed of battered walls evoking a sacred cave such as the one Le Corbusier drew for La Sainte-Baume. In contrast, the open-air altar beneath the draped concrete roof appears like the fabric tent of the Hebrew tabernacle[20] which Le Corbusier considered the origin of architecture, and repeatedly interpreted in the Pavillon de Temps Nouveau (1937) and the hyperbolic curves of the Phillips Pavilion (1958). The roof closely resembles the stressed skin membranes of tents and aircraft.[21] It has two thin concrete shells (6 cm each) held 2 meters apart by internal concrete girders and pre-cast beams. The originally intended structure of a metal truss with aluminum sheathing made the aerodynamic inspiration explicit. The great pivoting door retains this metal structure. Much of the drama of the building comes from this explosion into membranes and suspended planes of what first seems a solid mass of a building.

While buried beneath the illusion of tent and cave, the column is still of primary importance. Three walls have concrete columns imbedded in the rubble from the destroyed church. The southern wall is a concrete armature (of Modulor proportions) sprayed with Gunite. Both the slot of space below the roof and the single, exposed post by the outdoor altar make the columnar presence quite clear.

Given the activity of form, the wealth of imagery, and the complexity of structure, the interior of the chapel is striking in its subdued and empty quality. The ancillary chapels with their dramatic lighting are hidden. The floor slopes away, as does the roof. In the words of Tafuri, "a programmatic loss of center. . . [reveals] his art in search of its own origins."[22] The point of arrival is a point of departure.

ÉCLUSE DE KEMBS-NIFFER
1960–1962

Le Corbusier and Alain Tavès

ADDRESS
Canal de Neuf-Brisach
Embranchement de Huningue-
Rhin, Haut Rhin
Mulhouse 29 km, Colmar 60
km, Basel 25 km

ACCESS
The site is always accessible.
The customs station is open on
request of manager during
working hours which are
approximately 9–12:30 and
2–5:30 M–F.

DIRECTIONS
By car take A.36 from Mulhouse. Turn right on D.52 and
continue along the Rhine
toward Basel until D.468. The
lock is visible from the road on
the right. Buses leave the Mulhouse train station for Niffer
and Kembs about eight times a
day. (tel. 89.44.41.90). The
lock is just beyond Niffer,

At the initiative of M. Bouchet, the regional director for roads and bridges, Le Corbusier designed the customs house and watchtower for this lock on a branch of the Rhône-Rhine Canal.[23] The modest program on an extended site offered him an opportunity to elaborate on some favored landscape themes. As in many late works, Le Corbusier treated the flow of water as a significant if not mythic power. Here, the architecture dramatizes the level changes of the lock, the fall of the water, and the branching of the canal.

The vertical section of the structures and the designated path through them are mimetic of the site. The entry sequence first descends a flight of steps built into the hillside and then, from the machine room, ascends a stair case to the main floor at the level of the lock. The machine room chimney extends through the sod-covered roof to the height of the customs house as a vertical complement to the horizontal water and as a totem denoting the levels of the site. The watchtower is an enclosed fragment of a much larger vertical axis connecting the levels of the sluiceway. Its stairs continue down along the natural cliff to the lowest level of water.

The architecture also narrates the parting of the canal water. The watchtower establishes two distinct views from the two stairway flights on either side of the central concrete support, one toward the Rhine, the other toward the main canal. The views are joined in a continuous panorama from the lookout station, which is twisted off the orthogonal of the tower. Similarly, in the customs house, the twist of the roof and placement of the end columns create the impression that the building has been laterally pulled in two, creating a path between. The "columns" are actually drainpipes fed by the angles of the roof. The continuous rain water, divided into two streams by the roof, recapitulates the embranchment of the canal. From a distance, the V-shape of the roof engages a broad section of sky, drawing it deep into the crux of the building. This figure appears in other of Le Corbusier's work, most notably his project for the Errazuris house (1930). Here on the flat Alsatian plane, the diagonals also appear perspective lines leading to opposite horizons at either end of the canal.

As a water machine, the lock is intrinsically connected to the work of Le Corbusier, whose obsession with nature also extended to refashioning it as "machines for living." He was fascinated by water, its horizontal leveling, and the natural cycles to which it belongs. His oeuvre is filled with buildings on the edge of bodies of water, either manmade or suitably framed, the Heidi Weber Pavilion, the Unité at Nantes, the Assembly at Chandigarh, la Petite Maison at Vevey among them. The lock afforded an already complex situation to which Le Corbusier responded by reiterating its play between natural and constructed boundaries.

about a 35-minute bus ride. Get off at the Niffer town hall and continue walking in the direction of the bus route (D.468). The lock will be on your right.

LOCALE

The lock is south of a group of towns noted for their textiles, white wine and pork dishes. Closest accommodations are in Mulhouse, which boasts a comprehensive textile museum and a Rhenish Renaissance town hall. Colmar or Mulhouse make a base for an itinerary which includes Usine Duval and Ronchamp.

sections of the custom house

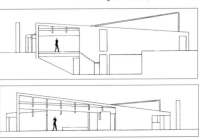

watchtower

23. Ragot and Dion, *Le Corbusier en France*, 185.

Le Corbusier, Iannis Xenakis; Fernand Gardien site supervision; André Wogenscky construction documents

ADDRESS
La Tourette
Frères dominicains
couvent de la Tourette
BP105 Éveux
69591 l'Arbresle-cedex

ACCESS
Open 10–12 and 2–6 except Sunday mornings April–June, Sept., and Oct. During Nov.–March, the only tour is at 2:30. For visitor information and tour schedule go to www.couventlatourette.com. To make reservations for the convent, write resa@couventlatourette.com. Tel 04.74.26.79.70, fax 04.74.26.79.99.

The commission for La Tourette, following soon after that for Ronchamp, was advocated by Father Alain Couturier, who considered Le Corbusier's avowed agnosticism secondary to the sacred value inherent in his architecture. For Le Corbusier, the commission was attractive as housing for a community for which he felt affinity. His initial statement of resistance toward the ecclesiastical commission, "I can't build churches for men who don't live there," was overcome by Couturier's brief "to house 100 hearts and 100 bodies in silence."[24] The cloister was to accommodate the intellectual and spiritual training of novice Dominicans near the cultural center of Lyon. As a consequence of Vatican II (1962–65), the original habitation of the convent was short-lived, and it continues today as a conference center for the order and the public.[25]

The architect's affinity for the project of a monastery ran deep. Le Corbusier had long before formulated his own social ideal based on the monastic balance of the individual and collective. He was inspired by youthful encounters with the Charterhouses of Galuzzo (a.k.a. Ema) and of Athos, whose sheer cliff is recalled in La Tourette's north face. He found Couturier's suggested model for the project, the abbey of Le Thoronet, equally compelling; its influence can be seen most particularly in the oratory. Moreover, Le Corbusier personally aspired to certain monastic values, including material simplicity, self-discipline, and silence. That this monastery was for the Dominican order was fortuitous in that, as Colin Rowe elucidates, "an architectural dialectician, the greatest, was to service the archsophisticates of dialectics."[26] The dialectic of the architecture emerges in intense contrasts of form, challenging the strict rendition of monastery typology.

A confrontation of the ideal and the material played a continuing role in the building's realization. Le Corbusier entrusted the design development of the building to the musician-engineer Iannis Xenakis with the words "it is pure geometry—a Dominican monastery. . . . it must be geometric."[27] The geometric rule of the building encompasses the underlying forms of prismatic solids, the application of Modulor measurements to many aspects of the interior, and the mathematically and musically derived window patterns. As conceived by Xenakis,[28] the pinwheel fenestration of the common rooms and classrooms are permutations of the golden section that unfold along the facade, similar to the combinatorials of his musical composition *Metastasis*, which he composed at the same time. In the corridor *ondulatoire*, or undulating glazing, the Modulor spacing of the concrete vertical mullions creates a continuously modulated effect of surface and light, much as the increments of the tempered scale create a shifting density of sound.[29] The *ondulatoire* geometry attempts to reveal the dialectic present within mathematics itself, between the incremental and the continuous, the rational and the irrational.[30] Similarly, the apparently static, rectangular south side of the church actually tilts in all directions, countering Euclidean form with optical distortions of depth and

DIRECTIONS

By car, take N7 from Lyon for 25 km to L'Arbresle. From L'Arbresle take D19 to Éveux. By train, it is approximately a 30-minute trip on the local line from the Lyon-Perrache station to L'Arbresle, direction Roanne. Trains run about once an hour with some longer gaps in the morning schedule. Check alternate local lines as well. Buses for L'Arbresle depart station Gorge-de-Loup. From the L'Arbresle train station the convent is a 2 km walk, uphill. Facing the hillside, take the road to the right, and at the intersection take the left toward Éveux. A sign marks the convent road.

LOCALE

The convent is located on the pastoral hillside above the town of L'Arbresle to the west of Lyon. A possible itinerary includes La Tourette on a day trip from Lyon and could encompass the town of Firminy-Vert to the south.

Corridor with ondulatoire *glazing*

rotation. The ear-shaped crypt has a constantly variable curvature constructed through incremental shifts of straight lines, which are visible in the concrete shuttering. As in the ruled surfaces of Ronchamp, the crypt reveals how the essentially two-dimensional Modulor and shuttered construction only approximate an algebraic curve.

Because Le Corbusier conceived the convent in steel which proved too expensive, and subsequently delegated the construction documents to André Wogenscky's office, the site supervision to Fernand Gardien, and the development of concrete technique to the contractors SET (Sud Est Travaux), some have concluded that he felt the material quality of secondary importance, "only ideas being transmissible."[31] The contractors at La Tourette were expert in the use of concrete for public infrastructure, but not its architectural application. Le Corbusier's concurrent work on Chandigarh, which occupied most of his attention, was similarly constructed in concrete of variable finish under sporadic supervision by the architect. Le Corbusier even chose to employ some of the detailing of India at La Tourette, specifically, setting the glass panels directly in the concrete in combination with a shuttered opening for air, called an *aerateur*. Entrusting the physical expression of his design to those building it was at once a logical acceptance of circumstance and a romantic act based on a neo-Gothic trust in the relation of the workman to the work. Le Corbusier wanted the words "here has passed the hand of man"[32] inscribed under a stairwell window made trapezoidal by mistake. The inconsistent rendering of abstract geometry through the individualized shuttering of rough concrete becomes a thematic duality of the building.

View of cloister with chapel roof

Despite its aura of worn handwork, much of La Tourette is prefabricated concrete, including columns, beams, and balcony facings. In fact, the precast structural grid developed by SET proved essential, in that it made the building affordable. The detailing joins primitive and sophisticated means rather seamlessly, just as Le Corbusier's late rhetoric pairs the archetypal with the new. Some of the brutish exposure of the mechanical systems is the result of poor coordination, but most of the contrasts in levels of finish are intentional. The interior walls are masonry block finished with sprayed Gunite or plaster. The floors are cast in place over ribs of hollow masonry, a technique Le Corbusier used in the villas of the 1920s to give the appearance of the flat slab.[33] The candle-like step lights are bare bulbs set directly in the concrete. The door to the church borrows the metal skin and shape of airplanes and ships. The shutters on the *aerateurs* are bent metal with an airfoil profile but the simplest of carved wood handles.

Below, from top to bottom: Ground, first, and third level floor plans

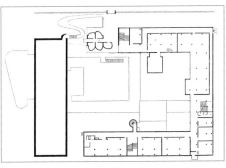

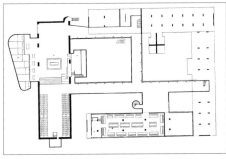

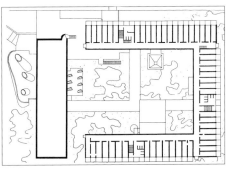

Le Corbusier's view of monastic life, as an "indissoluble binomial of the individual-collective," was in itself dialectical. At La Tourette he addressed the design of a type that was already an essential part of his architecture, having influenced the early *immeuble-villa* and the Unité d'habitation. In a perhaps ironic, reverse transformation, the cloister-inspired apartments of the Unité become the individual cells of La Tourette, the Unité corridors become the passages cutting across the traditional cloister. The sacred space of the church has its own binary relation to collective spaces assembled around the courtyard. The architectural systems enhance this social logic. The columnar system of the Dom-ino and the free plan it generates occur in the collective spaces of refectory, library and offices. The individual cells are walled, "tunnel-like"[34] spaces derived from the Citrohan house. Their columns are buried within the walls, as can be read from the short beam ends exposed in the strip window. The courtyard complex raised above the earth on pilotis opposes the sanctuary, which descends with the land so that, as Le Corbusier observed, "the lowest place becomes the highest, the highest the lowest."[35]

The canonical opposition of light and darkness appears here in the lucidity of secular space and the obscurity of places of faith. As Rowe suggests in a Hegelian vein, "negation becomes positive" in the darkness of the church.[36] Within this overarching structure of light are, however, a multiplicity of effects which resist easy categorization. Chapel and crypt have no less than five types of openings for light including the great "canons" which transmute light into floating discs of color. The fenestration of the secular spaces includes strip windows, the pinwheel glass wall, and the *ondulatoire* with its conceptually infinite effects. On the loggia wall of each cell is a concrete square in high relief as a measure of light and shadow.

Another prominent duality is that between architecture and nature: monastery and hillside are almost independent of one another.[37] Asserting that the project budget left no choice, Le Corbusier struck a line in relation to the horizon, and "hung" the floors of dormitory and collective space from it, letting the pilotis hit the ground where they may so that the building projects above the untended landscape. Cloister pathways disrupt the traditional courtyard garden, which appears on the roof. Neither captured nor cultivated in a cloistered garden, nature remains a thing for contemplation beyond the refectory window. Yet even the view of nature is often denied. Despite their symmetrical positioning, the courtyard corridors have one blank

Altar, with "canon" of light

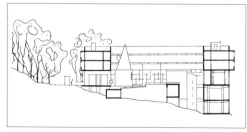

Section

Rooftop view

and one glazed wall. The perimeter corridors end in a window blocked by a concrete panel, which Le Corbusier called a "flower of ventilation." The traditional perimeter cloister is displaced to the roof as a solitary walk, but the parapet is built so high as to eclipse the very panorama it might have offered.

Though an obstruction to a promised delight, the parapet presents in its place the power of a constructed horizon punctuated by the vertical forms of chimney and bell tower. This room, open only to the sky, appears in other projects but, in the context of La Tourette, becomes a vehicle of detachment from the worldly. In its fabricated boundary is the spirit of the temples of the Acropolis which "drew around them the desolate landscape, gathering it into the composition"[38] through the horizon. According to Le Corbusier, the horizon is the "line of transcendental immobility" where mathematical order and nature coincide. In conjunction with its opposite, the vertical force of gravity, it reveals "the full power of a synthesis," a right angle that is "the sum of forces which keep the world in equilibrium."[39] While this line binds reason and nature it does so at an unfathomable distance. It is always present, never reachable, perceptible but not palpable, single but infinite and represents the boundary of the human condition as Le Corbusier found it.

24. Father Alain Couturier in Sergio Ferro et al., *Le Couvent de La Tourette*, 12.
25. Antoine Lion, "Continuité et Mutations au Couvent de La Tourette," in Prelorenzo, *La Conservation de L'Oeuvre Construite de Le Corbusier*, 91–99.
26. Colin Rowe, *The Mathematics of the Ideal Villa*, 194.
27. Iannis Xenakis in Ferro, *Le Couvent*, 81.
28. Xenakis, "The Monastery of La Tourette," in Brooks, *Le Corbusier*, 143–163.
29. Xenakis in Le Corbusier, *Modulor 2*: 326.
30. Evans, *Projective Cast*, 296.
31. Le Corbusier, trans. Ivan Zaknic, *The Final Testament of Père Corbu*, 83.
32. Le Corbusier in Ferro, *Le Couvent.*, ff. 81.
33. Ferro, *Le Couvent*, 98–103, 43–53; and Ford, *Details 2*: 211.
34. Rowe, *Ideal Villa*, 195 and Vincent Scully, *Modern Architecture*, 42.
35. Le Corbusier, *L'Art Sacré* 7.
36. Rowe, *Ideal Villa*, 197.
37. Le Corbusier, *Oeuvre Complète* 6: 42. "The convent is posed within the savage nature of the forest and the grasslands which is independent of the architecture."
38. Le Corbusier, *Towards*, 188.
39. Le Corbusier, *The City of Tomorrow*, 26–7.

**LA MAISON DE LA CULTURE
ET LA JEUNESSE (ALSO
ESPACE LE CORBUSIER)**
1959–1965

Le Corbusier, Stribick
engineers

ADDRESS
Rue de St. Just-Malmont
BP 40/ 42700 Firminy, Loire

STADE
1965–1968

Le Corbusier, André Wogenscky,
Fernand Gardien

ADDRESS
1, rue des Noyers
42700 Firminy, Loire

**CHURCH OF SAINT-PIERRE
DE FIRMINY**
1961–1970, incomplete

Le Corbusier, José Oubrerie

ADDRESS
Place-du-Mail

UNITÉ D'HABITATION
1968

Le Corbusier, André Wogenscky

ADDRESS
Les Bruneaux
47200 Firminy
Lyon 67 km, St Etienne 12 km

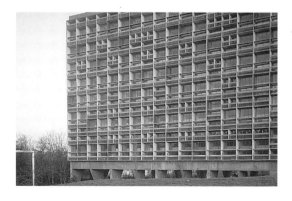

At Firminy, the bombings of World War II provided the prepatory clearing of the nineteenth-century industrial city that Le Corbusier often proposed in his urban projects. The overcrowded and substandard living conditions of the laborers and the pollution of the mines were notorious enough to earn the town the epithet "Firminy Noir" and immortalization in the writings of Zola.[40] Upon becoming mayor in 1953, Eugène Claudius-Petit, the former Minister of Reconstruction who had championed the Unité at Marseille, envisioned an alternative "Firminy-Vert" as a new enclave removed from industry and the nineteenth-century town on an open site surrounding a disused quarry. The rhetoric of Claudius-Petit resounded with the principles of CIAM and the Corbusian vocabulary of the Athens Charter. According to Claudius-Petit, Firminy-Vert would "a) lay the foundations for the renaissance of the human being, the family, the society, to effect an authentic revolution in the gestures of everyday life which would directly effect mothers and would largely determine the behavior of children; b) create the site, the everyday urban landscape, spaces, volumes, shapes and colors; to make the history of the town by means of utilitarian constructions seeing that nothing has been left of the town's past."[41]

As was often the case, entrusting the design of the new town to Le Corbusier proved too controversial, so that the Athens Charter entered the world through the designs of other architects, in this case André Sive and Michael Roux, Jean Kling and Charles Delfante. Firminy was initially regarded as a model of town planning because of the collaborative and interdisciplinary nature of the design team and the use of public consultation in the design process. Le Corbusier received the commission for a stadium and cultural center combined as a single building, followed by the Unité and finally the church. The pool complex was designed after Le Corbusier's death by Wogenscky.

While not the town plan per se, Le Corbusier's commission encompassed a site roughly the size of the capitol complex of India and contained the

ACCESS
Guided tours of approximately three hours leave M–F at 2:30 PM and weekends and alternative times by appointment from the Maison de la Culture/ Espace Le Corbusier. The tour visits the interiors of all the buildings including an apartment in the Unité and the works of the church. The larger site is always accessible for free. For additional information and reservations, contact the Espace Le Corbusier at espace.le.corbusier@ wanadoo.fr. Reservations can also be made at mairie@ville-firminy.fr. Tel 04.77.10.07.77, fax 04.77.56.47.37.

DIRECTIONS
By car, take Autoroute N88 Lyon-St Etienne-Le Puy from Lyon. Exit at Firminy following signs to Firminy-Vert, then to "Patrimonie Le Corbusier." From St Etienne, take A47 to Firminy and follow the signs. Public transportation from Lyon or St Etienne requires changes and can take over two hours. By train from Lyon Part-Dieu, go to St Etienne and switch to the St Etienne-Firminy line departing the local station Château Creux. From the train station at Firminy, take bus #23 Place-du-Breil to Firminy-Vert or walk along rue Jean-Jaurès to boulevard St Charles and then up the hill (20 min.). By bus from St Etienne-Bellevue, take the Firminy-Pont Cahney lines #1 or #2.

LOCALE
Firminy and the adjacent development of Firminy-Vert are at the center of the coal and iron mining district that encircles

St Etienne. Firminy-Vert is primarily residential. A possible itinerary centers on Lyon with day trips to Firminy and La Tourette.

40. Judi Loach, "Le Corbusier at Firminy-Vert," Raeburn and Wilson, *Architect of the Century*, 338–9.
41. Eugène Claudius-Petit in Le Corbusier, *Oeuvre Complète* 8: 11.
42. Anthony Eardly, *Le Corbusier's Church at Firminy*, 5. Le Corbusier mentions Santa Sophia and Stonehenge as sources of the development of the design for Firminy Church.
43. Ibid., 35.
44. Martin Purdy, "Le Corbusier and the Theological Program," in Walden, *The Open Hand*, 286–322.
45. See entry, Unité d'habitation at Marseille.
46. Loach, "Le Corbusier at Firminy Vert," in Raeburn and Wilson, *Architect of the Century*, 343.

Youth center roof

largest ensemble of his buildings outside of Chandigarh. He treated the project from the first as an urban landscape, reminiscent of an agora. The fabricated "history of utilitarian constructions" echoed with antiquity in the placement of monumental forms on the edges of the old quarry. The eventual separation of the cultural center as a "stoa" across from the stadium complex, and the addition of the Unité as a temple on top of the hill enhanced the allusion. Le Corbusier also envisioned an open-air stage for electronic spectacles, and an enclosed theater like an odeion, neither of which were built. Anthony Eardly finds an antique source for the church in the Telesterion at Eleusis, a connection made more pronounced by its pseudo-ruined state.[42] In accordance with the desires of the clergy, the church is located in the crater at the bottom of the hill, where Le Corbusier placed it to mark the major crossroads at the entrance to the site. Even incomplete, the church forges a connection to the raised stadium just behind it and the hills beyond. The buildings merge as an ensemble through their strict solar orientation along the east-west axis. Across the site, they establish a dialogue focused intently on each other and the landscape, less concerned with their relation to the intervening housing of Firminy than to a timeless, ideal city.

The cultural center owes its distinctive shape to the original program which incorporated the stadium seating at its base shaded by building above. The ministries of athletics and culture demanded the separation of the programs; but Le Corbusier kept the form and re-sited the building farther up on the ridge of the mine. The three levels within take advantage of the canted section and its relation to the slope: a lowest level of services and café, a primary section containing theater rehearsal and exhibit space at ridge level, and a mezzanine of offices.

The catenary roof was inspired by the expertise of the building engineers who had recently completed a suspension bridge. Pairs of cables are draped in a parabola between the two bearing walls, canted outward as an expression of the tensile struc-

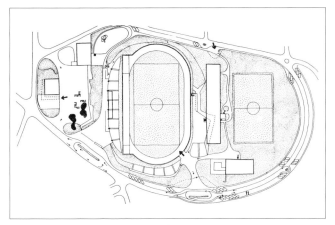

ture. The frieze of small rectangular openings at the top of the walls provides access to the tie rods which secure the cables and allow the tension to be regulated from the outside. The roof sheathing is of Celium auto-matted, cellular concrete plates, 10 cm thick, which rest directly on the cables as can be seen from the inside. The sculptural "gargoyles" at either end are roof drains toward which the roof panels slope. The "give" in this experimental structure has caused some problems over time and required renovation of the roof.

The form of the church descends from a much earlier design of Le Corbusier's for the chapel of Gabrielle de Monzie at Tremblay (1929) in which a cubic tower rises from a ramped base. The hyperbolic conical section of Firminy and its construction of thin-shell concrete were inspired by nuclear cooling towers Le Corbusier saw in India and employed as the roof in the Assembly at Chandigarh. The cone evokes in turn the mountains of slag in mining regions of France which Le Corbusier drew to resemble the pyramids of Giza in *When the Cathedrals Were White*.[43] It becomes the vessel of the sanctuary supported on a base of vestries. An exterior ramp leads directly to the space and the seating suspended within.

In the later part of his life, Le Corbusier considered it his goal to restore the sacred to the every day. Reluctant to build for an orthodoxy other than his own, he agreed to the commission of the Church in

end elevation Maison de Culture

1960 under pressure from his friend Claudius-Petit because its congregants were the working class of Firminy-Vert, the constituency and inhabitants of his other work there. Neither the plan nor the imagery of the church are strictly liturgical.[44] The eastern sun plays a determining role in the orientation of the light canon; and the geometry suggests the mystical transmutation of cube, pyramid, cylinder and cone. His late iconography based on a mythologically empowered nature appears elsewhere at Firminy, in the bas-relief on the youth center: a bull's head with the floating image of a feminine face, a human ear and a conch shell, four branches with leaves shaped like human heads. The real arena for his sense of the sacred is, however, the Unité.[45]

The apartment building at Firminy is the last completed Unité d'habitation, the great invention of Le Corbusier's late studio. At the time of this work at Firminy, largely in reaction to personal events including the death of his wife, Le Corbusier had radically shifted the structure and personnel of his atelier, peremptorily releasing the designers who had worked with him for years, and devoting the effort of his young team to the production of the Unités. A research component accompanied design, first in the sense that Le Corbusier treated the Unités as part of his ongoing study of the linear industrial city whether the commissions called for this planning or not. At Firminy, his original commission and study involved the disposition of three Unités in the district Chazeau, annexed to Firminy. In the end, the town completed only the single Unité of 414 units, 131 m long x 21 m wide x 50 m high; but looking west from the Unité one can see the site of the foundations for a second Unité. Research and development also tracked the working of the Unités at Marseille and Nantes.[46] The design for Firminy attempted to comply with the most frequent requests for more parking, a separate nursery school entrance, more public club rooms, bathtubs, broom closets, and loggias at the living room rather than bedroom level. Another area of constant study was the structure of the Unité. At Firminy, Claudius-Petit's request for fewer supports and greater transparency at ground level resulted in the placement of pilotis every other bay and the alternation of their angled profiles. The upper apartment structure of concrete slab and orthogonal walls rests on the "artificial ground" which is in turn supported by the pilotis. The stringent funding that played a determining role in all the Unités other than Marseille continued here, so that the small apartments and absence of a shopping street which Le Corbusier considered the real failings remained problems.

The shifting economy and political scene led to the replacement of Claudius-Petit by a communist mayor in 1970 and a critical reassessment of the capital expenditures of Firminy-Vert. The decline of the region's industry well into the next decade left the new town underpopulated and disused. The Unité in particular became an oversized burden, difficult and expensive to run. The town decided to "half" abandon it by installing Plexiglas walls at the middle of the building to close off the interior streets and apartments to one side. Since this rather surreal low point, the town has received the attention first of artists and architects who used the Unité as a site for installations, and then the public and regional authorities who have restored the cultural center and plan to complete the church. Oblivious to the critique of suburban sprawl lodged in the idea of the Unité, housing developments now blanket the hillside as evidence of a renewed economic prosperity that has transformed Le Corbusier's Firminy from an abandoned plan for the future to a patrimony.

UNITÉ D'HABITATION MARSEILLE

1945–1952

Le Corbusier, André Maisonnier with Jacques Masson, Roger Aujame, Felix Candilis, Jerzy Soltan, among others and ATBAT André Wogenscky, Vladimir Bodiansky and others.

ADDRESS
La Cité Radieuse
280, boulevard Michelet
13008 Marseille
Bouches-du-Rhone

ACCESS
Without a reservation, you can see the building from the gardens and the roof terrace. By appointment you can arrange to see a room furnished as it was originally. Tel 04.91.77.81.74. www.marie-marseille.fr. There is also a hotel, the Hotel Le Corbusier, in the building. www.hotellecorbusier.com. Tel 04.91.16.78.00.

DIRECTIONS
Take the Métro to Rond Point,

The Marseille block is the first built *Unité d'habitation à grandeur conforme*, although its social thinking pervades Le Corbusier's earlier writings and built work. The term *unité* had a profound philosophical resonance for Le Corbusier,[47] from his early dialectical formula of the "indissoluble binomial of individual-collectivity" inspired by the monastic community of Ema, to his postwar search for a dynamic unified measure in the Modulor. It first referred to the linear housing blocks on pilotis with interior streets described in *The Radiant City* (1930) and then to the rectangular slabs in proposals for Nemours, Algeria (1934) and Zlin, Czechoslovakia (1935). During the Second World War, Le Corbusier with François de Pierrefeu projected the reconstruction of France along the lines of the Unité in *La Maison des Hommes*, among other tracts. Specific postwar commissions for the towns of La Rochelle and St-Dié included Unités planned according to the principles of the Athens Charter, and the discussions of ASCORAL (Assemblé de Constructeurs pour une Rénovation Architecturale), a group of young architects chaired by Le Corbusier. In plans for both speculative and built projects, several Unités take their place among community facilities and garden apartments, although no such context was ever realized. For Marseille, in addition to the Unité, Le Corbusier envisioned a green city to replace the old port district.

As might be expected from the static surrounding Le Corbusier's promotions of his urban proposals over the years, the politics leading to the realization of the single Marseille block were complex. When Raoul Dautry, a friend and supporter of Le Corbusier, was appointed the first postwar Minister for Reconstruction and Urbanism, Le Corbusier hoped for a grand commission, on the scale of that for Le Havre which was handed to Auguste Perret. Instead, he received the intentionally limiting situation of housing under the new state provisions of ISAI (Immeubles sans affection individuelle), in the then communist city of Marseille. Met with opposition from many quarters, during a period of great financial and political instability, the project did receive the necessary support of seven successive city governments, and most importantly, from the next Minister of Reconstruction Eugène Claudius-Petit. Officially deemed "experimental" in order to free it from existing regulations, the Unité survived complaints from architects and inspectors that it violated building codes, and from doctors that it would mentally damage its inhabitants. Enormous delays, the five-year construction process, cost overruns, and confusions at the site added to the public antipathy toward the project and obscured its achievements. In its short life as public housing, the social program was never completed. As a private condominium it has consistently housed those appreciative of its intentions.[48]

Beyond the monastic ideal, which had limited application to daily and political realities, Le Corbusier's thinking relied on utopian models of the previous century. He drew especially from the "cottage-cooperative" of the Garden City model, and from the revolutionary, social-utopian models of Fourier's Phalanstery and Victor Considerant's Familistère.[49] The terms of these utopian models

which is the end of the line, and transfer to bus #22 which has a stop marked "Le Corbusier" beside the clearly visible building. From the train station, the trip takes about 35 minutes with good connections.

LOCALE
The Unité is located on a wide residential boulevard beyond the center of town. From Marseilles, an itinerary might include a drive to the mountain of La Sainte-Baume and a trip down the coast to Roquebrune and Le Petit Cabanon.

provided a frame for viewing contemporary divisions between suburb and the great European capital city. Le Corbusier prized suburbia's "sacred idea of the nuclear family,"[50] but criticized its confining role definitions. He saw the capitol city as providing the individual nomadic freedom within a context dense with choices, services and culture, but blighted by its lack of plan.

Le Corbusier's answer to this historical conflict of the individual and collective was the Unité. The "vertical-garden city" of the Unité promised "a phenomenon of architectural synthesis that suppresses waste, takes charge of the most burdensome domestic tasks, and organizes. It creates a productive social phenomenon whereby the individual and collective are equilibrated in a just redistribution of the functions of daily life."[51] Le Corbusier's nomenclature for the basic unit of this architectural synthesis is "the extended dwelling" (logement prolongé), referring to the services and facilities provided to the individual home through the collective. Within the community of 1600 (which was Fourier's ideal as well), the small family unit is predominant, but there are twenty-three types of accommodations, from bachelor studios and hotel rooms, to apartments for families of ten.

To emphasize the idea of the collective, Le Corbusier gave the communal services a physical presence within the building. In the early schemes, of which there were three for different sites in Marseille, the collective facilities were housed in separate buildings on the ground, but in the ultimate project they are absorbed into the Unité itself. Half-way up the block, identifiable through its band of vertical lamellas, is an interior commercial "street" (rue interior) intended as one immense store, but eventually filled with various professional offices, shops and services. Le Corbusier considered all the corridors as instruments of the collective. He even included these interior streets in his urban theory as the sixth in

Typical floor plans

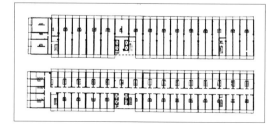

a hierarchy of seven ways of urban circulation. The overlap of the two-story apartments generates a skip-stop circulation system of corridors every third floor. The residual lobbies on the non-corridor floors become small club rooms. The quality of the interior streetscape is intentionally dark and subdued, to contrast with the illumination of the flats. The darkness is relieved by the individually colored and lit entrances with their various portals. These portals are the physical indicators of the intersection of private life and

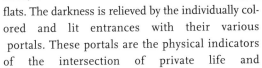

Lobby

collective service. Originally one door opened directly into the refrigerator for the delivery of ice, milk and groceries. Communal refrigerators (since converted to freezers) extended the capacity of the small home units. On the top floor is a nursery school with access to a roof garden that also supports a gymnasium, track, outdoor theater, and pool.

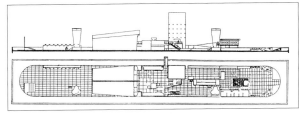

Roof elevation and plan

The sculptural park of the roof garden provides a collective context other than the simple quotidian, delving rather into the mythic. Le Corbusier's own description of its "Homeric"[52] quality seems to capture precisely a ritualistic aura more archaic than Periclean, with "raw material" and a "brutal order,"[53] totemic smokestacks and curved solarium like a ruin. The high parapet masks the immediate context, directing the view beyond to the mountains and the Mediterranean, siting the Homeric ship in an ancient landscape.

View of the roof garden

The rhetoric of archaic values pertains as well to the individual dwelling. The apartments, in the mode of the Maison Citrohan, are long and narrow walled boxes with double-height rooms opening onto a continuous balcony. In the most numerous "E" line, the bedrooms continue through the entire Unité

roof terrace

block to a loggia on the opposite side. Depending on the apartment's sectional relationship to the corridor, the kitchens and living rooms are alternatively located on the balcony or below it, although Le Corbusier and the inhabitants clearly favored the lower level entry. Larger apartments are assembled by adding bays of bedrooms. The entry sequence through the foyer kitchen to the living room is constant and essential as "the heart of life according to the most ancient traditions, folkloric or primitive (and French)."[54] The loggias facing east and west according to the solar cycle are porticos, "such as Socrates advocated" to provide "coolness in the summer and warmth in the winter."[55] The horizontal sun-break and balcony windows reassert this cultural symbiosis with climate by manipulating breeze and shade naturally rather than mechanically.

The kitchen of the Unité apartments might be the clearest moment of the confluence of the ancient and the new, a hearth bent from aluminum and steel. Le Corbusier entrusted its planning to Charlotte Perriand, who consulted also with Jean Prouvé. It is the most clearly modularized, uniform and prefabricated element in the Unité: the same kitchen occurs in all twenty-three types of apartments. In her research, Perriand looked to the efficiencies and also informalities of the American designs of George Nelson and Charles and Ray Eames. The kitchens share with them the materials of laminated metal and wood. The open relation of kitchen to living room across a two-sided cabinet was forward-looking at the time. Perhaps the area of greatest innovation was the mechanical systems and their integration into the Unité as a whole. Besides the refrigerator with ice portal, the kitchen had integral lighting, ventilation, and disposals for solid waste.

Apartment interior, ca. 1953

The sensibility of the furnishings combines the

folkloric and prefabricated. Perriand was largely responsible for equipment intended to be both flexible and precise, like the baby layette on the mezzanine and the rolling doors with blackboards between the children's bedrooms. She also designed the more rustic wood tables and chairs in the model apartments. Prouvé designed the prefabricated metal stair; Le Corbusier, a lamp for the dining corner. His office detailed the finish carpentry and its refined electrical services with aluminum and clear polystyrene fixtures.[56] Given the quantity of pieces required as well as the budget restraints, the quality of the woodwork is quite remarkable, especially in the window detailing and the paneling where some joints are exposed and others clad according to Modulor dimensions.

The structure and materials of the building oscillate between the seemingly primitive and the purportedly advanced. Poured-in-place surfaces are imprinted with sea shells of the Mediterranean, tables are cast with the locally handcrafted and authored tile of Philippe Sourdive. Out of this hybrid of technique, Le Corbusier fashioned a thick but permeable grid that serves as sun-break and loggia. The formerly prominent glass curtain occurs on the scale of the individual apartment, behind the concrete facade, and framed in wood. Whereas in the purist manner a single surface gave the illusion of layers or depth, here, to the mobile observer, the wall both reveals and dissembles its thickness, appearing alternately as an open grid, a series of colored planes and a dense mass. Once a transparent yet emphatic membrane, the wall is now occupiable. As such it brings the individual cell to collective expression.

Le Corbusier's described the strucural relation of cell to collective as a bottle rack in which individual, prefabricated bottle-like apartments would be inserted. With Jean Prouvé, he envisioned that the units would someday be assembled off-site like airplanes and then hoisted into place within the concrete frame. Other than along the corridors, the cells of the rack were left open to receive these conceptually packaged apartments. Although in the end the

47. Anthony Vidler, "The Idea of Unity and Le Corbusier's Urban Form," *Architect's Yearbook* 15, 225–235. Also Peter Sereyni, *Le Corbusier, Fourier and the monastery at Ema* in Sereyni, ed. *Le Corbusier in Perspective*.

48. The project monographs are Jacques Sbriglio, *L'Unité d'habitation de Marseille*, and David Jenkins, Unité d'habitation Marseilles.

49. Reyner Banham coins these terms for utopian models, "La Maison des hommes and La Misère des villes" in Brooks, *Le Corbusier*, 107.

50. Le Corbusier in Sbriglio, *L'Unité*, 19. Also, Le Corbusier *Oeuvre Complète* 5: 95, 192.

51. Le Corbusier in Jacques Sbriglio, "Unité d'habitation," in Lucan, *Le Corbusier: Une Encyclopédie*, 423.

52. Le Corbusier, *Modulor 2*: 304.

53. Le Corbusier, *Towards*, 211, 219.

54. Le Corbusier correspondence with Wogensky in Ruggero Tropeano, "Intérieur (aménagement)," Lucan, *Une Encyclopédie*, 201.

55. Le Corbusier, *Oeuvre Complète* 5: 95.

56. For furnishings, equipment and collaboration with Perriand see Tropeano, "Intérieur," Lucan, *Une Encyclopédie*, 200–206, also Sbriglio, *L'Unité*, 81–91.

57. Ford, *Details 2*: 187–8.

58. André Wogensky "The Unité d'habitation at Marseille," Brooks, *Le Corbusier*, 117.

59. Le Corbusier, *Modulor 2*: 233.

apartments were largely built on site, their construction did involve the systematic assembly of smaller fabricated parts and lighter materials. The apartment perimeter is a wood box of plywood sheathing and pine framing insulated with fiberglass or Isorel, and finished with gypsum board, oak panels and linoleum flooring. The mezzanines are framed of rolled, steel-edge beams and braked, sheet-metal secondary beams like C-studs which were designed by Jean Prouvé. To acoustically isolate the apartment structures, the steel is separated from the concrete rack by lead pads 10 cm thick.

The bottle-rack frame holding the apartments sits on a table or artificial ground, which is in turn supported by hollow pilotis that gather and dispense systems of supply and waste, and grant the whole a monumental identity. This idea in its incipient form appears in the Swiss Pavilion's steel matrix on concrete pilotis. While the diagram of table and bottle rack turned out to be a gross oversimplification of function, the rhetoric is carried out in the vertical service cores, which extend directly from the pilotis, the horizontal runs embedded in the artificial ground, and the concrete rack itself. As Edward Ford notes, whatever its acoustic and fabrication virtues, the idea of the bottle apartment independent of the rack is structurally redundant; the frame must be strong enough to stand without the apartments and the apartments sufficiently strong to stand without the frame.[57]

The most challenging aspect of the building became the collaboration required to combine a host of systems, many untested. To develop the engineering and construction details of the Unités, Le Corbusier created and affiliated with a separate office, ATBAT (Atelier de Batisseurs). It was headed by Le Corbusier's associate André Wogenscky and the Russian engineer Vladimir Bodiansky, who brought to the project his experience as a designer of aircraft and the "Mopin" building prefabrication system. Despite their

pilotis

ultimately stormy relationship, together the offices of Le Corbusier and ATBAT produced 2,785 drawings. As Wogenscky notes, this collaboration of architect and engineer was rare in France at the time.[58] Incorporated in the sequencing of construction and materials were experiments in efficiency and economy: the concrete frame served also as the building's own scaffold; the precast facings, as the form work for the structure poured behind.

exterior

The Unité was also the experimental site for the application of the Modulor. Le Corbusier's writings on the Modulor are long and contradictory, swerving between the mystical and the scientific. At the Unité, its qualities as a rational system of standardized measure predominate. Every element of the building can be described using the fifteen Modulor units illustrated in the stele of measure, the first stone, and the human figures inscribed on the building. The only exceptions are the brise-soleil frames misproportioned by mistake. To compensate, Le Corbusier decided to paint the bare exterior with "a polychromy so dazzling that the mind was forcibly detached from the dissonances, carried away in the irresistible torrent of major color sensations."[59] As he acknowledged, human error was an opportunity for inspiration and transcendence. The anthropocentrism of the Unité is its measure, its colossal stride, and the concrete finish which Le Corbusier likened to the human skin, showing its age and character through its flaws.

Le Corbusier

ADDRESS
Intersection of D80 and the
road to St Zacharie, Var
Marseille 30 km

ACCESS
The interior of this abandoned
roadside structure is currently
accessible. For further information contact the local tourist
office, tel/fax 04.42.62.57.57
or Conseil General Du Var,
tel 04.94.68.58.33.
www.tourisme.fr.

DIRECTIONS
By car from Marseille, take
A50 to Aubagne, D2 through
Gemenos and follow signs to La
Sainte-Baume as the road continues into the mountains. Just
east of the intersection with
D80 is the tourist office. The
building is beyond the tourist
office at the intersection of the
road to St. Zacharie with D95.

This small complex, thought to be artist studios and a gallery, was discovered and attributed to Le Corbusier in 1987 by Guillaume Jullian de la Fuente, chief architect of Le Corbusier's studio from 1958 to 1965, and Ann Pendleton-Jullian. They base their attribution on a series of sketches included in the archive,[61] as well as correspondence mentioning the project and the specifics of the site from Le Corbusier and Édouard Trouin, the force behind the projects at La Sainte-Baume.

While ideas of collage and assemblage permeate Le Corbusier's work, this building is a most literal realization.[62] The building is composed about the found objects of a corrugated metal barrack, concrete guard tower, and related stair that most likely date from World War II but were not necessarily built simultaneously. To these Le Corbusier added a linear bar of studios with individual entrances along the southern roadside, a foreground box with an undulating roof, and a long porch on the north. Exterior stairs, now mostly gone, connected the building fragments more compositionally than physically. The pieces remain distinct in their form and their references. As Pendleton-Jullian traces, the undulating roof has a source in Antoni Gaudí, whose work was of special interest to Le Corbusier. The individual studios suggest the crèche roof-top of the Salvation Army Refuge and the brise-soleils of his work in India. The barrack vault, besides its general value as an *objet-type*, resembles early Maison de Weekend schemes and the rooftop gym of the Unité at Marseille.

view looking west

The local population is familiar with the building.

Implicit in the design is a collective intent. The linear bars of individual units surround the barrack such that it becomes a central void understood as the communal space. Completed by the end tower, the plan echoes a monastery, the Corbusian model of the ideal community. The proximity to La Sainte-Baume suggests connections with its unbuilt pilgrimage village and hotel. The design of a shared existence out of discrete and pre-existing elements intimates a kind of "collage city,"[63] only fully articulated by those who followed the architect.

LOCALE

The building is in the hills before La Sainte-Baume, which is the site of a series of unbuilt projects proposed by Le Corbusier in 1948 for a cave shrine of Mary Magdalene and related pilgrimage village. The approach is steep and suitably spectacular. The region of the Var is a resort area with inns and camping grounds.

Another project based on the preservation of an archaeological fragment was to be located at the foot of La Sainte-Baume. La Bergerie de la Sainte-Baume (1951) was envisioned by Le Corbusier and Édouard Trouin as a wine bar and museum of Mary Magdalene. The stone walls of the existing but delapidated sheep pen were to be protected with an exterior coat of parging and a metal parasol designed with Jean Prouvé.[60]

60. Roger Aujame in Prelorenzo, *La Conservation*, 155. Also Robert Coombs, *Le Corbusier and Vernacular Architecture*, ACSA, 1995.
61. H. Allen Brooks, ed., *Le Corbusier Archive*, FLC 17766 and 17752.
62. For the building form and its sources see Ann Pendleton-Jullian, "The Collage of Poetics," *Design Book Review* 14: 33–8, also published as "Unknown Le Corbusier," *Parametro* 156: 53–61.
63. Colin Rowe and Fred Koetter, *Collage City*.

vault interior

Le Corbusier and Pierre Jeanneret; original sculpture by
Jacques Lipchitz

ADDRESS
503 route de l'Artaude
83220 Le Pradet
Toulon 15 km,
Le Thoronet 70 km

ACCESS
Views of this recently renovated
private residence from the surrounding roads are limited.
(View shown above is pre-
restoration).

DIRECTIONS
From Toulon, take buses #39,
#49 or #9 from avenue General
Le Clerc to the center of Le
Pradet. The walk to the villa
takes about 15 minutes. Continue along rue St David, which
becomes chemin de l'Artaude.
Opposite a new housing development, Le Verger de Beauvoir,
there is a private road with a

Le Corbusier cited the remote location of the
villa and the limitations of local craftsmen as the jus-
tification for this earliest departure from the pristine
surfaces of Purism. The guiding principles for this
shift had been outlined a few years earlier in his
proposition for the prototype Maisons Locheur,
named for the Locheur Laws (1929) which under-
wrote rural housing initiatives. In keeping with
the Locheur guidelines regarding local construction,
the prototype combined a masonry wall, dubbed
"the diplomatic wall," to be built by local craftsmen,
with prefabricated "dry" systems of windows,
steel frame, and zinc panels to be imported from
the industrial center of Paris. Despite the emi-
nence of the client, Hélène de Mandrot, patron
of CIAM, the first scheme for the house was a
slightly refined version of a Maison Locheur.
The client's decision to contract with a local
mason, Aimonetti, led to the use of stone in combination with a concrete frame sheathed in glass
and stucco, rather than the Locheur formula.[64]
The architect's use of local stone was in the end
problematic, however. Because Le Corbusier ignored

the stone's porous quality and chose to leave it exposed on the interior, the house was beset by damp as well as other problems to the extent that de Mandrot proclaimed it uninhabitable.[65] Le Corbusier then allowed "the beautiful stone of the region"[66] to be painted over.

The desire to expose the stone and the need to paint it over in a sense summarizes the intended confrontation between nature and artifice found throughout the villa. The naturalism of the villa is most evident in the exposed stone and in its siting. The house is wed to the hillside through a stone plinth forecourt, and organized according to the mountain view. Originally two sculptures by Lipchitz were placed to articulate the different experiences of the front of the villa and the expansive view behind. In many regards, this naturalism recalls Corbusier's early Swiss architecture. As in the chalets, the masonry walls and earthen terraces negotiate the hillside, creating an armature for the stucco walls. In the curve and countercurve of its podium stair, de Mandrot recalls in particular the terrace of Villa Jeanneret.

sign to that effect. The villa is the second house on the left along the private drive. It is not visible from the street. If you pass the camping grounds l'Artaudois on the chemin, you have gone too far.

LOCALE
Le Pradet is a small town less than half an hour outside of Toulon by public transportation. The terrain beyond the village is a high, gently rolling plain that provides many of the houses with dramatic views of the surrounding mountains. A possible itinerary includes a stop at Le Pradet on the way between Marseille and Le Corbusier's vacation cabin at Roquebrune.

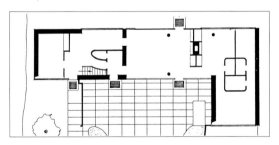

terrace level plan

At odds with these naturalistic qualities of Villa de Mandrot are the purist concerns typical of the Parisian villas. The ambiguities of the L-shaped plan slipping beyond the plinth but asymmetrically balanced by the guest house are purist strategies. The use of overlapping and shifted planes continues in the composition of walls and even the terrace table and steps. Where the stone of the facade is framed in steel, it appears as planar as the glass and stucco infill. Purism becomes an artifice overlaid on the natural materials and the landscape.

View of suspended veranda

64. Bruno Reichlin, "La Villa de Mandrot a le Pradet: Le dehors est toujours un dedans." 87–94.

65. Pierre Merminod, "La Villa de Mandrot: Diagnostic de la Degradation," in Prelorenzo, *La Conservation*, 131–9.

66. Bruno Reichlin, "La Restauration de la Villa de Mandrot," in Prelorenzo, *La Conservation*, 131–49.

67. Le Corbusier, *Oeuvre Complète* 2: 59.

68. Peter Blake, *The Master Builders*, 89.

This framing of the natural to intensify its experience was Le Corbusier's goal. As he described it: "The site offers the striking spectacle of a vast, unfolding landscape, and the unexpected nature of this has been kept by walling in the principle rooms to the view and by having only a door that opens onto a veranda, from which the sudden vista is like an explosion."[67] The intensified effects of surprise and reversal carry with it a sense of dislocation and of the surreal as well. As one critic observed of the framed stone "it looks almost more painted than real."[68] The promenade Le Corbusier described cuts directly through the house, such that the interior becomes a mere vestibule to the view; and the exterior forecourt becomes the displaced interior, equipped with dining table and a freestanding picture window. The displaced interior as an ambiguous realm of consciousness and desire is a common trope of surrealist painting. In distinction from the surreal, Le Corbusier reveals his devices as theatrical; the picture window is a stage flat, the suspended veranda has a ladder. The artifice of architecture is useful only so far as it returns us to the natural.

LE PETIT CABANON

1952

Le Corbusier, Jacques
Michelet, André Wogenscky

LA BARAQUE DE CHANTIER
1954, Le Corbusier

LES UNITÉS DE CAMPING
1954–1957, Le Corbusier

ADDRESS
Path parallel to Sentier du Bord
de Mer, Plage du Buse
06 Roquebrune-Cap-Martin
Menton 5 km, Nice 26 km

ACCESS
Visits on Tuesdays and Fridays
at 10 AM by registering at the
Office of Tourism at Cap-Martin
at least one day in advance.
Tour departs from the tourist
office, 218 avenue Aristide
Briand-Carnolès, open daily
9–1 and 3–7 in the summer.
From September to June, its
Saturday hours are 9–12:30
and 2–6, closed Sundays. Tel
04.93.35.62.87. www.roque-
brune-cap-martin.com. The
exterior and adjoining Etoile de
Mer are always accessible, a
9-minute walk from the Cabbé
railway station.

DIRECTIONS
Trains run regularly from Nice
to Menton and less frequently
to Cap-Martin. In summer,
buses run from the center of
Menton to Roquebrune and
Cap-Martin several times an
hour. Off season, take a 10-
minute cab ride from the Menton casino to the center of the
old village of Roquebrune.

The house is a 20-minute
walk from the station at Cap-
Martin along Promenade Le
Corbusier following the signs to
Étoile de Mer. Another scenic

Le Corbusier had a passionate attraction to the Mediterranean throughout his life, which he explained in part by tracing his own lineage from the Cathars of Languedoc. His wife actually came from the Provence region, from Menton, near Roquebrune. His introduction to this site began with visits to the publisher of *l'Architecture Vivante*, Jean Badovici, and the designer Eileen Gray at E.1027, the house she designed in 1927, just below Le Corbusier's cabin. The complex rivalry between Gray and Le Corbusier first came to a head when, unsolicited, he painted a mural portrait on her villa wall, much to Gray's distress.[69] After arguing with Badovici during a preparatory CIAM meeting held at the house in 1949, Le Corbusier began to stay at the neighboring restaurant, L'Étoile de Mer, and befriended the owner, Thomas Rebutato, who became the client for several unexecuted projects known as Roq et Rob. These studies for vaulted cab-

route beginning at the tourist office in the old village of Roquebrune follows avenue Virginie Herriot to Europe Village and around its garden wall toward the sea. Beyond a drainage station, the path divides. Take the right fork, which emerges on a cliff at the water's edge. Cross the bridge. To the left are the cabins and the gate to the property.

LOCALE
Roquebrune is a beautiful hilltown above the sea. Menton is larger and livelier with a notable Cocteau Museum. Eileen Gray's house, E.1027 now destroyed, was located just below the Étoile de Mer restaurant.

69. Peter Adam, "Eileen Gray and Le Corbusier," *9H: On Rigor*: 150–4; and Caroline Constant "Non–heroic Modernism of Eileen Gray," *JSAH* 53: 278–79. Beatriz Colomina, "Battle Lines: E.1027" in Agrest et al, *The Sex of Architecture,* 167–83. Also for Le Corbusier's unapologetic description of the murals see Le Corbusier, *New World of Space,* 99.
70. The monograph on the projects is Bruno Chiambretto, *Le Corbusier à Cap Martin.* See also Chiambretto "Cabanon" and "Roq et Rob," Lucan, *Encyclopédie,* 81–3, 353.
71. Le Corbusier, *Towards,* 203, 70.
72. Constant, "Non-heroic Modernism," *JSAH* 53: 269.
73. Chiambretto, *à Cap Martin,* 39–42.
74. Le Corbusier, *Modulor* 2: 244.
75. Le Corbusier to Charles L'Epplatenier as recounted by Francesco Passanti.

ins grouped in the manner of a Mediterranean village also produced, most notably, the idea for a new structural system of component metal angle called Le Brevet, or "226 x 226 x 226," after its Modulor dimensions. In the end, the only series built for Rebutato were the five prefabricated wooden camping units in a simple shed form, erected by the client on concrete pilotis to accommodate his boule court. To keep costs down, they were built with screen rather than the intended wood plank, and many of the details were left out. In exchange for the design and construction of the camping units, Le Corbusier bartered from Rebutato a small lot contiguous with the restaurant, on which he erected his own vacation cabin and studio.[70]

For his own vacation retreat, the only house he ever built for himself, Le Corbusier suppressed the will to invent, and instead selected from the preexisting. The two sheds, a log cabin for dwelling and a flat plank studio for working, are truly *objets-types*, those banal found vessels he depicted in his paintings. He called his studio "La Baraque de Chantier," a worker's shed from a construction site. The log cabin shell was actually a kit which he had prefabricated like the five camping units in Ajaccio, Corsica, by Charles Barberis and then customized on the interior according to Modulor dimensions. Le Corbusier investigated the mass production of the cabin, enlisting Jean Prouvé to design the hardware and fittings and Barberis to streamline its construction.

Le Corbusier's cabin is simultaneously *objet-type* and archetype. In its intentional rusticity, it suggests the image of primitive hut pervasive in Enlightenment theory as the original dwelling. Le Corbusier rejected the related propositions that the stone column derived from the tree and that classical architecture evolved from the hut, contending rather that they were both "pure creation of the mind." The cabin manifests his "attraction for both the savage and the Parthenon, distant as they are in their degree of order and understanding."[71]

The relation of the rustic hut to the pristine white box of Gray's E.1027 below is ideological in view of Le Corbusier's classical theory and his criticism of Gray's alternative functionalism as "not really modern."[72] In his postwar years, a utilitarianism, seen here as a spiral of function and form boxed in logs, became his vision of meta-modernity. The log cabin is parasitically attached to the side of the Étoile de Mer lot in a manner unexpected of either an archetypal hut or white temple, but allowable within this late utilitarianism.

The design of the cabin interior synthesizes functions, furnishings, and surfaces into a helicoidal progression of relationships based on Modulor number. The overall volume of 366 cm x 366 cm is divided into four equal rectangles of 226 cm x 140 cm spiraling around a central square of 86 cm.[73] Each rectangle is devoted to a basic function, such as bathing, resting, or eating, and its related equipment, such as sink, bed, or table. The equipment is often integrated with an architectural element such that the sink is a wall, the ceiling is storage. Le Corbusier orchestrated views across the cabin with near and far, high and low points defined by the furnishings.[74] At three places along the spiral, through carefully adjusted openings, this interior landscape connects with views to the outside.

Cabin and shed have identical geometric relations to the outside and the cliff, with their roofs slanting toward the sea, except that their doors are on perpendicular faces. A path connecting them emphasizes a suggested ninety-degree rotation. Together they recall a much earlier definition of Le Corbusier: "One obelisk, that's nothing. Two obelisks—that's architecture."[75] Because they occupy the entire depth and height of the small terrace, a simultaneous view of building and sea is impossible except from the center of the cabin looking out a window framing the horizon. As Le Corbusier repeatedly suggested in his late buildings, between cabin and sea there is no middle-ground.

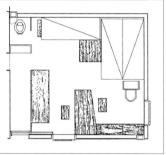
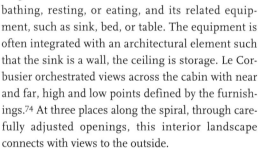

Plan of log cabin

Entry door to cabin

GRAVE OF LE CORBUSIER AND HIS WIFE, YVONNE GALLIS

1957

Le Corbusier

ADDRESS
Roquebrune Cemetery
Chemin de Pancrace
06190 Roquebrune-Cap-Martin
Alpes Maritimes

ACCESS
Public cemetery open daily

DIRECTIONS
The cemetery is a half-hour
walk uphill from the Roquebrune tourist office. The most
picturesque route is up the
chemin du Pontet, past the
chapels of St Roche and la
Pausa to the town château.
Just before the château, take a
right on chemin de Pancrace.
The cemetery is on your left. Le
Corbusier and Yvonne's grave is
beyond the second arched
gateway on your right as you
climb the central terrace.

LOCALE
See Le Petit Cabanon

Le Corbusier designed the grave in 1957, the year of his wife's death. He died 27 August 1965 while swimming in the Mediterranean just below the Petit Cabanon. The tombstone presents the most consistent and compelling aspects of his cosmos: prismatic solids, natural objects, and the ever-elusive horizon line. Within the four-square plot stands a hollow cylinder as a feminine vessel for Yvonne and an ambiguous angular solid for Le Corbusier. His headstone simultaneously suggests primitive shed, a cube or plane rotated about a horizontal axis, a sloped perspective. The horizon appears again in the bright stripes on the enamel nameplate. Embedded in the plinth are their respective signs of faith, Yvonne's cross and Le Corbusier's seashell. But looking up from the grave to the Mediterranean, it is clear he intended the unframed landscape to be a final testament.

QUARTIER MODERNE FRUGÈS

1925–1928

Even before he tested his purist notions in the design of Parisian villas, Le Corbusier proposed a scheme for a Contemporary City of Three Million Inhabitants.[76] In this scheme, a wide greenbelt separates a central city of business from an industrial district and from garden communities for the working class. The workers' settlements imagined by Le Corbusier are more like suburbs economically dependent on the city of business than independent towns, but they are still in the tradition of the nineteenth-century British Garden City. In their depiction as Mediterranean-styled houses along orthogonally ordered streets with garden lots, they also owe a great deal to the residential district of Tony Garnier's Industrial City.[77]

Early in his career, Le Corbusier had the opportunity to test a fragment of his working-class community outside an urban center, thanks to the patronage of Henry Frugès, an enlightened industrialist, artist and man of letters who was impressed by the young architect's writing and work at the Salon d'Automne in 1922. Frugès sought to stabilize his sugar-cube factories' workforce by building housing:

Le Corbusier and Pierre Jeanneret

ADDRESS
rue Le Corbusier, rue Henry. Frugès, rue des Arcades 33600 Pessac
Bordeaux 7 km, Arachon 57 km, Lège 50 km

ACCESS
Neighborhood of private residences visible from street. One of the houses is now La Maison Municipale Le Corbusier/Musée Frugès, 4 rue Le Corbusier 33600 Pessac. Open Wednesday–Saturday 10–12, 3–6 and Sunday 3–6 (except July and August). Tel 05.56.36.56.46, fax 05.56.55.49.00.

DIRECTIONS

From Quai Richelieu in downtown Bordeaux, local buses on line P run along avenue Jean-Jaurès to Quartier Frugès. The stop is just beyond avenue des Acières at Place du Monteil. To reach Lège continue from Pessac east on the Bordeaux-Arachon road.

LOCALE

The center of Bordeaux has many neoclassical monuments of note. Its two- and three-story housing stock from the eighteenth century recalls in its volume and severity Le Corbusier's work at Pessac. In nearby Lège, Le Corbusier built a group of houses for Frugès as a dry run for Pessac which have been severely altered. The countryside of the Gironde is also the site of a water tower in a stripped-down neoclassical style designed by Le Corbusier as part of his work for SABA, an engineering and building concern. Also see entry on Château d'eau.

76. See entry Pavillon de l'Esprit Nouveau.
77. For the Garden City tradition and Le Corbusier's early urbanism see Le Corbusier, *La Construction des Villes*, and H. Allen Brooks, *Le Corbusier's Formative Years*, 482–9.
78. Abbé Laugier in Le Corbusier, *The City of Tomorrow*, 74.
79. Brian Brace Taylor, "Le Corbusier at Pessac," in Walden, *The Open Hand*, 163–85. Also see Brian Brace Taylor, *Le Corbusier et Pessac*.
80. For color at Pessac see Mark Wigley, *White Walls, Designer Dresses*, 216–218, 222 and Lionel Favier, "Volume et Couleur: Liberté et Ordonnance dans Le Jeu de L'Espace Construite," in Prelorenzo, *Le Corbusier et La Couleur*, 67–79.
81. Le Corbusier in Favier, "Volume et Couleur," Prelorenzo, *Le Corbusier et La Couleur*, 70.

first as a prototypical dwelling, Maison du Tonkin in Bordeaux, then in a small development of houses at Lège, and finally in a community of over one hundred units at Pessac.

Pessac reinforced Le Corbusier's assessment of the modern condition created by the First World War: the problem of housing shortfalls, the potentials of industry. He linked the design of the houses to their intended production according to the principles of Taylorization, the scientific study and management of industry for increased efficiency. Le Corbusier intended the wall panels, windows and doors as mass-produced and standardized elements fitted to reinforced concrete frames. The non-bearing panels were to be mattresses of straw, a cheap and plentiful material of good insulating value, finished with a sprayed coating of concrete. The standard window was a strip of alternating square and half-square bays with two sub-units: a single square window and a square flanked by two half-squares.

This systematic approach extended to the treatment of space as well. Related more to the paradigm of the Maison Dom-ino than to the figural identity of the Maison Citrohan, the plan has no single configuration; rather there are a variety of houses built from two basic spatial units, a square cell of 5 m x 5 m and a rectangular half-cell. The cell was based on Le Corbusier's research into dimensional minimums of vernacular housing. The attempt to create an enriched housing typology by assembling modular volumes from standardized elements derived from the thinking of Le Corbusier's contemporaries such as Mies van der Rohe, and also from Le Corbusier's favored seventeenth-century theorist, Abbé Laugier, who likewise recommended "wild variety in layout, uniformity in detail."[78] Within the houses, the idea of variety had to do with the potential flexibility of the rooms. The plans tend to have compact utilities as a core between large, square rooms with little space devoted specifically to circulation or other functions. The varieties of housing types include triplex "towers" of two units; "arcades" of duplex units connected to one another by arch-covered terraces;

single residences with workshops on the ground floor; "quinconces" in which two attached units alternate between street and garden entrance; and similarly arranged Z-shaped terrace houses.

In the siting of these houses, Le Corbusier drew on established traditions of urban composition—from the picturesque of Camillo Sitte to the classical of Laugier—and also references to the thirteenth-century gridded and arcaded new towns (*villes neuves*) of southwestern France.[79] The original project included a more formal sector with a broad avenue leading to a square plaza bordered with housing, recalling the design of these *villes neuves*. The sector as built has a central garden axis through the terrace units which is interrupted by the cross axis of single residences, and framed by the row of towers and an arcade along an angled cul-de-sac.

Axonometric of built sector

The most radical device in the urbanism of Pessac was its spare geometric uniformity (although it is perhaps no more severe than the neoclassical housing of Bordeaux which it recalls) and the polychromy developed in response to it. Under pressure from Frugès, Le Corbusier painted the different sides of the houses pale green, blue, and red ochre. While he and Ozenfant had developed a theory of color in purist painting, the houses at Pessac present the first extensive play of color in his architecture.[80] As Le Corbusier saw it, they "applied an entirely new concept of polychromy, pursuing a clearly architectural goal: to model space. . . in a word to compose with color as with form." The planes of color "suppress volume (weight) and amplify the surface (extension),"[81] working as counterpoint to both the sculptural mass of the houses and the perspectives constructed through the plan. According to Le Corbusier, the role of each color is exact: "burnt sienna to establish fixed points, the fair ultramarine blue to make the lines of the buildings fly into

Z-shaped terraces

Towers and terraces

the distance, the pale green to mingle certain sectors with the vegetation, and finally the white facades as a standard of appreciation."[82]

Pessac was neither completed according to its original plan nor inhabited as intended. Bureaucratic and technical problems abounded during construction. The inadequacy of the site's drainage and sewage facilities delayed occupation of the project for years. In his zeal to Taylorize the building process, Le Corbusier insisted on using a cement spray gun for coating the wall panels that the workers could not operate. Eventually, after bringing his Parisian contractor to Pessac at great expense, he changed the infill wall construction to traditional masonry, also at great expense. By the time he prevailed upon Minister de Monzie to let him complete fifty of the houses under a new housing provision, not only did the dwellings cost too much for workers to inhabit, but Frugès had suffered a nervous breakdown and moved to Africa. At first, a few daring bourgeois families moved to the settlement. The Locheur Law (1929) eventually made it possible for workers to live there as tenants.

For one brief moment, the empty project planted with fruit trees and painted pastel colors attracted international acclaim and visits from people like Mies van der Rohe and E.S. Rasmussen. But Rasmussen wrote in 1926 that despite the evocative nature of the objects, "the value of Le Corbusier's architecture for the future will be entirely dependent on his conception of the task of this architecture. If the program is wrongly conceived, then no matter how ingenious the solution, (the houses) will not express our times."[83] Events revealed Rasmussen's doubts to be well-founded. The occupants began to add to the cubic houses the pitched roofs and windows typical to Bordeaux. In a sense, even these ostensible effacements fulfilled Le Corbusier's assertion that "rational construction based on

Terrace houses

the use of component blocks does not destroy individual initiative."[84] In response to the changes, Le Corbusier commented, "You know, it is life that is always right and the architect who is wrong,"[85] recognizing the paradox of an architecture so severe that the inhabitants want to transform it, so flexible and blank that they can.

The transformation of the houses reached a peak by the seventies when they were documented in a classic of its era, *Lived-in Architecture* by Phillipe Boudon, which treated Pessac as a controlled experiment measuring the limits of Modernism in the face of individual and social psychology. Now, a generation later, due to a complex of motives which include Le Corbusier's historical stature and a shift in demographic base, Pessac is encountering yet another transformation, restoration back to an original condition for the "middle-class gentleman of the time."

82. Le Corbusier in Wigley, *White Walls*, 216.
83. E. S. Rasmussen, "The Architecture of Tomorrow?" in Serenyi, *Le Corbusier in Perspective*, 90.
84. Phillipe Boudon, *Lived-in Architecture: Pessac Revisited*, 35.
85. Ibid., 2.

CHÂTEAU D'EAU

1917

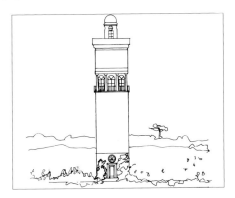

Le Corbusier

ADDRESS
rue Pierre-Vincent
Podensac
Gironde

ACCESS
Visible (dome never built). To visit interior contact "Groupe des cinq," tel. 05.56.08.78.71

DIRECTIONS
Take N.113 from Bordeaux to Toulouse. The water tower is on the left before entering the village of Podensac.

This work was commissioned by Le Corbusier's first patron in France, SABA (la société d'application du béton armé), an enterprise of Max Dubois. It is Le Corbusier's first built work in France after Villa Schwob. In keeping with his other work of the period, the structural armature for the classical form is concrete handled with the finesse of his mentor, Auguste Perret.

VILLA LE SEXTANT
(MAISON AUX MATHES, MAISON L'OCÉAN)

1935

Le Corbusier, Pierre Jeanneret

ADDRESS
17, avenue de l'Océan
17570 La Palmyre-Les Mathes
Charente-Maritime

ACCESS
Visible from street. Office de
tourisme de la Palmyre, 2
avenue de Royan. Tel
05.46.22.41.07, fax
05.46.22.52.69.
www.tourisme.fr; contact@la-
palmyre-les-mathes.com

DIRECTIONS
Take D.25 from Royan. From
center of Mathes, the house
is another 4 km in La Palmyre.
The road to the house from
Les Mathes, rue du Caplet,
changes its name several
times but reaches La Palmyre
as avenue des Mathes. It
meets a major traffic circle
and emerges as avenue de
l'Océan. The house is less
than 500 m from the Atlantic.

For the daughter of Albin Peyron, who as Commander of the Cité de Refuge was patron of Le Corbusier's most technically ambitious work, the architect created the most modest of his houses to date. A summer beach residence, it is largely a roofed porch, with all rooms opening onto a continuous veranda. Except for the two fireplaces, it is unheated. Le Corbusier explained his choice of vernacular materials and forms as the natural adaptation of his interest in prefabrication to rural circumstances, a thematic interest dating from the Maisons Locheur (1929). Here he designed walls of fieldstone, timber framing and infill panels of glass, plywood and asbestos cement in such a way that the three systems could be erected independently and without architectural supervision. In fact he never visited the site, although the villa's strong resemblance to neighboring barns suggests a familiarity with the region. Le Corbusier explained the atypical butterfly roof with pipes running along its center ridge as an architectonic solution to heavy rainfall. The orientation of the house to the east, with the blank stone facade toward the street, served as protection from the ocean winds and provided privacy for the porch to the west.[86]

On this updated regional model, Le Corbusier imposed purist composition and tectonic ambiguity. The masonry box of a barn is pulled apart into two L-shaped walls controlled geometrically through a composition of squares. The diagonal opposition of solid and void, wall and porch across the center of the house derives from a standard purist diagram. Here the center is marked by the sign of a navigator's sextant and a projecting stone slab. The box is shattered materially as well as formally into masonry fragments woven together through the timber frame and infill panels. Set back from the face of the stone, the strip window and rolling doors define a continuous plane behind the equally planar masonry. Consequently, the stone appears both a weighty, load-bearing material and a surface that does not even touch the roof it was intended to support.

In applying purist principles to a stone barn, Le Corbusier modified his original purist polemic linked to the machine-age through its smooth white walls and floating volumes. Whereas in his purist villas, the illusion of transparent planes required that stucco conceal the cinderblock beneath, here the architectural illusion depended on the simultaneous expression and contradiction of the physical properties of the wall. Le Sextant presents the possibilities of an alternative architecture characterized by tectonic expression and sensual primacy of materials. This alternative was not an isolated incident in Le Corbusier's oeuvre, dating to his rustic Swiss chalets and early admiration for the bricks and cement of Roman ruins. Along with Villa de Mandrot (1930) and Maison de weekend (1935), Le Corbusier developed in the 1930s a self-critique and a critique of an increasingly troubled industrialized world.[87]

Public transportation via bus from Royan takes 40 minutes. Service is spotty. Off season it runs only on Wednesdays (for the market). More frequent service runs to La Tremblade which is 3 km from Mathes. Taxi service is available from Mathes to La Palmyre.

LOCALE
La Palmyre is a summer beach resort that caters to families of campers. Most facilities are closed off-season. The larger coastal town of La Rochelle has hotels which remain open all year. The intermediate countryside is quiet and agricultural, dotted with small villages boasting Romanesque churches.

Ground floor plan (top); Balcony on rear facade (bottom)

86. Le Corbusier, *Oeuvre Complète* 3: 135–7.
87. Frampton observes that Le Sextant was designed on the eve of World War II, *Modern Architecture*, 427.

UNITÉ D'HABITATION DE REZÉ
(LA MAISON FAMILIALE) 1952–1955

Le Corbusier, André Wogenscky;
Séchaud et Metz engineers with
consultation of Lafaille and
Freyssinet

ADDRESS
44 Cité Maison Radieuse
44400 Rezé

ACCESS
Public access all day (free
admission). Reserved tours
organized by the town hall
(for a fee) depart on Tuesday,
Thursday, and Saturday mornings. Tel 02.40.84.43.84.
The fiftieth anniversary of the
recently renovated building in
2005 is documented on
www.maisonradieuse.org,
tel 02.40.84.42.30.

DIRECTIONS
From the train station in
Nantes, the tram and bus lines
#31 Petit Chantilly/Trentemoult
or #37 Le Pelletin/Rezé-les-
Nantes, have a stop near the

La Maison Familiale was the second Unité built and
the first to serve the organized working class, whom
Le Corbusier envisioned as its proper tenants. The
project began with the interest of a lawyer from
Nantes, Gabriel Chereau, who revived La Maison
Familiale, a private cooperative composed primarily
of laborers and foremen from the port of Nantes,
who in turn commissioned the building.[88] Le Corbusier considered this commission by users as a
mandate for the Unité and an opportunity to continue to refine the model.[89] In fact, the variations
from the Marseille block were largely driven by budget constrictions imposed by a national housing policy (Habitations Bon Marché) and took the form of
smaller apartments, diminished social amenities,
and reduced attention to sculptural qualities of portico and roof garden. The building is smaller than
that at Marseille, with 294 apartments as opposed to
330, and has fewer variations in apartment type.
More significantly, double-height living rooms were
eliminated and bedrooms extended over them. The
clients rejected the interior commercial street, a facility that Le Corbusier believed vital to the Unité's

social life. On the other hand, his studio resisted the mayoral request to incorporate a large school on the roof, which they believed belonged in the public realm and would deconsecrate the internal life of the building. The rooftop school as built is a large kindergarten for which Le Corbusier devised a facade of colored windows like "optical glitter."[90]

Besides the social program, the structural and material program also underwent reformulation. Le Corbusier's studio refined the detailing of the glass and wood exterior wall, the Modulor construction of the brise-soleil panels, and the surface of the exposed concrete which they finished with a pebble aggregate. A box frame of precast concrete slabs replaced the "bottle rack" system of Marseille. Whereas at Marseille, a structural grid separate from the apartment cells sits on a base of pilotis, here the plate-like pilotis are actually the cross-walls of the apartments brought down to the ground to act as bracing as well as supports. The stair towers also act as stiffeners. A "château of cards," as Le Corbusier called the building, it has no columnar skeleton; rather the "shoebox of slabs" which defines each apartment is also the structure.[91] Within the individual apartment shell of concrete is a layer of acoustic isolation of fiberglass mattresses and then a finished sheathing of wood and wallboard. This "shoebox" tectonic carries with it a spatial organization: a three-dimensional matrix that is fixed rather than free in plan and section. Consequently, forty years after its construction, the anomalous structure of plates developed faults and required a complete overhaul that is now complete.

La Maison Familiale's most distinctive feature is its siting. Several of its feet dip into an ornamental lake that fills an old red granite quarry. While the siting accentuates the building's resemblance to a ship, it also suggests another source of fascination for Le Corbusier: the prehistoric stilt dwellings found in lakes of central Europe which are echoed in his Citrohan house project for a seaside villa (1922–27). Like an expanded version of these dwellings, the "family house" is both raised above and immersed in nature. The bridge which crosses the lake is Le Corbusier's

building called Maison-Radieuse. From the tram station, the walk is less than ten minutes along rue de Château to boulevard Le Corbusier or "La Bouvardière" as it is called.

LOCALE
Rezé is a small community just across the Loire from the city of Nantes, principal city of Brittany. Nantes has both neoclassical and contemporary architecture of note. A possible itinerary continues from Nantes to the coast and Maison le Sextant outside La Rochelle.

pilotis in lake

88. Sbriglio, *L'Unité*, 148–50 and Ragot et Dion, *Le Corbusier en France*, 140–43.
89. Le Corbusier, *Oeuvre Complète* 6: 188; Le Corbusier, *Architectural Review* 3: 327.
90. Le Corbusier, *Oeuvre Complète* 5: 166.
91. Le Corbusier, *My Work*, 272.
92. Le Corbusier, *Creation is a Patient Search*, 273.

Interior view of stair tower

deliberate, symbolic proof that this type and its suggested landscape provide a viable economic alternative to the modern suburb. He described how its 1,400 inhabitants passed over the 1.83 meter-wide bridge daily without discomfort. "Authorities require three kilometres of roads, communications, water and gas in (suburban) family houses. Here there is a bridge over water. Impossible to cheat. 50 meters long. That's all."[92] The Unité now hovers above the extended suburb it was envisioned to replace.

CITÉ OUVRIÈRE

1917–1919

This commission for clockmakers now known as Réveils Bayard was probably connected to Le Corbusier's contacts in La Chaux-de-Fonds. The intended plan of 46 dwellings of three types of double-houses reflected Le Corbusier's early research into picturesque traditions. While the axis was formal, the site itself was slightly irregular and the housing followed its trapezoidal outline. The plan was reviewed in British and American periodicals of the time as a "French Garden Hamlet."[93]

Only one of the smallest type "C" houses was built, however: a one-and-a-half story building that contains two identical dwellings, each with a gabled roof and dormers. A central stair dividing first-floor living and bedroom symmetrically leads to two bedrooms on the attic story.[94] Le Corbusier wanted to construct the houses of hollow concrete blocks manufactured on site, but in the end was asked to use traditional bricks and brick detailing. The modified vernacular vocabulary of the house only thinly veils the typological link between the Cité Ouvrière and the startling abstraction of the garden town of Pessac.[95]

Le Corbusier

ADDRESS
rue Raphaël-Hennion
Saint-Nicholas-d'Aliermont
Seine-Maritime
Dieppe 13 km, Rouen 65 km

ACCESS
Half of the double-house maintains its original exterior detail. It is visible from the street.

DIRECTIONS
The house is at the intersection of route d'Envermeu, D.49, and route Saint-Nicholas-d'Aliermont, D.56, with rue Raphaël-Hennion. It is east of Dieppe by route D.1 and D.54.

LOCALE
From Paris the trip is under two hours.

site plan

93. Brooks, *Formative Years*, 481–5.
94. Ragot et Dion, *Le Corbusier en France*, 194.
95. Taylor, *Le Corbusier et Pessac*.

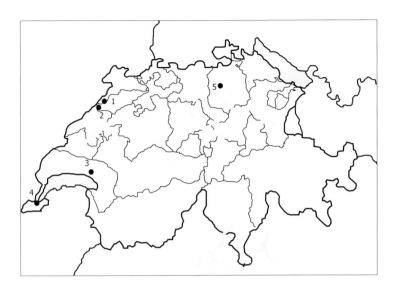

SWITZERLAND

1. La Chaux-de-Fonds
   Villa Fallet
   Villa Stotzer
   Villa Jacquemet
   Villa Jeanneret
   Cinéma La Scala
   Villa Schwob
2. Villa Favre-Jacot, Le Locle
3. La Petite Maison, Vevey
4. Immeuble Clarté, Geneva
5. Centre Le Corbusier
   (Heidi Weber House, La Maison
   de L'Homme), Zürich

Le Corbusier with René Chapallaz; decoration by students from the local School of Art and L'Eplattenier. L'Eplattenier is credited particularly with the color scheme, Le Corbusier with the branch designs.

ADDRESS
1, chemin de Pouillerel
2300 La Chaux-de-Fonds

ACCESS
Private villa visible from street

DIRECTIONS
Take bus #10 to the chemin de Pouillerel or take bus #1 to rue du Nord and climb the hillside steps.

LOCALE
See Villa Stotzer. The thatched house of L'Eplattenier designed by René Chapallaz in 1902 is across the street.

Le Corbusier was eighteen years old when his mentor at the School of Art, Charles L'Eplattenier, obtained this commission for him and arranged for the established architect René Chapallaz to supervise the project. L'Eplattenier often sought design commissions that involved the participation of his students. In this case, the execution of the house was to serve as an introduction to the subject of building as well as an opportunity to apply lessons in ornamentation. The client, Louis Fallet, was a small designer and manufacturer of watches, a member of the board of the School of Art and a supporter of L'Eplattenier's ideas. While the house is imbued with Le Corbusier's spatial sense, it is above all a testament to L'Eplattenier's search for an art and architecture appropriate to the region of the Jura mountains at the moment industrialization began to threaten the craft culture.[1]

Sympathetic to the authors and principles of the Arts and Crafts movement, L'Eplattenier advocated respect for local culture, materials, building methods and landscape. In this spirit, Le Corbusier's first house incorporates features of a Swiss chalet and vernacular architecture: overhanging eaves, complex gables, and the clear disposition of materials according to their structural role. References to specifically Jura types are minor. There is a typical rusticated stone base of yellow Neufchâtel stone and an expressed, heavy timber frame with infill stuccoed panels. The building is placed like most of the houses of the region—major axis and gable toward the view—but with a heightened sensitivity to its site. The land drops away beneath the house so that the entrance level is high on the hill and intimately scaled, while the south facade is vertical and imposing. The living room opens onto a balcony dramatically suspended over the slope. The plan likewise follows the tenets of the Arts and Crafts movement and Hermann Muthesius in its separation of workshop, living and sleeping areas and its organization about the surprisingly lofty space of the stairwell in the north gable.

entrance

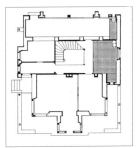

Ground floor plan

L'Eplattenier's curriculum, *dessin et composition décorative*, is most clearly expressed in the ornament. The villa is draped with imagery of the indigenous fir tree, the sapin. The orientation of the trees, with mullions placed like branches reaching up and eaves carved as pine cones hanging down, reflects John Ruskin's emphasis on direct observation of nature for both its form and symbolism. Most of the ornament has a degree of abstraction in accordance with a belief in the spiritual connection of nature and mathematics. Following the precepts of the grammar books of Owen Jones and Charles Blanc, and the more mystical texts of Henri Provensal, L'Eplattenier had his students extract the essential forces of natural forms by drawing their geometric structure. In the Villa Fallet, for example, pine boughs are depicted as compositions of cubes. Most significant is the fluid profusion of drawing using the *sgraffito* technique of applying color to wet plaster. In the manner of Art Nouveau and Jugendstil, equal weight is given to figure and ground, to branches and the spaces between them, creating a unified surface. Cut into this surface are windows with brackets fastened to the wall. Le Corbusier described it as "a true carpet in the tectonic tradition of [Gottfried] Semper."[2]

pinecone stair newel

1. For Le Corbusier's formative influences see: Geoffrey Baker, *Le Corbusier: The Creative Search*; H. Allen Brooks, *Le Corbusier's Formative Years*, Charles Jencks, *Le Corbusier and the Tragic View of Architecture*; Paul Turner, *The Education of Le Corbusier*; Mary Sekler and Paul Turner in Walden, *The Open Hand*; and Jacques Gubler, "Villa Fallet," in Frank Russell, *Art Nouveau Architecture*.
2. Geroges Baines, "La Maison Guiette à Anvers," in Prelorenzo, *La Conservation de L'Oeuvre Construite*, 56.

VILLA STOTZER
1907-1909

Le Corbusier with René Chapallaz

ADDRESS
6, chemin de Pouillerel
2300 La Chaux-de-Fonds

ACCESS
Private residence visible from
street

DIRECTIONS
See Villa Fallet

VILLA JACQUEMET
1907-1909

Le Corbusier with René Chapallaz

ADDRESS
8, chemin de Pouillerel
2300 La Chaux-de-Fonds

ACCESS
Private residence visible from
street

DIRECTIONS
See Villa Fallet

In form and program as well as in their historical circumstance, Villas Jacquemet and Stotzer can be grouped as a single entry in Le Corbusier's work. The architect designed them in tandem while in Vienna, on a European tour that had also included Italy and Budapest. As in the case of Villa Fallet, René Chapallaz advised the younger architect, completed the drawings and then supervised construction, this time on the basis of drawings and models mailed from Vienna.

Still under the sway of L'Eplattenier's search for a national romanticism, Le Corbusier was unsympathetic to the Viennese School, which he dismissed as an architecture of "cement and tin."[3] His influence was instead the experience of the Gothic, filtered through the eyes of John Ruskin's *Mornings in Florence* which was his traveling companion. According to Le Corbusier, the rusticated and overhanging stonework of the medieval Bargallo appears in the bases of these two houses. However, this probity in the use of materials and its restraining influence on ornament came as much from Le Corbusier's clients as from Ruskin. Jacquemet in particular rejected the Art Nouveau aspects of Le Corbusier's first design, requesting a scheme closer to L'Eplattenier's own house which incorporated typical Jura elements. The motif of the pine tree of Villa Fallet still figures in the eaves and windows, but massing and a bold treatment of structure and surface displace pattern as the means of expression. The voluminous dormers are like foliage, the wooden supports like branches. The bearing masonry with extended side walls derives from the Jura farmhouse via L'Eplattenier. This structural essay includes the use of reinforced concrete built according to the Hennebique patent for the floor slabs, terraces and supporting brackets. Surprisingly, the use of concrete in domestic architecture was not uncommon in the region at this time.[4] The non-bearing walls have a plain stucco rather than sgraffito finish in keeping with Ruskin's preference for "a freshly laid surface of gesso" over "most pictures painted upon it,"[5] an anticipation of the modernist preference for the bare surface.

LOCALE
La Chaux-de-Fonds, the birthplace of Le Corbusier, has many points of related interest. The town library, Bibliothèque de la Ville at 33, rue du Progrès, has a marvelous collection of his sketches, correspondence, and memorabilia, which is accessible to scholars who request permission in advance. Le Corbusier's teacher, L'Eplattenier, was involved in the design of several murals and buildings in town, including his own thatched house on chemin de Pouillerel, the Crematorium, the Museum of Fine Arts, and the paintings in the post office.

The town retains many of the features that exerted an influence on Le Corbusier in the late nineteenth century. Like Le Corbusier's own first city plans, La Chaux-de-Fonds is rationally ordered according to a preconceived plan. Following a fire in 1794, the town was rebuilt on a grid with a major avenue and pleasant town squares, one with a sculpture by L'Eplattenier. Two of Le Corbusier's buildings, the Cinéma La Scala and the Villa Schwob, are located downtown on the grid. The other four houses he designed are located on a hillside path above the commercial center. At the time they were built, the neighborhood was a more rural colony of houses belonging to the intelligentsia. Today, nature is still close at hand in the forest paths that begin just behind Villa Jeanneret.

3. Baker, *Creative Search*, 118; also Brooks, *Le Corbusier's Formative Years*, 139.
4. Brooks, *Le Corbusier's Formative Years*, 129–46. This is the definitive account of the Swiss period.
5. John Ruskin, *The Seven Lamps of Architecture*, 83.

The two villas had nearly identical patrons who requested similar programs. Relatives of Le Corbusier's first patron, Louis Fallet, both clients shared his progressive bourgeois views and artistic interests. Stotzer taught mechanics related to watches; Jacquemet was a polisher of cases among other trades. With the commission, Le Corbusier began to think of the hillside as a potential extended site of an artisan colony. For economic reasons, both clients requested houses containing two apartments designed to appear as a substantial single residence. The solution called for flats with a living-dining room on the south, bedrooms on the north, service wings on the east and west under hooded bay windows, and an entrance hall half-submerged within the main block of the house. Rather than use the repetitive conditions of the program to explore varied solutions, Le Corbusier formulated a modest typology. This attitude was to characterize his design approach throughout his career.

The difference between the villas is related to their sites and siting. Jacquemet on the gentler slope has the more placid appearance. The curved profiles of its stone piers ease its transition to the ground. The horizontal coursing and windows on its south side and the folded peak of its roof counteract the thrust along the major axis down the hill. Like a covered bridge, its vestibule spans the one abrupt drop in the terrain. If Jacquemet has the Ruskinian character of the Lamp of Beauty, then Stotzer is Power. At Stotzer, the composition exaggerates the verticality of its slope, from the tilted roof to the cut in the high stone podium leading to an elaborate stair. In a quiet polemic, Le Corbusier joins ideas that are more often dialectically opposed in his later work, the invention of type and the uniqueness of site.

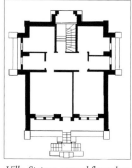

Villa Stotzer, ground floor plan

VILLA JEANNERET

1912

ADDRESS
12, chemin de Pouillerel
2300 La Chaux-de-Fonds

ACCESS
Private residence visible from
street. "La Maison Blanche"
has been awarded a 2005
Getty Foundation preservation
grant and is slated to become a
center for architecture and
design exhibitions, seminars,
and concerts.

DIRECTIONS
The villa is a short walk up the
hillside from Villa Fallet.

LOCALE
See Villa Stotzer.

In 1911, after a journey to eastern Europe and Greece, Le Corbusier reluctantly declined an offer from his former employer Auguste Perret to work on the Théâtre de Champs Elysées and returned to La Chaux-de-Fonds to head a new section of the local art school at the request of his master Charles L'Eplattenier. On his return, Le Corbusier also established his own design firm closely allied to Les Ateliers d'Art Réunis, decorative workshops run with his former schoolmates. Between 1912 and 1917 he designed three houses, Villa Jeanneret-Perret for his parents being the first, but he supported himself primarily as a decorator of domestic interiors.[6]

The house is substantial, with work space for Le Corbusier and accommodations for himself and his brother on the ground floor; music salon, living, and dining on the middle entrance level; and private quarters for the parents at the top. The cost far exceeded the modest resources of his family. With the depression in the watchmaking industry, his father's

6. Nancy Troy, *Modernism and the Decorative Arts*, 112. Troy places Le Corbusier in relation to the world of Parisian decorative arts at the turn of the century.

7. Brooks, *Le Corbusier's Formative Years*, 308–328.

8. Troy, *Modernism and the Decorative Arts*, 161.

9. Ch-E Jeanneret (Le Corbusier), *Étude sur le movement d'art décoratif en Allemagne* of 1911, a study commissioned by the art school in La Chaux-de-Fonds to examine the industrialization of German craft.

enameling business often struggled, and they relied on his mother's income as a piano teacher. They sold the house at a disastrous loss seven years after construction.[7]

The Villa Jeanneret-Perret is the first of Le Corbusier's works to reject the chalet style for a restrained classicism filtered through an array of sources both antique and contemporary. The interiors of the house represent a genre of this "classical eclecticism" which Le Corbusier had encountered in Paris among the *coloriste* decorators. The house had an assembly of furnishings in a stripped-down Empire style, some designed by Le Corbusier and others procured on his intermittent visits to Paris. The Jeanneret's sold the house in 1919 to a man named Jeker, whom Le Corbusier similarly advised to buy antiques in the style of Louis XVI and Directoire, chairs of his own design, and a purist painting.[8] This preference for a culture of artifacts additively assembled persists in his mature work as well, notably in his own apartment.

The sources for the architecture trace the itinerary of Le Corbusier's introduction to the classical. The exterior color of the house connects it with a Mediterranean tradition encountered in his travels, earning it the local sobriquet "*la maison blanche*." The central piano salon defined by four columns suggests classical precedents from

view of upper terrace

Pompeii to Palladio. The neoclassicism of Peter Behrens' Villa Shröder, Josef Hoffman's villas at Käasgraben and through them, Frank Lloyd Wright's Winslow house are possible sources for the attic-story windows, floating hip roof and axial planning. During his previous European tours, Le Corbusier had met with Hoffman, worked with Behrens and encountered the 1910 Wasmuth edition of Wright. The modernity cloaked within all these sources occurs here as well in the structural core of concrete columns carrying steel beams and in the concrete window frames. The plan is open, the windows expansive. Le Corbusier may have even entertained the use of a flat roof for the villa, but rejected it under pressure from L'Eplattenier and out of the need to collect roof water in the absence of municipal supply.

Le Corbusier's ambivalence toward bared industrial production emerged from his first-hand study of the Germans, whom he felt, as a response to an emerging machine age, turned to the classical in the absense of a native tradition.[9] In 1911, traveling from Berlin to the East with the book *Les Entretiens de la Villa de Rouet* by Alexandre Cingria-Vaneyre, Le Corbusier expanded his argument for a Swiss classicism. At Villa Jeanneret, he adopted in modified form Cingria's thesis that the French-speaking Swiss, or Suisse-Romande, descended from Mediterranean peoples and thus should have a regional architecture reflecting classical values of pure, geometric shapes distinct from nature. He intended the villa as a reconsideration rather than a rejection of regional style.

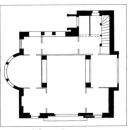

Ground floor plan

At Jeanneret-Perret, the white villa is wedded to the region through its siting. It engages the Jura hillside on three different levels through a sequence of spiraling terraces. The entrance path is carved through these plateaus, as well as built upon them. Even in this accommodation to the local terrain there are echoes of a classical, Acropolitan ascent up a mountain and around the building, but the gestures are particular. The profile of the cuts and protuberances along the path tend to be curved and part organic. The rotated apse carved from the terrace, the winding stair, the arc of the bay window and the wavelike profile of the final patio create a sequence of curve and counter-curve around the static symmetry of the box. In Le Corbusier's later, purist work, abstract descendants of these undulating shapes appear within the buildings as representations of nature, but at Jeanneret they seem to emerge from the landscape itself.

view to lower terrace

Le Corbusier and René
Chapallaz

ADDRESS
52, rue de la Serre
La Chaux-de-Fonds

ACCESS
Public cinema accessible during evening showings only. For the price of admission you can see a movie as well as what remains of Le Corbusier's design. The front wall has been completely rebuilt, and all interior finishes changed. The basic plan remains intact, however, and some of the original rear elevation is still visible beneath the addition of a cantilevered projection booth.

DIRECTIONS
Take bus #10 from the train station to the corner of rue de l'Ouest, or walk.

Frustrated by the nature of his design commissions in La Chaux-de-Fonds which were primarily interiors, Le Corbusier wrote Max DuBois that "it is very very odd: all my studies have been on the subject of reinforced concrete and yet I have barely cast twenty cubic metres of it. And while I have never studied interior architecture, preferring merely to look at it, lo and behold it has constituted all my work in 1913!"[10] The design of Cinéma La Scala at last afforded him the opportunity to construct a public, long-span building which included the material. Originally, the commission to transform the existing theater into a cinema belonged to René Chapallaz, the supervising architect for Le Corbusier's earliest houses, who designed the theater plan, structure and interiors, at least schematically. After wooing the client, Le Corbusier gained the commission for the design of the facades, ostensibly through a public competition. In the finished building, laminated wood arches designed by Hetzer of Zürich span the 16 meter interior and support a pitched timber roof. A seven-meter-deep reinforced concrete balcony is cantilevered over four slender columns.

Le Corbusier's contribution to the project seems to be the facades, despite Chapallaz's claims of total authorship. As the architect of record, it was Le Corbusier who was sued by the client when melted snow infiltrated through the eaves.[11] Le Corbusier claimed this experience spurred his research into flat roof slabs with internal drainage, first used at Villa Schwob.

The original elevations, only the rear of which remains, were romantic-classical in character, with gestures recalling Ledoux and Schinkel.[12] The motif of an arch within a pediment appeared in both, but varied in size and placement. Taken together they suggested a narrative related not just to the classical tradition but also to modern cinematic projection across a theater interior. On the front, an expansive arch flanked by colossal pilasters and two miniature temple fronts rose above the cornice, accentuating the flatness and screen-like quality of the wall. The rear had an actual depth created by layering the pyramidal stair in front of the wall. On the surface of this stair was inscribed a small, low arch seemingly conceived at a great distance from the front arch and consequently diminished in size according to the laws of perspective. This telescoping effect appeared also in the relation of the small rear pediment to the roof line and the small lunette to the arch below. While the current, cantilevered projection booth is an awkward addition to the rear, it makes literal the idea of projection and enlargement across the distance of theater.

The cinema's romantic rational character rather than its cinematic effect may dominate reading of the building now, but to the local population of La Chaux-de-Fonds of 1916 and to Le Corbusier, it had radical qualities. The local paper even called it "cubist" in response to its abstraction. To illustrate the placement of movie posters on the facade, Le Corbusier placed a drawing of a Greek in peplum in the right bay, and a bomber advertising a World War I news reel in the left.[13]

LOCALE
See Villa Stotzer. The cinema is in the center of town.

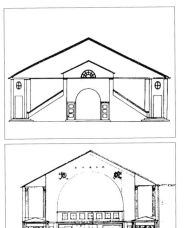

Original elevations: front (top) and rear (below)

10. Joyce Lowman, "Corbusier as Structural Rationalist," *Architectural Review* 160: 956,229.
11. For the project history see Brooks, *Le Corbusier's Formative Years*, 415–24.
12. Brooks also proposes Louis Sullivan's Farmer's Bank, in Owatonna as a source, Ibid., 424.
13. Jacques Gubler, "Charles-Édouard Jeanneret, 1887–1917, ou l'accès à la practique architecturale," in Lucan, *Le Corbusier: Une Encyclopédie*, 229.

Le Corbusier; construction supervision by Marcel Montandon; decorative panels by Léon Perrin

ADDRESS
167, rue du Doubs
2300 La Chaux-de-Fonds

ACCESS
Accessible upon arrangement. Ask in advance at the tourist office (near the train station) to arrange a visit. The villa was bought by la Société Ebel, the Ebel watch company, as a public relations center in the mid-1980s and subsequently restored by the Neuchâtel architect Pierre Studer with decoration by Andrée Putman. In 1996 it underwent a second minor renovation.

DIRECTIONS
The house is in a residential

The Schwob family were industrialists involved in the finishing of watch cases, intellectuals, and patrons of the arts. Le Corbusier knew them as part of an artistic and social circle whose activities and members are documented in the novel *Le Concert sans Orchestre* by Jean-Paul Zimmerman (1936). Le Corbusier appears in the novel as the musician Félix Courvoisier. Prior to the commission of the villa for Anatole Schwob, Le Corbusier had executed interior decoration for various members of the family, including a smoking room for Anatole.[14]

The client asked for a house similar to the Villa Jeanneret-Perret, but in a 1914 article entitled "Renewal in Architecture," Le Corbusier had publicly abandoned his previous commitment to a regional architecture of the Suisse-Romande in favor of more progressive rationalist arguments linked to the French and the international scene. This shift in thinking is most clearly stated in the construct of the Maison Dom-ino (1914) by Le Corbusier, with the Swiss engineer Juste Schneider and concrete manufacturer Max DuBois, as a building system that could replenish housing stock destroyed in the war. Villa

Schwob incorporates the spirit if not techniques of the Dom-ino system: slender reinforced concrete columns supporting smooth slabs, including a flat roof which serves as a roof garden, large expanses of glass which are a consequence of the nonload-bearing walls, and a freely flowing arrangement of plan. While the Dom-ino was intended as a site-prefabricated system of flat slabs, here the concrete was more traditionally poured with coffered slabs which were then smoothed over. A 4 x 4 grid of columns defines a variation of a nine-square plan at the center of the house which is extended by apsidal bays likewise framed in concrete. Other technical innovations at Schwob which follow from the potentials of the Dom-ino frame are the system of internal drainage from the inclined roof slab, and the circulation of heated air through the brick exterior cavity walls.

neighborhood on the eastern edge of the town grid. It is a 20-minute walk from the bus station along rue de la Fusion, then downhill on rue de Doubs; or take bus #1 (Recorne), stop at Villa Turque as it is known locally. Ebel SA headquarters (through which access is arranged) is also located down-town at 113 rue de la Paix, tel 41.32.912.31.23, fax 41.32.912.31.24, marketing@ebel.ch.

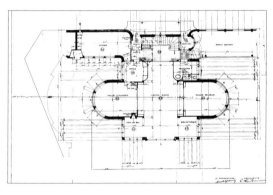

ground floor plan

The structural system, the client's expanding program, increases in square footage, and superior materials resulted in cost overruns which nearly doubled the budget of the house. The final project called for a three-story house with maids rooms, guest rooms, a solarium and terrace on the pent-house; bedroom suites on the mezzanine; and salon, library, and entrance zone of service functions on the main floor. Le Corbusier upheld that the yellow glazed bricks ordered from Lausanne were the most beautiful manufactured in Switzerland. Despite the cost far in excess of traditional masonry and the law-suit between architect and client that eventually ensued, Le Corbusier maintained great faith in the system, proudly announcing Schwob as one of the first concrete villas in Europe.

front

The rationality of the Dom-ino did not contradict the classical aspects and sources of the villa in the mind of Le Corbusier. As Paul Turner has demonstrated, contained within the Dom-ino itself are an idealized trabeation and the classical geometry of the golden section.[15] Besides Le Corbusier's usual references to the contemporary classicism of Behrens and Hoffman, in the Villa Schwob there are traces of his employer Auguste Perret and the Théâtre des Champs-Elysées. Scholars have traced antecedents back to Palladio's Casa Cogollo,[16] and even to the Swiss classical tradition.[17] There are also seraglio qualities and massing reminiscent of the Byzantine architecture Le Corbusier had admired on his "Journey to the East"—hence its local nickname Villa Turque. In the spirit of Perret's classical rationalism, these sources are rendered abstractly with an emphasis on their pure, geometric qualities. The facades are composed using a proportioning system of angles based on the golden section in the manner of Auguste Choisy. Le Corbusier published drawings of the facades in the book *Vers une architecture* (1923) as an illustration of the power of these "regulating lines" to control surface. The geometry of the volumes is also "pure." The pilasters on the apses are half-cylinders like the apses themselves. The most pure, most blank, yet most inexhaustible element of the house is of course the great front facade, a seemingly weightless screen on to which can be projected a variety of meanings.

In his interpretation, Le Corbusier filters the modern through the antique and vice versa, suggesting that the classical is prescient of a machine age. The entablature of three bare planes of concrete at Schwob is an homage to what Le Corbusier called

14. For building history see Brooks, "Le Corbusier's Formative Years," 425–460 and Tim Benton, *Six Houses* in Raeburn and Wilson eds, *Le Corbusier Architect of the Century*, 58-60.
15. Turner, "Romanticism, Rationalism and the Dom-Ino System," Walden, *The Open Hand*, 37.
16. Colin Rowe, *The Mathematics of the Ideal Villa*, 32.
17. Brooks, *Le Corbusier's Formative Years*, 463.
18. Le Corbusier, *Towards a New Architecture*, 217.

the "machined perfection" of the Parthenon, its appearance of "naked, polished steel."[18]

The character of the house exceeds its classical sources through intense contrasts in size and placement and the sense of instability they create. In elevation, the extreme delicacy of the porch plays off the severe quality and scale of the wall behind. The small oval windows seem even more oddly proportioned in relation to the overblown entablature. The huge, chiseled cornice wraps the volumes, in an effort to offset the tendency of the massing to disintegrate into an assemblage of parts—front plane, apses, cubes and corners. On the interior, a similar tension exists between the primacy of the central cube and the lateral pull of the cross axes. From the perspective of the entrance hall, the salon appears a unified and luminous volume with a strong axis leading to the garden. Once in the room, however, the balconies and apses seem to slice the room apart.

The house was built in record time, less than a year. Still, before it was complete, Le Corbusier had left La Chaux-de-Fonds for Paris and a new architectural office underwritten by DuBois' French companies, Societé d'Applications du Béton Armé (SABA). Le Corbusier carried with him his ideogram of modernity, the Maison Dom-ino, but he left behind in Schwob an equally significant experiment in which the Dom-ino's plastic potentials are rendered with complexity.

main salon

Le Corbusier, with decoration
by Léon Perrin

ADDRESS
6, côtes des Billodes
2400 Le Locle
La Chaux-de-Fonds 8 km

ACCESS
Private residence visible from
access road

DIRECTIONS
A local train runs frequently
from La Chaux-de-Fonds and
takes 10 minutes. Walk west
along the road in front of the
station, following signs to the
museum and hospital. After
crossing the train tracks, where
the hospital road turns back up
the hill, continue west to an
unmarked drive lined with
trees. This is the entrace to the
villa. The côte des Billodes is
off the rue des Billodes just
beyond the small railroad

Simultaneous with the design of Villa Jeanneret, Le Corbusier received the commission of a substantial villa for the owner of a major watch factory. As at Jeanneret, the architecture renders the Jura regional style in terms of the classical heritage of the Suisse-Romande. Again, there is what Goethe might call an "elective affinity" for Le Corbusier between this Suisse-Romande and the German architecture which uses classicism as its cultural filter. Grander in site and scale and more formal than the Villa Jeanneret, the house has moments reminiscent of K. F. Schinkel and Peter Behrens's Villa Cüno.[19]

Regionalism finds expression here in a composition of classically conceived geometric solids that accord with the spirit of the site. Overt references to the nature of the Jura are vestigial, as in the abstracted pine cones traced on the pilaster capitals by Le Corbusier's friend from art school Léon Perrin. More significant to the house's character is the negotiation of the slope. A sequence of rooms from forecourt to the rear terrace establishes a horizontal datum for the shifting play of terraces and floors. For example, the entry is in fact at piano nobile level; the front balcony window is off the third-floor bedroom. The plan provides several intermingled promenades, each articulated with leitmotifs such as columned porches and cylindrical volumes. The promenades begin with the approach to the villa, at the pre-existing coach house, and move along the retaining wall of the terraced drive. The geometry of this court is quite complex: the circle described by the paving does not align with that described by the building; the wings of the building are asymmetrical in relation to each other and the court; the ground tilts. The resulting form is highly gestural, indicating one path into the house and another movement of eye and body beyond the house and down the slope. Here, as later in the Villa Savoye, the movement of the car, and its turning radius determined the dimensions of the drive.

At this time, Le Corbusier and L'Eplattenier were immersed in urban studies and proposals for La Chaux-de-Fonds, using the methodology of Camillo Sitte as a corrective for what they perceived as the impoverishment of an overly rationalized plan. La Chaux-de-Fonds had been rebuilt on a grid after a devastating fire in the eighteenth century. Sitte's idea of site, based on mobile perception, could have served as a source for the villa as well. Stanislaus von Moos identifies the forecourt with a contemporaneous design by Le Corbusier for the plaza in front of the train station of La Chaux-de-Fonds.[20] It was not the last time that Le Corbusier was to traverse manmade and natural landscapes, urban and domestic scales with a single form.

bridge. There are some good views of the villa from rue des Billodes.

LOCALE
Le Locle is a manufacturing town, neither as large nor as prosperous as La Chaux-de-Fonds, but similar in landscape and feel. Le Corbusier's client, M. Favre-Jacot, owned the town's largest operation, the Zenith watch factory, and a lot of local real estate. There is a watch museum and a museum of fine arts in the town.

19. Stanislaus von Moos, *Elements of a Synthesis*, 17.
20. von Moos, "The Monument and the Metropolis," *Columbia Documents* 3: 115–39.

LA PETITE MAISON

1923–1924

Le Corbusier, Pierre Jeanneret

ADDRESS
Villa le Lac
Route de Lavaux
CH-1802 Corseaux
Geneva 78 km, Lausanne 19
km, Montreaux 7 km

ACCESS
Open Wednesdays 1:30–5 or
by appointment, except
December–February, when
visits can be arranged
through the town hall,
tel 41.21.925.4011, or
through www.athenaeum.ch,
tel 41.21.921.4602. The
house is administered by the
Fondation Le Corbusier,
tel 41.21.923.5363.

DIRECTIONS
By train Vevey and the adjoining town of Corseaux are a half
hour from Lausanne and an
hour from Geneva. Service
runs hourly. From the train
station at Vevey walk west in

Le Corbusier designed this modest vacation house for his parents just before his father's death. His mother spent time there throughout her life as did his brother, Albert Jeanneret, a composer who used it as a studio. Many photographs survive of family gatherings in the garden. The house contains custom furnishings and also personal artifacts of the family such as Mediterranean pottery and an elaborate wood desk designed by the architect earlier in his career.

Despite its personal program and private demeanor, the house played a public role in the "controversy of the window" waged between Auguste Perret and Le Corbusier in Parisian journals of 1923.[21] In brief, Le Corbusier asserted that the major positive consequence of Dom-ino concrete frame construction was the strip window, which could continuously and conveniently distribute light within an interior where it was most needed, at eye level. At Vevey, this window is the rhetorical center piece of the house, "*l'acteur primordial.*" In his book on the house, *Une Petite Maison*, Le Corbusier presents the window as the inevitable and scientific response to the first "given," the sun, its zenithal path, and its relation to "the horizontal eye."[22] This resulting window is a south-facing, eleven-meter-long slash in the wall, which bears no strict relationship to the division of rooms.

Auguste Perret, a father of concrete construction and mentor to the young Le Corbusier, dismissed the strip window as decorative and contrary to use. For him, the horizontal window destroyed the definition of interior space by eliminating threshold and eclipsed the experience of exterior space by cropping the view of foreground and sky. It degraded all perspectives into cubist composition.

The house at Vevey follows directly from this argument of the horizontal window. Le Corbusier described its plan in similarly mechanistic terms as a "dwelling machine." He claimed that the precise functioning and dimensioning of its parts resulted in efficiency and spatial economy. A gear of form at the center generates the uses along the box. Many of the elements operate like machine parts. The bedroom wall opens to reveal storage cabinets built below the floor. The table and lamps are instrumental extensions of the window that slide along the south wall.

The structural and material system which allows for both the window and the dwelling machine is predictably a version of the Dom-ino. Driven in part by budgetary constraints, the system has a homely translation: supports are metal pipe columns filled with cement; the roof is concrete made by the

the direction of Lausanne on avenue General Guisan, which becomes route de Lavaux. The house is on the lake side of the road about 20 minutes from the station and just beyond the Nestlé Headquarters.

LOCALE
Vevey is a resort town on the shores of Lake Geneva (Lac Leman). When Le Corbusier built his little house, only an old Roman road connected it to the sleepy village. Today the major thoroughfare to

strip window

Lausanne runs right through the town and in front of the house. Still, the terraced vineyards that spill down the Alps to the lake are spectacular; you can view them from the funicular that runs from the town center.

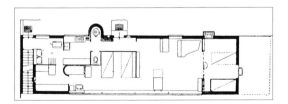

plan

lost tile process; the walls are hollow concrete block plastered. While the primitive rendering of the rhetorically high-tech system was intentional, the primitive detailing was not. Several seasons after its completion,

front door from route de Lavaux

21. Bruno Reichlin, "Une Petite Maison on Lake Leman," *Lotus* 60: 59–75.
22. Le Corbusier, *Une Petite Maison*, 5. All entry quotes by Le Corbusier are from this book.
23. Edward Ford, *The Details of Modern Architecture* 1: 235.

all-too human cracks in the stucco skin arose, probably from the detailing of the parapet without metal coping. In generous self-defense, Le Corbusier treated the occurrence as a scientific study in aging and nature. He covered the south wall in a corrugated metal, which likewise combined allusions to high and low-technologies, vernacular farm buildings, and airplane cockpits. In a restoration of 1945, the south wall was also covered, because of cracks from hydrostatic movement beneath the basement.[23]

The shock of the little house is in its siting, which makes the argument for Perret as strongly as the strip window argues against him. A masonry wall wraps the site along the edge of the road and the edge of the lake, and creates an outdoor room mediating between the house proper and the landscape at large. Into the south portion of this rough wall is cut a "square window" providing a controlled view of the lake "which will not overpower the senses." This of course is Perret's window, reframing the lake which is first seen through the strip. The entire promenade as drawn by Le Corbusier culminates in the distant view of the lake through this window and the foreground still-life of dining table and pottery vessel set before it. The last room of the house is darkly painted and lit only from above as a caesura from the view and the garden scene.

garden window

door to garden

The idea of foreground and distant views pertains also to the house's real and imagined sites: the foreground garden whose plantings Le Corbusier describes at length, the middle ground map which he draws showing the lake at the center of train routes to all European capitals, and the distant Mediterranean which was his obsession. The remote site of the Mediterranean becomes apparent in the low-slung, perimeter rubble wall with picture window. Together they give the house a vernacular villa aura.

Le Corbusier wrote that he and Pierre Jeanneret went in search of the "perfect site" for this house with the completed plans in their pocket, and that they found at Vevey a piece of land "which fit it like a glove." The generative plan contained the idea of a dwelling that could fully express itself only in relation to its desired landscape. The strip window of the house needed the aedicule in the rough stone wall, the machine its garden.

IMMEUBLE CLARTÉ

1931

Le Corbusier and Pierre Jeanneret with Charlotte Perriand

ADDRESS
2, rue St Laurent
Geneva

ACCESS
Apartment building with some
professional offices. Public
areas accessible. The building
is now a registered monument
and may be toured by arrangement with the government
agency Architecture au Service
des Monuments et des Sites,
tel 41.22.327.4532,
fax 41.22.327.5130,
www.geneve.ch/dael, and is open
on Journée du Patrimoine each
September.

DIRECTIONS
Rue St Laurent is a five-minute
walk from the Rond-Point de
Rive. Bus #6 or tram #16 pass
close by.

LOCALE
The building is located on the
southeast side of town, in a
pleasant neighborhood not far
from the Museum of Natural
History.

Between 1930 and 1932 a shift occurred in Le Corbusier's urban thinking, not away from his faith in
the power of the plan, but away from the concentric
and limited Contemporary City toward a more egalitarian and expandable Radiant City. The housing of
the Radiant City stressed economy and standardization, whereas that of the Contemporary City had
focused on providing the elite classes living at the
city center with a luxurious lifestyle. Gone were the
villa apartments (*immeuble-villas*) of the earlier city
with their alternating cells of duplex apartment and
hanging garden. In the Radiant City, everyone was to
live in long, horizontal blocks of flats. Basic to the
character of these blocks were their orientation to the
sun, their glass sheathing, roof terraces and pilotis all
providing the inhabitants with the immediate and
"essential joys of sun, space, and green."[24]

Le Corbusier with Charlotte Perriand envisioned
the city's standardized apartment of fourteen square

meters per occupant in some detail. Influenced by CIAM's 1929 discussion of *existenz minimum* (minimum dwellings) and by the contemporary Soviet architecture which Le Corbusier encountered on his trip to Moscow in 1930, the plans stressed the flexible use of rooms of small dimension with built-in equipment instead of furniture. As in the earlier Weissenhof double house, thin sliding partitions of a *wagon-lit* replaced traditional walls so that spaces could be combined according to family need.[25] The soundproofing of the apartments insured individual privacy, while the communal services of the blocks assured daily comfort.

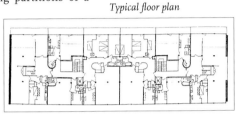

Typical floor plan

The Immeuble Clarté is an explicit and particular rendering of this moment of thinking between Le Corbusier's city planning schemes. The first design proposed by the architect had duplex apartments derived from the *immeuble* model but disposed along double-loaded corridors (*rue intérieurs*). It was the client, Edward Wanner, who critiqued the scheme according to standards that were in fact coincident with the Radiant City but also tuned to the reality of the site and the traditions of bourgeois housing in Geneva: "I have received your scheme whose idea is acceptable but not perfect. In fact there are three main defects: 1) Orientation; 2) Corridors of twelve meters without any lighting whatsoever. This is certainly bothersome . . . the disposition of the plot absolutely does not allow comparison to the general case; 3) The apartments are too big. . . ."[26] The final design, which accommodates Wanner's suggestions, has eight apartments per floor of various plans, some duplex. While the apartments remain commodious, they incorporate features of the Radiant apartments such as sliding partitions and built-ins. Access to the apartments is from two skylit stairwells detailed in glass block so that the "essential joy of light" filters through the build-

View of stairwell

Detail of facade at street level

24. Le Corbusier, *The Radiant City*.
    See also entry Pavillon de l'Esprit
    Nouveau.
25. Christian Sumi, "Clarté," 100–1
    and Arthur Rüegg, "Équipment,"
    132–3, in Lucan, *Encyclopédie*.
26. Christian Sumi, "Il Progetto
    Wanner," *Rassegna* 3: 42. Also see
    Christian Sumi, "Wanner," in
    Lucan, *Encyclopédie*, 477–8.
27. Christian Sumi, "The Immeuble
    Clarté," in Palazzolo and Vio, *In
    the Footsteps of Le Corbusier*, 177.
28. Wanner in Sumi, "Il Progetto
    Wanner," *Rassegna* 3: 42.

ing. In lieu of hanging gardens, and once more at the suggestion of Wanner, the units on both sides of the building face uninterruptedly onto balconies which serve also as sunbreaks for the glass walls below. The orientation remains rhetorical, with the primary axis aligned along the cul-de-sac and a severe avenue facade that registers the architect's dissatisfaction with the existing city street. In the photographs of the *Oeuvre Complète*, Le Corbusier and Lucien Hervé staged evocative scenes of mothers and children in remote and blissful inhabitation.

A metals manufacturer, Edmond Wanner also encouraged Le Corbusier's thinking in terms of standardization and prefabrication. As a consequence of Wanner's interest and capabilities, the building is the first in which Le Corbusier uses a steel frame and no concrete. The steel supports a subframe of wood and interior finish layer of wood and plaster. From the windows and wall panels to the framing, the building is designed according to an unvarying module. Wherever possible, the modularized elements were fabricated in quantity off-site and then assembled "dry." The balconies served as a kind of in-place scaffold for assembly. All the parts in steel, which include awnings, balconies, columns and hardware, are detailed with thin profiles, smooth casings and welded connections underlining the sense of light construction. A relatively untested combination of material and technique, the building has required major restoration.[27]

The Immeuble Clarté is Le Corbusier's first apartment house and first "*maison à sec*," and as such represents a first opportunity to experiment with some of the housing principles from his urban plans. The urban thinking is fluid, situated simultaneously in the Radiant, the Contemporary, and the real city of Geneva. As Wanner predicted, this hybrid situation "does not allow comparison to the general case but leads rather to the resolution of a specific case,"[28] and the building's particular qualities.

CENTRE LE CORBUSIER
(HEIDI WEBER HOUSE, LA MAISON DE L'HOMME)
1967

Heidi Weber's patronage began when she impulsively traded her Fiat to a friend in exchange for a collage by Le Corbusier. She subsequently held an exhibition of his paintings in her design showroom despite the architect's apt warning that the work wouldn't sell. Unwilling to disappoint, she told him that all the work had sold and then bought them herself. Elated by his "success," Le Corbusier told her to double the price of the paintings, whereupon they became in great demand.[29] Heidi Weber then proposed a museum to house his art along with residential amenities for display purposes and for her own use.

Initially skeptical, Le Corbusier warmed to the project as he considered it in his own pre-established terms of a "synthesis of arts" and "house of man." Le Corbusier conceived synthesis as a perceptual experience of the mobile body with regard to "this equipment: two eyes which can only see ahead."[30] By directing the viewer through a relatively open architecture on a rotational path, he felt that space, art, and the body would achieve a form of symbiosis.

Le Corbusier, Jean Prouvé, André Wogenscky

ADDRESS
Höschgasse 8
Zurichhorn Park, Zürich
110, A Postfach, CH-8034

ACCESS
Open July–Sept., Saturday and Sunday 2–5 or by arrangement, info@centre-lecorbusier.com. www.center-lecorbusier.com. Because of the extensive glazing and surrounding open space, it is possible to get a good sense of the interior even when the building is closed.

DIRECTIONS
The tram up Seefeldstrasse passes Höschgasse; but the forty-minute walk from the center of town along Seefeld Quai is nice.

Synthesis was a lifetime goal and the focus of his exhibit pavilions for Paris, Japan, and India, the Carpenter Center, and the unbuilt Palais Ahrenberg which resembles Weber House. "La Maison de l'Homme" is a particularly French and Corbusian locution that defies literal translation. Le Corbusier explained it as an "example of dwelling. . . constructed on the scale of man for the disposition of man."[31] The curiosity of this last building of Le Corbusier is that it is neither a house (there is no bedroom) nor a museum per se.

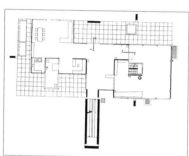

ground floor plan

The intentional confusion of domestic shelter and public exhibition found in this pavilion/house is thematic to the work of Le Corbusier. In his own myth of origin in *Vers une architecture (1923)*, he tells the same story of the primitive nomadic tent twice, first for the house and then for the temple. He called much of his institutional work "palace," that ambiguous place where private life is a matter of public ceremony. He also bonded this palace to the more intimately domestic in his rubric, *"une maison—un palais."* The architecture of Weber House plays freely with these categories. The building offers glancing views across its dimensions so that all its internal functioning is exposed. The buried section contains the public auditorium and a mausoleum-like chamber labeled "shelter." Derived from Le Corbusier's exhibition projects, the monumental umbrella appears here more as a sign of domestic roof and pediment. While neutral in their geometry, the cubes define the most homey scale. They derive from the Le Brevet structural system developed by Le Corbusier and Jean Prouvé[32] according to the smallest Modulor dimension of habitation for a single, six-foot man with an outstretched arm, or 226 cm. A shallow moat surrounding the entire building protects the inhabitant but reinforces her exhibit value.

The confusion of the program is masked by a tectonic clarity. The purity of tent-like roof, hut-like cubes and cave-like cellar raises structural language to the plane of archetype.[33] The subterranean chamber recalls Le Corbusier's proposed cave shrine at La Sainte-Baume. The ramp is a trace of his brutalist concrete from the previous decade in a structure that otherwise uses metal for its visceral expression of lightness. The provenance of the umbrella roof within Le Corbusier's work is the mythic tent, the built tents of Pavillon de Temps Nouveau (1937) and the Phillips Pavilion (1952), and the umbrella of Porte Maillot (1950). While not literally textile, its plate structure approximates a stressed skin, and its shape suggests the folding of material.[34] The cube frames are a system of small, built-up members, akin to the stick assembly of some primitive huts. A single length of steel angle bolted together in cruciform sections acts both as structure and sheathing frame. The members have an identity and simplicity that is visually important, where in truth they take different horizontal and vertical loads and could be sized differently.[35] The panels of enameled metal, backed with insulating polystyrene, act as a stabilizing sheathing within the framework.

Only in their interaction do the three distinct structures engage the complexity of the program. The cubes suggest an organic architecture of adjoined identical units (fully realized in the Venice Hospital project) that values cellular growth over predetermined and complete form. Through the use of reveals and shadows, the panels seem to float within their frames and slightly above the ground, emphasizing the independent nature of their entire system. The umbrella and ramp control the spread of this expandable fabric as if to represent how ceremonial culture controls our quotidian drives. On every side, a column or water leader, roof or moat define the limits of the house within the nature of the park. In a choreographic move reminiscent of Villa Savoye, that other summary "house of man" in nature, the ramp at the center of the grid causes a shift in the structure which in turn disrupts the axis of entry. In his final built work, Le Corbusier offers us yet a new formulation of *Et in Arcadia ego*.[36]

29. Michael Peppiatt, "Celebrating Le Corbusier in Zurich," *Architecural Digest* (March 1991): 54-58.
30. Le Corbusier quoted in Arnaldo Rivkin, "Synthèse," in Lucan, *Une Encyclopédie*, 388.
31. Heidi Weber quoted by Pierre-Alain Crosset, "I Clienti di Le Corbusier," *Rassegna* 3: 34–38.
32. Also known as "226 X 226 x 226," Le Brevet was developed for the housing at Roq et Rob.
33. Deborah Gans, "Structural Archetypes in the work of Le Corbusier," TSAR Tulane (1992): 117-122.
34. Ford, *Details* 2: 207.
35. Ibid., 215.
36. Edwin Panofsky suggests that the statement "I am in Arcadia" is spoken by Death, and that the pastoral tradition of Virgil similarly introduces tragedy into utopian Arcady through the dissonance of human suffering and superhumanly perfect surroundings; the tragedy is nevertheless softened by its projection onto a mythical future or past. Edwin Panofsky, *Meaning in the Visual Arts*, 299–301.

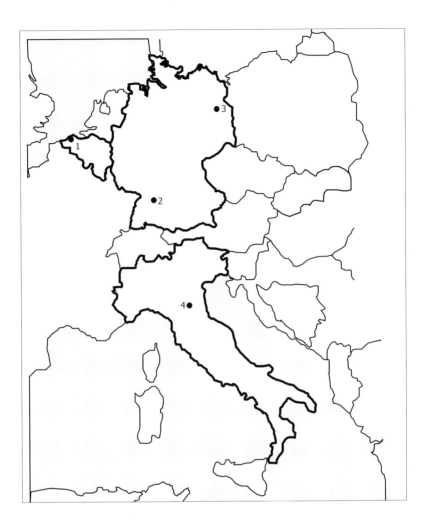

EUROPE

1. Maison Guiette, Antwerp
2. Houses of the Weissenhof, Stuttgart
3. Unité d'habitation, Berlin
4. Pavillon de l'Esprit Nouveau, Bologna

Le Corbusier and Pierre
Jeanneret

ADDRESS
32, Populierenlaan
(avenue des Peupliers)
2000 Antwerp, Belgium
Brussels, 52 km

ACCESS
Private residence clearly visible
from the street

DIRECTIONS
From Brussels-North station,
trains depart for Antwerp
approximately twice an hour.
From the Antwerp train station,
take one of several local buses
including #17 and #27, or
tram line #2. Get off several
blocks beyond the Kleine Ring-
weg where Eglantierlaan
crosses Vare della Faillelaan.

LOCALE
Maison Guiette now stands
beyond the circumferential
built in the 1960s at the
edge of a pleasant residential
neighborhood. Visitors might
spend time touring the rest
of Antwerp, birthplace of
Peter Paul Rubens and Henry
Van de Velde, or visit Maison
Guiette on a half-day trip from
Brussels or Lille.

1. For the correspondence with Guiette see Georges Baines, "La Maison Guiette à Anvers" in
Prelorenzo, *La Conservation de
l'Oeuvre Construite de Le Corbusier*,
39–63.
2. Le Corbusier, *Oeuvre Complète* 1:
137.
3. Le Corbusier, Decorative Arts of
Today, 76.
4. Baines, "La Maison Guiette," in
Prelorenzo, *La Conservation*, 47.
5. Yves-Alain Bois and Bruno Reichlin, *De Stijl et l'architecture en
France*.

The painter René Guiette commissioned Le Corbusier to build him and his family a "pretty house"
in the manner of the architect's Atelier Ozenfant and
Pavillon de L'Esprit Nouveau.[1] The built project subscribes more to the spatial and structural formula of
the Citrohan 2 prototype of 1922, adapted to a standard Antwerp lot, 6 meters wide and very deep. As in
the Citrohan model, the "free facade" with generous
strip glazing is limited to front and rear, whereas the
parallel sides have columns embedded within largely
solid, though non-bearing walls. Similar to its model,
the posts of the concrete frame fall between the narrow bay for the linear stair and the wide bay for the
living quarters, freeing the non-bearing walls for
streamlined curves. The double-height studio with
balcony, used as the living room in the Citrohan, is
returned to an authentic role as a painting studio on
the top floors. According to Guiette's wishes, the living room is on the ground floor facing the garden,
thus eliminating the Citrohan pilotis. Because of the
site's depth, the typical Citrohan plan of two rooms
facing front or back gives way to a linear sequence of

three rooms, with the middle one looking onto a side garden in the manner of both European and American townhouses. Le Corbusier acknowledged the resemblance when he described the Guiette stair as the "Jacob's Ladder" of the tenement in Charlie Chaplin's movie *The Kid* (1919).[2] Still, other than the Weissenhof exhibition house, Guiette remains the purest rendition of the Citrohan and an illustration of Le Corbusier's rhetoric regarding the type. "There is no shame in living in a house without a pointed roof, with walls as smooth as iron, with windows like those of factories. And one can be proud of having a house as serviceable as a typewriter."[3]

The compositional qualities of the house belie its functional description. In fact, during the belabored construction process, the builder and site architect Smekens aggressively lobbied the owner to eliminate features he felt useless and overly determined by aesthetics. The balanced asymmetry of the windows and the independent planes of awning and balconies owe something to the de Stijl compositions of the period, but the insistent cubic volume is particular to Le Corbusier. Whereas de Stijl architecture explodes volumes, Le Corbusier's approach suggests interpenetrating volumes beyond the literal relations of rooms, but within the confines of the cube. For example, the vertical strip and the horizontal window below the balcony both suggest continuous slots of space. The front studio window describes both a void cube and a plane of glass passing continuously from the top to the bottom of the building. As he explained in one of many letters of description, declamation and pleading to Guiette, "conforming to our principles, we have sought to realize an *envelope* [emphasis Le Corbusier] of house which is very unified, very calm, containing (without exterior protuberances) a complex and supple plan."[4]

The polychromy of the house also reflects de Stijl influences.[5] Their shared intent was to shape space through color, rather than surface material. The polychromy for this project played an important role, as Guiette was himself a colorist. Le Corbusier insisted on specifying the palette on site which he

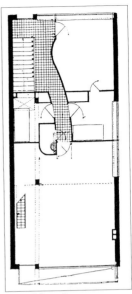

Second floor plan

Section

6. Le Corbusier in Baines, "La Maison Guiette," Prelorenzo, *La Conservation*, 58.

7. Le Corbusier in Mark Wigley, *White Walls, Designer Dresses*, 238.

8. Le Corbusier in Baines, "La Maison Guiette," Prelorenzo, *La Conservation*, 55.

accomplished during his single visit in May of 1927. The interior palette was "ultramarine blue, light and dark cerulean blue, yellow ochre, burnt sienna, burnt ochre, rose (with sienna and white) and light English green for the terrace."[6] The burnt sienna appeared on walls parallel to the stair, the other colors reserved for perpendicular planes.

In contrast to the variegation of the interior, the exterior color in its very monotony has a unique place in Le Corbusier's oeuvre. Le Corbusier had earlier criticized the de Stijl use of color on the exterior for the "effect of camouflaging; it destroys, disarticulates, divides and is opposed to unity"[7]—a statement he would soon retract at Pessac, where he employed color to define planes. At Guiette, in search of unity, Le Corbusier draped the entire volume in an "elephant gray pulled from the blue stone from which it was composed," giving it "a good rough granite effect."[8] As city regulations demanded that cladding be a natural material, Le Corbusier's typical cement finish contained particles of the blue stone.

Design and construction of the house was an extended and difficult process, with budget and technique a recurring issue. Le Corbusier was dissatisfied with the executed gray. Smekens changed the cladding material, from a modular, pre-clad plastered wall panel (*pan de pierre*)—in keeping with the panel of glass (*pan de verre*)—to a more traditional, cement plaster finish which later disintegrated.

In 1988, architect George Baines completed a thoroughly researched restoration of the house, and in 1993 he designed a studio addition. Baines took great care to remain true to the dimensions and regulating lines of the original design, maintaining the slender window profiles despite the addition of double glazing. The interior color scheme is faithful to the sketches and codings preserved by René Guiette and the traces of paint found on the original wall. Baines also devised an exterior cladding similar to the intended clad plasterwork, using plaster-covered insulating panels. The only, rather provocative, change Baines made was to the exterior color—white now replaces the ever elusive "elephant gray."

HOUSES OF THE WEISSENHOF

1927

In 1925, the German Werkbund, a national academy and workshop dedicated to the revitalization of art through industry, held its second international exhibit at the Weissenhof. The exposition included temporary pavilions and an enclave of experimental housing intended to be permanent. As the first such exhibit after World War I, it served a national purpose as well as the agenda of the Werkbund. The intention as announced by Mies van der Rohe, the exhibit director and president of the Werkbund, was to "call upon the leading representatives of the Modern Movement to take their own approach to the problem of the modern dwelling."[9] He asserted that the solution required rational planning, economic construction using all available methods, and high aesthetic quality. In keeping with the alliances of the Werkbund, which mediated between issues of aesthetic form and functional determinism, Mies' pretensions were to a unity of spirit, a movement, not a style, formulated through the international diversity of the chosen architects. However, the final roster and production was perhaps neither as diverse as the initial rhetoric nor as unified as its eventual sum-

Le Corbusier and Pierre Jeanneret; Alfred Roth, site architect

ADDRESS
Am Weissenhof 30
D-7000 Stuttgart 1
Basel 150 km, Zürich 230 km

ACCESS
Private residences visible from the outside; the double house is slated to be a museum as of 2005—with one house in original condition. The Weissenhof Architectur-Galerie sells guides to the complex and holds exhibits 11–3 M–F, 10–6 weekends, tel 07.11.25.79.187, weissenhof.immodulor.de

DIRECTIONS
From opposite the main train station, at bus stop Kuntsacademie take #43 bus in the direction Killesberg. It is a ten-minute ride to the top of the Weissenhof

hill. The complex will be on
your right.

LOCALE
From the top of the Siedlung
one has a fine view of
Stuttgart, with its picturesque
vineyards within the city fabric.
The city has many other buildings notable in relation to the
Modern Movement including
the Zeppelinbau by Paul Bon-
atz and Celle Schoal by Otto
Haesler. In the wake of the
Weissenhof, Stuttgart built several other projects of municipal
housing during the 1930s, the
Wallmer Siedlung, the Schön-
bühl Siedlung and the Wangen
Siedlung on the Inselstraase,
all with buildings by Richard
Döcker. More recently it has
become home to the Kuntsmu-
seum by James Stirling.

A walk through the Weis-
senhof places Le Corbusier's
architecture in the context of
contemporary proposals: the
Germans Peter Behrens, Walter
Gropius, Mies van der Rohe,
Josef Frank, Adolf Rading, Lud-
wig Hilberseimer, Hans Poelzig,
Hans Scharoun, Max and
Bruno Taut, and the Stuttgart
representatives, Richard Döcker
and Adolf Schneck; the Dutch
Jacobus Johannes and Pieter
Oud; the Swiss Mart Stam; and
the Belgian Victor Bourgeois on
an adjoining site.

9. Mies van der Rohe in Richard
Pommer and Christian Otto, *Weissenhof 1927 and the Modern
Movement in Architecture*, 132.
This is the authoritative history.
See also Karin Kirsch, *The Weissenhofsiedlung*.
10. The Weissenhof buildings were
used as exemplary of modern architecture in the exhibit held at the
Museum of Modern Art and in the
related publication *The International Style* by Henry Russell
Hitchcock and Phillip Johnson, the
exhibit curators.
11. Pommer and Otto, *Weissenhof*
40–45.

mation as "The International Style," so called by
Alfred Barr.[10]

Mies was responsible for laying out the site and
unifying principles to assure the *siedlung*, or neighborhood, would be a harmonious ensemble. His site
plan differs from the modern *zeilenbau* planning
which came to predominate in the 1930s, in which
houses are arranged in a grid oriented for light and
air without regard to topography. In contrast, his
plan is an almost picturesque arrangement respon-
sive to the contours of the hill in the mold of the
earlier Werkstatte colonies such as the Kustler-
Kolonie of Darmstadt. He created a series of garden
terraces for the individual buildings each with its
own yard, view, and pedestrian paths. There were no
pretentions to create a model community in a social
sense, although there was some conscious representation of women as the primary client for domestic
invention.[11]

Of the rules controlling the individual buildings,
the flat roof was the most controversial. It engendered
a bitter debate with the local Stuttgart school over its
aestheticism unsupported by *sachlichkeit*, or objec-
tivism of even the vernacular. The local architects and
Heinrich Tessenow eventually withdrew in relation to
this issue. Quite late during construction Mies suggested the principle of "lightness" (not "whiteness").
While predominant, this did not exclude Le Corbusier's use of pink and pastel elements on his single-
family house or even the vivid palette of Hans
Scharoun. More at issue was the size and cost of the
dwellings which were luxurious compared to the typical municipal project and therefore either criticized as
elitist or defended as an attempt to raise the standard
of living. The technical specification set out by Mies
favored the standardization of the element, such as the
window, rather than the whole, thus protecting the
individuality of the single-house design. Techniques
included hollow block of volcanic stone and framing
in iron or wood with some use of poured concrete.

Le Corbusier's inclusion in the exhibit was
assured from early on by the adamant support of
Mies and others who considered his writings a pub-

lic if not unifying voice for Modernism. Within the complex orchestration of the site plan by type and architect, Le Corbusier was honored with the prime spot, a beacon to the city. His contributions to the exhibit were the single and double houses and also the texts to accompany them. It is in reference to the houses that he coined the term the "Five Points" to enumerate a technical and aesthetic agenda for the reinforced concrete frame: "a roof garden for the top of the house, pilotis beneath it, a free facade on the outside, and maximum illumination through strip windows."[12] His text for the exhibit presented the houses as a standardization of elements calculated to satisfy the uniform physical needs of the human being, but deployed with an "absolutely revolutionary freedom" to provide a wide variety of dwellings for the spectrum of "moral types."[13] In demonstration of these moral varieties, he described two different scenarios for living in his projects at the Weissenhof within a unified palette of construction.

12. Le Corbusier and Pierre Jean-neret, *Zwei Wohnhäuser*, 5–9.
13. Le Corbusier, trans. Christian Hubert, "The Significance of the Garden-City of Weissenhof, Stuttgart," *Oppositions* 15/16: 202.
14. Ibid., 203
15. Ibid., 203.
16. For contemporary journalistic response see Pommer and Otto, *Weissenhof*, 85.
17. Ibid., 135.

rear of single-family house

The single-family unit is Le Corbusier's most literal rendering of his prototypical Maison Citrohan. Here he emphasized, along with its spatial and material modern efficiencies, its character as a "dwelling that derives from the primitive hut a certain force and a certain simplification in its manner of living."[14] A double-height living room dominates the plan, organizes the facade, and determines the major axis from front to back. At the rear of the box is a sleeping balcony with kitchen tucked below. On the roof are the children's bedrooms and requisite garden. The maid's quarters and service area are inserted beneath the pilotis. Circulation is in a slot of space along the building edge extending onto a small balcony. According to Le Corbusier, this architecture was to provide for a kind of nuclear family life focused on a large communal

Single-family house, ground floor plan

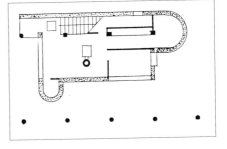

space around a hearth. The only private spaces are the bedrooms, arranged in a clear hierarchy. The curves and angles of the few interior elements, such as the mechanical shaft and hearth, formally enrich this "simplified order."

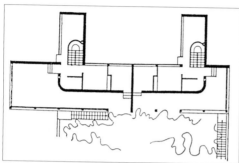

Two-family house, ground floor plan

The "transformable double-house" employs a variant program, plan, and structure in accordance with the character of its imagined inhabitants. In contrast to the stable centrality of the single-family house, flexibility dominates both plan and social relations. In place of the Citrohan structure of columns embedded in the wall, here the Dom-ino system of concrete slabs cantilevered beyond the column leaves the grid exposed. The front columns are steel rather than concrete, a response to Mies' specifications. In lieu of a three-level vertical arrangement, all the family dwelling spaces are axially arranged on the single floor; only the maid's chamber is again at the ground level. Le Corbusier described the house as "a sort of sleeping-dining car combined with equipment for day and for night."[15] He had planned to design new, compact and light-weight equipment out of bentwood and metal, but was forced by time and budget to make use of *objet-types* such as Thonet chairs. By day, the space is delineated but not divided by the columns, concrete built-in cabinets, and desks. By night, sliding partitions at the metal columns divide the continuous room into a series of sleeping cells along a narrow corridor leading to a shared toilet, as in a *wagon-lit*. The idea was of an expandable house to which more bays could be added like cars on a train—hence the placement of the stairs perpendicular to the body. The party wall, which does divide the plan and the two families, is repressed on the exterior except for the curious metal flag within the continuous window. The insinuated merged identity of the families, the internal shifting conditions of intimacy allowed by the plan, and the low bathroom partitions shocked the public.[16]

Le Corbusier's work is distinguished from the other projects at Weissenhof by the clarity of parts in their precise relation to the landscape. The houses are solitary in their unimpeded views, but social in their adjoining turf. They back onto a shared garden which is the sole representation of their community. The pilotis allow the garden to flow uninterrupted. The metal posts of the two-family house seem to rise out of the cliff itself. The painted pastel shades labeled "space, sky and sand" further bespeak the architect's intent to compose architecture with nature and to consider the horizon as both a natural and constructed event.

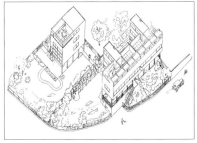

axonometric

Reactions to the exhibit were varied.[17] Le Corbusier, then as now, was criticized for an abstract aestheticism in rendering function, social narratives, and technological realities. In the final accounting, his houses were the most costly on a per-square-foot basis and the most difficult to lease. (The double-house was eventually rented to a single tenant). In general, supporters praised the *siedlung*'s appearance of unity in the landscape, and the pioneering of new types. Criticism regarded the romantic use of technology, the willfulness of the cubic form, the functional inadequacies of the planning, and the focus on a bourgeois clientele. Mies blamed the building industry and the municipal authority blamed Mies for the poor construction quality, excessive cost and late completion of the *siedlung*. More serious was the emerging antipathy to the new architecture as a whole in the climate of Nazism, which paradoxically transformed the *siedlung*'s studied lack of political definition into an emblem of Allied capitalist democracy. Only because the German Army High Command chose the Weissenhof hilltop as the site for its new headquarters was the *siedlung* saved from total demolition by the war.

UNITÉ D'HABITATION BERLIN-CHARLOTTENBURG
(LE CORBUSIER-HOCHHAUS) 1958

Le Corbusier and André
Wogenscky

ADDRESS
Flatowallee 16
Berlin-Westend

ACCESS
Public areas of the apartment
house are accessible. To
make reservations to stay
at the Unité, contact
mail@domizilberlin.de,
tel 49.30.20.9811 or
49.17.06.91.4672.
www.domizilberlin.de,
www.corbusierhaus-berlin.de

DIRECTIONS
The closest stop is the S. Bahn
Line S75 or S9 to Olympiasta-
dion; also U. Bahn Line U2 to
Olympiastadion Ost.

LOCALE
The Unité lies in the city center
district Charlottenburg of former West Berlin. Le Corbusier's
Unité is surprisingly far from
the Interbau development in
the Hansa Quarter. The Unité is
located on the hill above Heer-
strasse, not far beyond the
Theodor-Heuss-Platz.

Thirty years after the Weissenhof Exhibition in
Stuttgart, Le Corbusier, among other architects
involved in that experiment, had another call to present Europe with models of mass housing for postwar reconstruction. In this case, the destruction of
World War II had almost obliterated the historical
city. The Citizens' Administration of Berlin mandated the reconstruction of the Hansaviertel in conjunction with an international exposition of
architecture that would test ideas of housing, industrial production, and urban patterns. Organized as
the Interbau of 1957, the site plan by G. Jobst and W.
Kreuer along green-city principles incorporated disparate buildings by an international roster of architects from fourteen countries including Alvar Aalto,
Walter Gropius, and Bruno Taut.

The housing exhibited the restoration of modern values interrupted by Nazism in conjunction
with their modification. The Unité is a case in point.

Given the innovation in a project such as Aalto's,[18] the continuity in Le Corbusier's thinking between the single house of the Weissenhof from 1927 and the apartment of the Unité is striking. Yet, its grand social and material organization reflects a thirty-year gestation that Le Corbusier felt only the Unité fulfilled.[19]

Appropriate or not to the site and mandate of the Interbau, Le Corbusier's choice of the Unité for Berlin was inevitable in that the type constituted the major focus of his French studio at the time. To cope with its grandeur, the organizers capitulated to his request for an honorific but distant location on the crest of the Olympic Hill outside the limits of the Interbau proper.

Despite his commitment to the Unité as type, Le Corbusier was dissatisfied with the building at Berlin, to the extent that he renounced it. The communal facilities and the internal market street that he felt crucial to the social functioning were missing; but they are missing in a number of the built Unités. The source of his discontent was above all the German builders' resistance to the use of the Modulor, Le Corbusier's system of measure.[20] In the aftermath of World War II with building materials in short supply, industry in shambles, and construction dependent on labor and craft rather than uniform products and techniques, Germany developed UNI norms for unified measure. As Benevolo observes, "in this way it was possible to build single elements in small series, with the certainty that they would always be made to fit together in the actual assembling"[21] whether the building at hand was traditional or contemporary. Le Corbusier felt the Modulor a far superior solution to these problems in that it was dynamic as well as standardized and correlated to the human body. Unable to convince his collaborators to deviate from German industry standards, he abandoned some Modulor measures, increasing the floor-to-floor heights by as much as a meter. The building had a large program to begin with, such that the reproportioning exaggerated its already hefty girth and undermined the Corbusian sense of balance.

18. For a comparison of Aalto and Le Corbusier see Kenneth Frampton, *Modern Architecture*, 200.
19. See entry Unité d'Habitation at Marseilles.
20. Benevolo, *History of Modern Architecture* 2: 738.
21. Ibid. Also see Peter Blake, *No Place Like Utopia*, who describes watching Le Corbusier draw colored camoflauge to cover his misproportioned spandrels within minutes of seeing the building. 223–26.

PAVILLON DE L'ESPRIT NOUVEAU

1925, 1977

Le Corbusier and Pierre Jeanneret; reconstructed in 1977 under the direction of Giuliano Gresleri with José Oubrerie.

ADDRESS
Piazza Costituzione,11
1-40128 Bologna

ACCESS
The pavilion is now a facility of Oikos, an association of academic institutions and industry. To visit, call Padiglione Esprit Nouveau, tel 39.051.35.6068, fax 39.051.35.3624 or Oikos, tel 39.051.27.0344, mail@oikoscentrostudio.com

DIRECTIONS
Local Buses run frequently from downtown Bologna.

LOCALE
The pavilion is next to the Museum of Modern Art, on fair grounds located in a quarter of planned workers' housing.

Fifty years after its demise, the Pavillon de l'Esprit Nouveau was reconstructed in Bologna as the French contribution to an international building fair. The project was the idea of Giuliano Gresleri, sponsored by the arts magazine *Parametro*, financed by a group of manufacturers, and facilitated by the Le Corbusier Foundation. Occurring in the mid-1970s, at the height of postmodern meditations on the nature of history, the reconstruction of this temporary pavilion known primarily through its photographic record was an indicator of a complex reframing of the Modern Movement.[22]

As Gresleri points out, Le Corbusier always intended the reconstruction of the pavilion, which was originally commissioned as an exhibit for the International Exposition of Decorative and Industrial Arts held in Paris in 1925. From the first and until the Exposition administration demolished it against his will in 1926, Le Corbusier sought a client who would buy the *maisonette* dwelling unit of the pavilion and re-erect it as permanent housing near Paris. This use of the exhibit pavilion as a demonstration house and its machine-age appearance set it at odds with most of the Exposition, with the exception of the similarly modern Russian exhibit of Konstantin Melnikov and the "City in Space" of Fredrick Kiesler. The majority of French exhibitors favored instead the popular classicism of Art Deco.[23] Le Corbusier sought to demonstrate the irrelevance of decoration to art, to the problems of postwar urban housing, and to the new domesticity available through industrial production.

As Le Corbusier explained in *Les Arts décoratifs d'aujourd'hui*, the Pavillon de l'Esprit Nouveau was to demonstrate a comprehensive vision inclusive of the single object, the fragment of the existing metropolis, and the new city in its entirety. Attached to the *maisonette* is a rotunda with dioramas of the apartment buildings and urban schemes to which the *maisonette* belonged, the Voisin Plan for Paris and the Contemporary City for Three Million. On the one hand, the single standardized element by its repetition defined the metropolis; on the other hand, the urbanism was a determining factor of all details. Le Corbusier wrote, "the culture of today is an urban culture: both the senses and the mind of urbanized man, be he employed or employer, are quite different from those of the pre-machine-age citizen."[24]

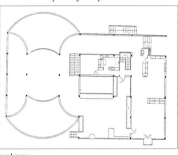

plan of the pavilion

CONTEMPORARY CITY FOR THREE MILLION

Scientifically detailed by technicians, implemented and administered from above, the *Ville Contemporaine*, or Contemporary City was to combine nature and modern industrial culture in a single urban form. The geometric patterning of the plan, based on the figure of the double square, is an expression of its ideal of unity.[25] Within this complete environment, functions and corresponding populations are separated according to zones. At the heart of the city stand twenty-four cruciform, glass office towers for the heads of industry, finance, science and the humanities, each sixty stories high and eight-hundred feet apart in a continuous park. At night the zone is devoted to entertainment, with a

22. Giuliano Gresleri and Silvio Cassará, "What can we learn from the rebuilt Pavillon de L'Esprit Nouveau," *A + U* (Sept. 1980): 3–26. Also see *Parametro* 49/50.
23. On the Parisian context see Nancy Troy, *Modernism and the Decorative Arts*, chapter 4.
24. Le Corbusier, *L'Esprit Nouveau.*, 21, quoted in Gresleri and Cassará *A + U*: 22.
25. Anthony Vidler, "The Idea of Unity and Le Corbusier's Urban Form," *Architects' Year Book* 15: 225–235.

night club on top of each tower. On the outskirts of this zone are the municipal and administrative buildings, and the museum and university. Throughout is a tiered circulation system of vehicular roads, park promenades and elevated pedestrian malls with cafés and stores. At the center is an inter-modal, multilevel transportation nexus crowned by a landing plaza for airplanes, reminiscent of the drawings of the Italian futurist Antonio Sant'Elia. From this focus run the grand arterial thoroughfares. Of this plan, Le Corbusier wrote, "a city made for speed is made for success."[26]

Beyond the business center are residential neighborhoods for those who work in the towers. In concept, they responded to the problems of contemporary Paris with a two-pronged agenda: increased density of dwelling simultaneous with increased exposure to light, air and open space. The two housing configurations are a twelve-story perimeter block and linear blocks with set backs (*bloc à redents*). Both configurations have communal services, including house cleaning, a gourmet kitchen, and recreational facilities to free the individual from daily drudgery. The influence of the utopian dwellings from Charles Fourier's Phalanstery and Victor Considerant's People's Palace can be seen, particularly in the linear blocks.

Outside the city of business, beyond a wide greenbelt, is an industrial zone which includes both the manufacturing districts and the residences of the citizens who work in them. In these outlying communities, the former slum dweller lives in low-rise garden apartments reminiscent of the English Garden City and Tony Garnier's *Cité Industrielle*, but structured more as suburbs than as independent towns.

The politics of this city are unclear. As in Henri-Saint Simon's utopia based on the organization of industry, "the administration of goods replaces the government of men."[27] The individual within this hierarchical collective is, according to Le Corbusier, a "modern nomad"[28] without property, who receives the "essential joys of nature" and products of tech-

26. Le Corbusier, *The City of Tomorrow*, 179.
27. Robert Fishman, *Urban Utopias in the Twentieth Century*, 163–213, and Le Corbusier, *City of Tomorrow*, 301.
28. Le Corbusier, *City of Tomorrow*, 231.

nology regardless of class, and further benefits according to his position of responsibility.

VOISIN PLAN

Le Corbusier typically sought support for his projects from the captains of industry whom he envisioned eventually realizing the principles of his utopias. The Plan Voisin is named for the automobile company who helped fund the pavilion.

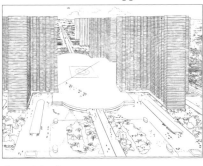

Voisin plan, airport and surrounding glass towers

While seeking cures for the ills of Paris, Le Corbusier took inspiration from some of its glories: the boulevards of Baron Haussmann, the squares of Louis XIV, the romantic landscape of Adolphe Alphand and the power of Jean-Baptiste Colbert. It was in the spirit of these historic acts of bold destruction and monumentalization that he proposed to raze over three square-kilometers of existing urban fabric on the right bank of the Seine to create a great park. As in the Contemporary City, within the park are glass towers for business surrounded by luxury dwellings and connected by a tiered system of circulation. Selected monuments, including the Louvre and humbler private houses, are conserved as garden follies. He speculated that the plan would attract international concerns to its centralized facilities, thus solving national financial woes.

VILLA-APARTMENT

For Le Corbusier, the ideal coupling of individual and collective life was represented in the Carthusian Monastery of Ema which he had encountered at the age of eighteen on his first travels through Europe. The *immeuble-villa*, or villa-apartment, is the Corbusian decendant of this monastic model on many levels. At Ema, the monks lived in duplex cells surrounded by L-shaped gardens, here reconfigured as the L-shaped dwelling bordering the square terrace with its

Detail of the immeuble-villa

captured tree. The individual cells at Ema were then disposed around a cloister garden, here mirrored in the relation of *immeuble-villa* to courtyard and urban park. This exhibition house is luxurious by monkish and even Corbusian standards, 2,900 square feet including terrace, but it demonstrates a secular purification of life through industrial production.

According to Le Corbusier, the pavilion illustrated "how, by virtue of the selective principle [of standardization applied to mass production], industry creates pure forms."[29] He posited that the progress of industrialization mimicked a Darwinian natural selection whereby the new is tested and perfected through repeated use and manufacture. Le Corbusier had previously addressed issues of mass-produced housing in the Maison Citrohan, which is the source for many aspects of form and technique here: the duplex organization, consistent design module (in this case five meters square), industrial sash glazing. For the structure of the pavilion, Le Corbusier employed his favored concrete frame, clad with wall panels of pressed straw called Solomite which were then waterproofed with oil-based paint and coated on site with cement using a spray gun manufactured by Ingersoll-Rand. This was the technique intended but abandoned at Pessac (1926). The current reconstruction again abandons Le Corbusier's experiment for concrete and polystyrene panels which mimic the Solomite in thickness, finish and permeability.[30]

The interior furnishings were also industrial equipment refined through standardization to fulfill human need. The Thonet bentwood and laboratory flask "vases" passed the scrutiny of Le Corbusier's own selective standards as equipment for living. In fact, several of the pieces were customized with new standards for the exhibit pavilion rather than bought off the shelf, such as the metal table fabricated by L. Schmittheisler, a hospital equipment company, the metal doors made by the Ronéo office equipment company, and even the specially dimensioned Maple club chairs.[31] The storage units (*casiers standards*) designed by the architect were inspired by the effi-

29. Le Corbusier, *Oeuvre Complète* 1: 104 and Le Corbusier, *The Decorative Art of Today*, xiv–xix.
30. Giuliano Gresleri, "Le Pavillon de L'Esprit Nouveau: Reconstruction versus Restauration," in Prelorenzo, *La Conservation*, 99–109.
31. Mary McLeod, "Architecture or Revolution?" *Art Journal* 43: 2, 132–147, Arthur Rüegg, "Équipment," in Lucan, *Une Encyclopédie*, 126–130; and Le Corbusier, *Almanach d'Architecture Moderne*, 160–90.
32. Le Corbuiser, *Almanach d'Architecture Moderne*, 145.

ciency of Ronéo files and Innovation luggage. The tubular metal stair had its origin in factory and agricultural use. Several of the pavilion suppliers advertised in Le Corbusier's journal *L'Esprit Nouveau* in rhetorical spreads written by the architect. Some, including Ingersoll-Rand, and Frugès the builder of Pessac, were patrons of the exhibit pavilion. The purpose of the exhibit was to demonstrate that industry and free enterprise could cooperate to create a marketplace of classless goods affordable by all, if only consumers could abandon their irrational distinction between furnishings and tools.

Le Corbusier argued not that style and pedigree were irrelevant but rather that "the law of economy— commercial selection—conferred on industrial objects what could be called style."[32] He called these elements of style *objets-types*. Although they were expendable—in contrast to art of lasting and individual value—they were the subject of contemporary modern art, and of the purist paintings on the wall by Le Corbusier, Ozenfant and Léger. As in the work of Adolf Loos, the manufactured *objet-type* is recognized as modern folk-culture, analogous in spirit to the pavilion's anonymously crafted Berber rug, a suitable possession for the "modern nomad." Scattered through the original display were also stones and shells, reminders of the ultimate parallelism of natural and man-made order. The rendering of the interiors as a montage of sources unified by "the principle of selection" describes the inhabitant, *l'homme poli vivant dans ce temps-ci* ("the gentleman of the times") supposedly anonymous but clearly the projection of Le Corbusier himself.

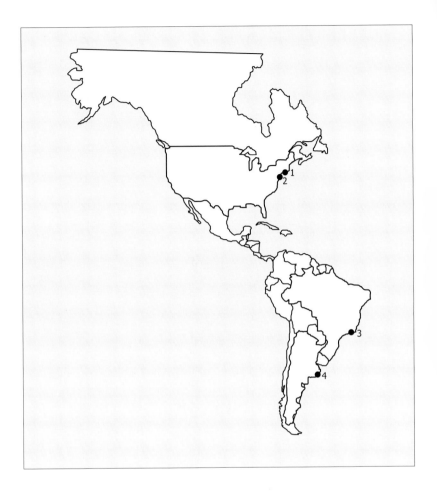

AMERICAS
1. Carpenter Center for the Visual Arts, Cambridge, Massachusetts
2. United Nations Headquarters, New York, New York
3. Brazilian Ministry of Education and Public Health (Palácio Gustavo Capanema), Rio de Janeiro, Brazil
4. Maison Curutchet, La Plata, Argentina

CARPENTER CENTER FOR THE VISUAL ARTS

Le Corbusier and Guillaume
Jullian de la Fuente with
Josep-Lluís Sert and Assoc.

ADDRESS
Harvard University
24 Quincy Street
Cambridge, Mass. 02138
Boston 8 km

ACCESS
The center is open M–S
9–4:45 and Sundays 2–11:30
during the academic year.
To confirm other hours and
exhibitions contact
tel 617.495.3251.
www.peabody.harvard.edu/
museum_carpenter.html,
www.ves.fas.harvard.edu.

DIRECTIONS
Subway stop Harvard Square,
Red Line. Walk through
Harvard Yard to Quincy Street.
Carpenter Center is between
the Fogg Art Museum and the
Faculty Club.

Le Corbusier openly stated his desire to make the Carpenter Center a didactic statement of principle for two reasons. First, it was to be his first and only building in America, a country that had repeatedly thwarted his ambitions on a larger scale. Secondly, the official building program was to create a place for communication among the arts and, as he put it "the connection between mind and hand,"[1] ideas he held dear. Le Corbusier's own art informed and inspired his architecture. He spent every morning in the painting studio in his home before crossing town to his architectural office at rue de Sèvres. At Carpenter Center, the significance of synthesis became thematic to the design problem. He acknowledged the message might not be legible, especially given the complexity of the building required by the site. But, he maintained, "a difficult site generates a hermetic solution giving pleasure to somebody who knows what underlies it."[2]

Underlying the building is a half century of his work. Much as his late painting *1923–1953* revisits an early purist still life,[3] the Carpenter Center presents a kind of revisionist history. Designed just following

La Tourette and the Capitol Complex at Chandigarh, the building reinvests *béton brut* with qualities of the early Dom-ino. Smooth slabs are cantilevered over slender, round pilotis. The column capitals necessary to the stability of the two-way slab are buried in a cavity for mechanical services between the lower structural slab and the finished floor above. Abandoning what in America would appear an "artificial primitivism"[4] as Le Corbusier called it, the concrete finish is smooth and precise. In fact, the finish of the building depended less on the prowess of American industrial production than on a sophisticated level of quality control in a work that at some points approached handicraft. Each narrow piece of smooth, grained formwork, each tapered end of the brise-soleil, each pencil-line inverted V-joint between panels required individual inspection. The pilotis vary in diameter according their load, requiring corsets of densely packed metal reinforcing in some of the most slender. The result of the calibrated dimensioning and finish is a supple and rarefied version of the horizontal space of the free plan.

As in India, the building combines the Dom-ino structure with the thickened screen wall of brise-soleil. By now, Le Corbusier had rejected air-conditioning as wasteful and unhealthy, the cause of rampant American sinusitus, although he accepted its eventual incorporation into the building. The direction, depth and form of the brise-soleils vary according to their orientation to the sun. The exposed glazing to the north, called *ondulatoire*, has fixed concrete fins placed in a rhythmic Modulor arrangement. The resolution of these window elements in relation to the Dom-ino occurs in different ways throughout the building. Perhaps most elegant is the wall of the western studio where the interior curve defined by the brise-soleil is subtly graded in relation to the exterior slab. Whereas in India, the thick sunscreen typically extends like a curtain to the ground, here it appears suspended in the air, except for a single fin that stands "as a fir in the forest"[5] of the front courtyard.

LOCALE
Carpenter Center is located on the main campus of Harvard University, just across from Harvard Yard. Critical of American planning in general, Le Corbusier was enamored of the American campus, which he considered Virgilian and radiant. He valued Harvard's campus as a successful exercise in order and was awestruck by the view from University Hall of the students changing classes along the campus pathways. The University boasts buildings by Charles Bulfinch, H. H. Richardson, Richard Morris Hunt, Walter Gropius, Josep-Lluís Sert, James Stirling and others. The university information office, on the corner of Holyoke Street and Massachusetts Avenue, provides campus maps and offers tours.

Quincy Street approach

1. Le Corbusier, *Oeuvre Complète* 7: 54.
2. Edouard Sekler and William Curtis, *Le Corbusier at Work*, 61, 104, "dans le paysage et formant paysage."
3. Ibid., 249.
4. Le Corbusier in Sekler and Curtis, *at Work*, 167, 302.
5. Le Corbusier in Sekler and Curtis, *at Work*, 164.
6. Sekler and Curtis, *at Work*, 104.
7. Le Corbusier, *Manière de penser l'urbanisme*, 144.
8. Fred Koetter in *Oppositions* 19/20, 218.

Le Corbusier's buildings, like his paintings, do not simply respond to nature; they construct it. He declared this idea at the Carpenter Center, describing it from the first as a "landscape within a landscape,"[6] in reference to the literal interaction of architecture and garden on the roof terraces, and to the imagistic forest of pilotis within a climbing topography. The concretization of light and shadow in the brise-soleil is also part of this landscape. There is a more symbolic presence of the sun in the skewed skylights set within deeply hued ceilings according to specific solar angles. The sine curve of the ramp is Le Corbusier's diagram for the path of the sun in the twenty-four-hour day, which, in the English translation of *When the Cathedrals Were White*, he dedicated to America. For Le Corbusier, landscape is inclusive of the city which he saw as the interaction of man with the natural environment at a large scale. If he could not make America conform to his optimum ratio of 12% building to 88% greenery,[7] he would at least represent the terraced architecture and multi-tiered circulation routes as a bold figure within the conventional urban frame of the given site. This landscape is best apprehended by the moving body and eye from the privileged positioning of the ramp. Le Corbusier intended the ramp as the main entrance to the building and the path from the Yard to future University development. Its summit at the center by the gallery still serves as the entrance into the deep space of the building, like the deep space of a painting.[8] As in his paintings which marry bottles to buttocks to hillocks through their shared contours, the Carpenter Center joins building to body to landscape in the metaphoric lungs of studio astride the circulatory system of the ramp, and through the synthesis of light and shape perceived in motion.

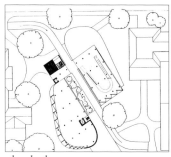

plan, level 3

UNITED NATIONS HEADQUARTERS

1945

Le Corbusier's love/hate relationship with New York City was first consummated with his visit in 1935 on a lecture tour devoted to his ideas of a Radiant City. He returned in 1946 aboard a liberty ship as chairman of the postwar French mission on Architecture and Urbanism, this time armed with not only his urban plans but also his new tool of the Modulor, which he refined on the boat ride over.[9] He admired New York's ten-mile-long avenues for automobile circulation but decried the congestion caused by skyscrapers that were "too small" to allow for surrounding parks, and a central park that was too big. His impressions of this first trip are found in his book *When the Cathedrals Were White*.

For Le Corbusier, the United Nations represented one more frustrated attempt "to create a point

The International Committee of Architects for the United Nations: Australia, Gyle Soilleux; Belgium, Gustave Brunfaut; Brazil, Oscar Niemeyer; Canada, Ernest Cormier; China, Ssu-ch'eng Liang; France, Le Corbusier; Sweden, Sven Markelius; USSR, Nikolai Bassov; United Kingdom, Howard Robertson; Uruguay, Julio Vilamajo. Chairman: Wallace K. Harrison. B. J. Barnes, George Dudley, Kevin Roche, John Johansen, Roger Aujame, Bill Lyman, Oscar Nitzchke, Jerzy Soltan among others

ADDRESS
First Avenue between 42nd and 48th streets
New York City

ACCESS
Tours run daily except January and February when they run Monday through Friday. Tours depart every half hour 9:30–4:45, weekends 10–4:30. For additional information or arrangements for groups of 12 or more contact tel 212.963.8687. Tours take approximately one hour. www.un.org/tours.

DIRECTIONS
Walk from Grand Central Station or take the 42nd Street bus east to First Avenue. The E train stops at 53rd Street and First Avenue.

LOCALE
The United Nations Headquarters is located in midtown Manhattan on the East River, within walking distance of many of the towers that made

an impression on Le Corbusier. From the United Nations, walk west on 42nd Street to the former Daily News Building (1930, 1958) at no. 220 by Howells and Hood, the Chanin Building (1929) at no. 200 by Sloan and Robertson, the Chrysler Building (1930) at Lexington Avenue by William Van Alen, the former Bowery Savings Bank (1923) at no. 110 by York and Sawyer, and across the street, Grand Central Station (1913) by Warren and Wetmore, with a tower addition by Gropius and Belluschi (1978). At Fifth Avenue and 47th Street is Rockefeller Center, which housed the U.N. Design Team offices.

on the globe where the image and meaning of the world may be perceived and understood."[10] He had earlier imagined that point both with his doomed entry in the League of Nations competition (1927) and later design for the Mundaneum (1929) which combined an international political forum with a cultural center. In his initial outlines for the United Nations project, Le Corbusier joined the Mundaneum program with an alternative urbanism of his Radiant City. For this "city of international bureaucracy," as he called it, Le Corbusier and others on the site selection committee suggested a site twice the size of Manhattan in virgin landscape where the delegates and their families would live and work. They circled around estates of Westchester and the former World's Fair grounds in Flushing Meadow, Queens, before settling for a smallish ten-square-mile piece of industrial property on the edge of Manhattan as the closest they could get to "the center of the world."[11] The property was owned by William Zeckendorf who had hoped to develop it as X-City, schematically envisioned by Wallace Harrison as apartment towers perpendicular to the river and a centerpiece of two curved slabs straddling a glowing "blob" for the Metropolitan Opera and Philharmonic halls, heliport, and yacht club.[12] Through Harrison's connection, John D. Rockefeller bought the property from Zeckendorf and donated it to the United Nations. Unlike Zeckendorf's dream, the program for the United Nations on the site was limited to the working quarters for the United Nations: library, cafeteria, assembly, conference areas, and a dominant square footage of offices for the Secretariat. Le Corbusier's frustration stemmed ultimately from the limitations inherent in the project, as well as from departures in the finished building from his design. The United Nations was to be, after all, an addendum to the island of Manhattan rather than its apocalypse.

A team collaboration over a period of months produced some thirty schemes, but Le Corbusier was the design force by virtue of his early rendering of the project and also by the extent to which his thinking of the previous thirty years permeated the shared axioms of the group. Le Corbusier had suggested a different group, one that included Alvar Aalto, Mies van der Rohe and Walter Gropius, who could have confronted his assumptions more forcefully; but Harrison did not want to deal with "too many geniuses."[13] The most significant critique in the process, encouraged by Harrison, came from Oscar Neimeyer, Le Corbusier's protégé.

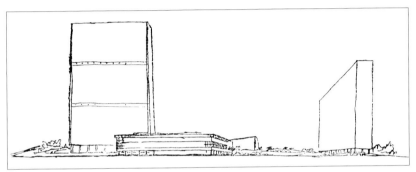

Le Corbusier's design sketch (23a)

Le Corbusier's initial presentation of the building was a Secretariat in a single tower above a low square volume of the Assembly, placed on a largely open site which was anchored at the far end by another slab. Crystallized as scheme no. 23a, Le Corbusier claimed authorship of the U.N. on the basis of its outlines, which he later redrew in his sketchbooks to more closely match the final project. During the collaborative design process, the site which Le Corbusier initially bermed along First Avenue became increasingly open to the city and the water. The scheme suggests an elaborate sequence of spaces moving from the General Assembly entrance on the avenue, through the building, ending in a great ramp to a dock. As in other institutional buildings by Le Corbusier, the fluid circulation of spaces and forms at ground level are balanced against the static slab of offices. In this case, as Lewis Mumford observed, through its size and position, the technocracy of the Secretariat, rather than the political forum of the Assembly, seems the U.N.'s symbolic voice, ironically or otherwise.[14] The ultimate scheme, no. 42, divides the single volume of assemblies proposed by

9. Le Corbusier, *Modulor* 1: 52–54, 113–15.

10. Paul Otlet in Le Corbusier, *Oeuvre Complète* 1: 190. See also Stanislaus von Moos, *Elements of a Synthesis*, 243.

11. Secretary General Lie's mandate in George Dudley, *A Workshop for Peace: Designing the United Nation's Headquarters*, 16. This is the comprehensive documentation of the building design process.

12. Rem Koolhaas, *Delirious New York*, 286.

13. Dudley, *A Workshop for Peace*, 43.

14. Lewis Mumford in Paul Goldberger, *New York: The City Observed*, 132.

15. Koolhaas, *Delirious*, 281.

Le Corbusier into a composition of wings wrapping the Secretariat as suggested by Neimeyer's scheme no. 32.

After the unanimous acceptance of scheme no. 42, much to Le Corbusier's dismay, Wallace Harrison was entrusted with the execution of the project. The built version retains the outlines of the accepted plan but reinterprets the intended relations, in part because the budget was reduced by twenty million dollars and the building shrunk accordingly. The large end of the wedge intended as seating became a vast lounge; the theater of the General Assembly became subsumed within the volume it was intended to define, and the entrance to the project shifted perpendicular to the street. Stylistically, the building is rendered with a technical elegance that belongs to Harrison, rather than with the physical and symbolic weight of Le Corbusier's late architecture. As Harrison confessed, he just couldn't imagine Le Corbusier detailing the curtain wall.[15]

BRAZILIAN MINISTRY OF EDUCATION AND PUBLIC HEALTH (PALÁCIO GUSTAVO CAPANEMA)

1936–1943

Le Corbusier as consultant to Lúcio Costa, Oscar Niemeyer, Carlos Leao, Alfonso Reidy, Jorge Moreira, and Ernani Vasconcelos

ADDRESS
Palácio Gustavo Capanema
Ruá da Imprensa 16
20030 Rio de Janeiro

ACCESS
Open workdays year round. By special request, visitors may see the original office of the Minister, which houses the Candido Portinari Museum. The fourth floor library is open to the public. Direct inquiries to Fundaçao Nacional Pro-Memúria Library on the eighth floor. Tel 21.220.1490.

DIRECTIONS
From the beach areas such as Ipanema, take any bus marked Castelo downtown to Avenida Presidente Antonio Carlos. It is easiest to get off at Praça dos Estados Unidos, cross to Rua Pedro Lessa and walk west. The metro stop is Esta ço Cinelandia. From the beach by car, follow signs to Centro and along the *aterro* landscaped by Roberto Burle Marx to Castelo and Avenida Presidente Antonio Carlos. At its intersection with Avenida Nilo Pecanha is a municipal parking lot. The ministry is three blocks south.

LOCALE
The neighborhood of ministries is called Castelo, in reference to Castle Hill, which was removed in a wave of urban renewal starting in 1920.

The establishment of the Ministry of Education and Public Health was part of the program of the industrialized technocratic welfare state envisioned by the regime of Getúlio Vargas which came to power in 1930.[16] The Minister of Education and Health, Gustavo Capanema, supported Lúcio Costa in his modernist reform to the curriculum at the Escola Nacional de Belas Artes so that, when the legally required competition for the building design awarded a neoclassical entry, Capanema mandated the building be exempt from the process and appointed Costa as architect. Costa gathered in turn a group of architects under the sway of the Five Points and *Précisions,* and arranged for Le Corbusier to come to Rio for six weeks as a consultant on this

Despite their neo-classical facades, many of the surrounding buildings date from the post-renewal period. Local points of interest include the ABI, Brazilian Press Building (1936) at the corner of Ruá Araujo de Porta Alegre and Ruá Mexico by Marcelo and Milton Roberto; the National Library (1910) of General Francisco Marcelino Souza Aguiar, and the National Museum of Beaux-Arts (1908) both on Avenida Rio Branca; the Municipal Theater (1906) by Francisco Oliveira Passos on Praça Floriano; and the Academy of Letters (1978) by Marcelo and Milton Roberto.

project and on the Ciudade Universitaria. Although the European architect's thought pervades the project to such an extent that he receives credit for the design, the building also represents a first achievement of *Brasilidade*, the native search for the authentically Brazilian.

Le Corbusier's contribution to the project included his encouragement to freely explore the premises of the modern as well as the Brazilian in the effort to assimilate them. The initial scheme by Costa's team was U-shaped and strictly functionalist. The presence of Le Corbusier led to a series of schemes of looser, asymmetrical composition on an open plaza. After studying various arrangements of horizontal office slabs and individually expressed exposition halls on two sites, the team arrived at the T-shaped plan of a sixteen-story tower on pilotis for the offices and a lower cross combining the public parts of the program. The building depends on attributes typical of Le Corbusier's thinking: the concrete frame, its flat roof gardens, non-bearing glass walls, and "free" interior plans. Also characteristic of Le Corbusier is the definition of the auditorium as a distinct wedge-shaped volume. With particular contribution from the young Niemeyer, in the course of refining the project, the Brazilians raised the pilotis from four to ten meters so that the light and low volumes truly flow beneath the elegantly extended office slab. They also shifted the project from the street to the center of the site.

Despite Le Corbusier's limited participation over the six years it took to realize the building, the Ministry represents an important moment in his oeuvre as the first realization of the brisesoleil, or sunbreakers. Le Corbusier's work in the late thirties showed a growing concern with architecture's relation to climate and a growing dissatisfaction with the mechanically dependent, hermetically sealed glass

groundfloor plan

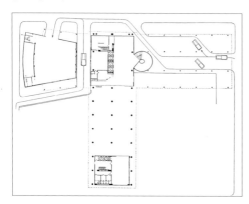

enclosures of his invention. The Ministry tower combines operable windows behind a concrete screen. It was the Brazilian's idea to make the horizontal shutters adjustable and paint them light blue. Ever in search of scientific exactitude, Le Corbusier protested that the shutters be fixed to an "optimal" angle for the site's latitude based on azimuth. Upon its completion, G. E. Kidder Smith hailed it as "the most advanced building in the Americas,"[17] in response to its formal qualities, rather than to its construction by unskilled labor.

For the Brazilians, the achievement of the Ministry was its mixed allegiance to the International Style, their modern state, and native tradition. Like Le Corbusier, the architects initially viewed the new technocracy positively as an enlightened and cultured patron. Encouraged by Le Corbusier, they viewed the building as a synthetic work of art incorporating the garden design and rugs of Roberto Burle Marx, the figure of youth of Bruno Giorgi, roof sculpture by Antonio Celso and the native "azulejo" or mosaic of Carlo Portinari. They included a sculpture by Lipchitz to assert the link of regional to European artistic consciousness. The Brazilian team at the time did not polemically distinguish the colonial from indigenous tradition, so that the cladding alternates fluidly among native carioca, granite, and Portuguese faience tiles. The purist elements of the plan such as the curved lobby stair are imbued with a "highly sensuous native expression"[18] which derives most directly from the Spanish Baroque tradition but was understood simultaneously as authentic. In one of the happiest of his collaborations, Le Corbusier's ideas found fresh expression in a culture he admired and in a new school of Brazilian architects. It is interesting to view Niemeyer's later contribution to the United Nations as the exportation of this flourishing movement to North America and to Le Corbusier himself.

16. The authoritative source is Elizabeth Harris, *Le Corbusier Riscos Brasileiros*.
17. Bruce Goodwin and G. E. Kidder Smith, *Brazil Builds: Architecture New and Old 1652–1942*, 27.
18. Goodwin and Smith, *Brazil Builds*, 16.

MAISON CURUTCHET

1949–1954

Le Corbusier, Roger Aujame
and Bernard Hoesli with site
architect Amancio Williams

ADDRESS
320 boulevard 53
Barrio el Bosque
1900 La Plata
Argentina

ACCESS
The house is the headquarters
of the Colegio de Arquitectos
de la Provincia de la Buenos
Aires (CAPBA). It is open
Monday through Friday,
10–2:30. To confirm times
and for additional information
contact tel 221.482.2631,
fax 221.421.8032,
www.capba.org.ar.

DIRECTIONS
From Buenos Aires, La Plata is
an hour trip by bus on the
Costera Crolla line departing
the Retiro bus terminal or by
train departing from Constitu-
ción station for La Plata. Once
in town, several buses run near
the house, destination Stadium
de Estudiantes de La Plata, or
walk 20 minutes to the end of
boulevard 53, across from the
stadium on a dead-end street
where Calle 53 meets Paseo
del Bosque.

LOCALE
La Plata, the capital of the
province of Buenos Aires, is a
small city about one hour from
the Capital Federal by car. It
is a planned town of the late-
nineteenth century on a square
grid with intersecting diagonals. The many parks help
define its character.

The small residence and office for the surgeon
Pedro Domingo Curutchet fills a typical urban lot in
a South American setting. As was repeatedly the
case, Le Corbusier accepted the relatively minor commission in relation to hopes of realizing a master
plan: in this instance his *Plan Directeur* for the city
of Buenos Aires, designed without commission in
1938 and accepted for official study in 1949. Le Corbusier's involvement with Argentina extends even
earlier to his lecture tour of 1929, later published as
Précisions, and two other unexecuted domestic projects, the Villa Ocampo and the Villa Martinez. Outside of Le Corbusier's urban agenda, the architect
and client had a mutual attraction. Curutchet was the
inventor of a surgical method which he termed the
"axi-manual technique," involving the repositioning
of the hands in surgery and the related design of
ergonometric instruments.[19] He placed his scientific

research within a larger attitude toward life which he described as "modern" in terms consonant with those of Le Corbusier. For both men, the hygienic and functional were understood as components of art, in particular the art of Mathyla Ghyka, Igor Stravinsky, and Paul Valéry, among others. In accepting the commission, Le Corbusier, wrote,

> Your project is characteristic of a small residential house, which has always interested me. Your program: the house of a physician is extremely seductive (from a social point of view). Your site is well located, and offers favorable conditions. In short, having established a plan for Buenos Aires in 1938–9 which is now being considered by the government, I am interested in producing for you a small masterpiece of simplicity, conformity and harmony, all within the limitations of an extremely simple construction, with no luxuries, as is typical of my work.[20]

Executed at a great distance from Paris, over an extended period during which the economic stability of Argentina was variable, the house would never have been completed without the dedication of Argentine architect Amancio Williams. Known and respected by Le Corbusier, Williams participated in the design development and construction documents and the first phase of supervision. His detailing lends a particular quality to the house. He developed the strip windows as unframed glass panels which slide in wood tracks attached to the concrete sills. For the garage gate, he designed a counter-weight and wheel that rolls uphill. To the bathrooms, he contributed a radiator whose grid of exposed pipes also serves as a towel bar and dryer. To achieve the flat slab of the Dom-ino, he developed a purposefully hidden floor cavity, in which the profile of posts and beams occurs on the upper side of the structure, between the smooth bottom surface of the slab and the finished floor above. He also suggested the rotation of the stair to its present location.

A falling out with Curutchet over costs and delays led to Williams' departure and the brief employment of construction supervisor Simón

19. Alejandro Lapunzina, *Le Corbusier's Maison Curutchet*, 35–37. This is the authoritative history of the house.
20. Le Corbusier quoted in Lapuina, *Maison Curutchet*, 38.

Ungars who summarily changed several features of the architecture to Curutchet's dismay. In a functionalist critique of the house's planning, Ungars simplified the curves of the bathrooms, substituted high walls for low partitions between the bedroom and bath, lowered the partition between guest room and living room, and reoriented the stair landing and the adjoining space.[21]

Le Corbusier's design combines the strategies typical of his earlier Parisian townhouses with an emerging naturalism. As in the Parisian villas, figural tropes like the curved bath enclosures, sculptural hearth and ramp are organized as a free plan within the slender column grid. The rear residence is a "cubic house" in the lineage of Maison Cook (1925). The entire site is likewise separated into four

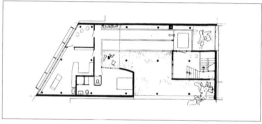

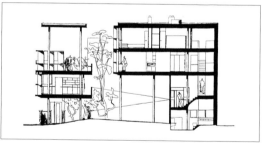

Le Corbusier's original design for the mezzanine floorplan (top) and section (bottom)

parts in plan and section; the office is separated from house, the vehicle from the pedestrian across the central axes. Optical diagonals across the cube, such as from front door to roof terrace, and diagonal paths such as the ramp, weave the plan and section together.

The naturalism of the house differs from the primitivism of Villa Sextant (1935) or Maisons Jaoul (1952). As a climatically inspired adaptation of Purism, it is most closely akin to the Ministry of

Education in Rio (1938) and the first scheme for Villa Baizeau (1929). For the tropics, Le Corbusier developed a vocabulary of forms to engage the idea of sun and wind that included the brise-soleil wall and parasol roof or *baldaquin*. Additionally, at Curutchet he made use of the local vernacular house plan, dubbed the "sausage," which places the house in a U-shape about a shady interior court.[22]

The brise-soleil of Curutchet is an independent and taut screen dimensioned according to the Modulor. It relates to the surfaces of Purism and also to the walls of neoclassicism on which ornament similarly inscribes geometry. Although Le Corbusier never saw the site first hand, Curutchet provided detailed contextual information, so that the architect understood that his screen would be read against the pilastered facade of the neighboring colonial house as a related but evanescent frame of the architecture. In place of the environmentally taut envelope of both the purist and neoclassical house, the enclosure of Maison Curutchet is rethought as a sequence of layers that moves across the entire depth of the site, allowing for the penetration of eye, air, and nature. Curutchet doubted that the tree called for at the center of the courtyard would thrive, but it did.

In the process of opening up the house to the climate and views of the park across the boulevard, Le Corbusier introduced an intense formal ambiguity in the conception of the wall that lends the house a surrealist air. The massive doorway is set in a wall that is basically imaginary, defined only by the mesh fence. The office brise-soleil appears to float despite its obvious weight. Ungar's failed attempt to rationalize the house is a testament to the architecture's profound play between the optical and material in resistance to a reductive Modernism.

21. Lapunzina, chapter 2 of *Maison Curutchet*.
22. For Le Corbusier's description of vernacular Buenos Aires see *Precisions*, 210.

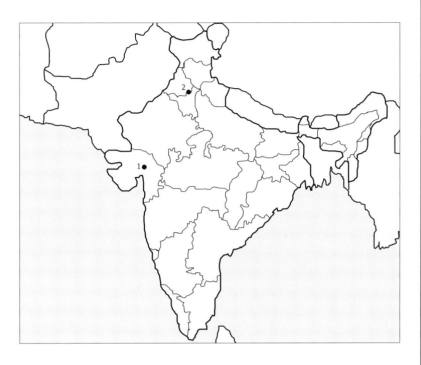

INDIA

1. Ahmedabad
  Millowners' Association Building
  Villa Sarabhai
  Villa Shodhan
  Museum of the City
    (Sanskar Kendra)
2. Chandigarh
  Palace of Justice (High Court)
  Palace of Ministries
    (The Secretariat)
  Palace of Assembly
  The Monument of the Open
    Hand and the Depth of
    Consideration

The Tower of Shadows, The
  Geometrical Hill, and The
  Monument to the Martyr
The Yacht Club
College of Art
College of Architecture
Museum
Art Gallery (Museum of the City)

MILLOWNERS' ASSOCIATION BUILDING

Le Corbusier, Balkrishna Doshi,
Jean-Louis Veret

ADDRESS
Ashram Road
Ahmedabad, Gujarat

ACCESS
Accessible during business
hours

DIRECTIONS
The building is on the main
drag of Ahmedabad well within
walking distance of Nehru
bridge; but it is set consider-
ably back from the street and
so is easy to miss. Current
landmarks are a large apartment building adjacent, the
bank across the street and the
state textile store on the same
side of the street and slightly to
the north.

The millowners are a group of textile industrialists
related by caste, religion, and blood and distinguished by their use of wealth for philanthropic and
cultural concerns. They were Le Corbusier's patron
in Ahmedabad, commissioning houses, their headquarters and the museum. Le Corbusier understood
that the association building was to be a meeting
place for an intimate group of families of wealth and
class, a private clubhouse with a certain symbolic
and institutional role. He described it as a "small
palace," in line with his long-standing notions of *une
maison—un palais* and his grandest house, the Villa
Stein at Garches.[1]

As in his villas of Ahmedabad and Paris, the primary luxury of the building is its space. The Millowners' is one of the most empty of Le Corbusier's
buildings, a fact that is not readily apparent from
the drawn plans. This emptiness suggests the pavilions of Indian palatial architecture as well, where the
only walls are the perimeter marble screens. At
Millowners', the few columns, partitions and stairs
create a seeming compression and expansion of
space as the visitor alternately looks straight through

the building to the Sabaramati River or encounters obstacles that lengthen and elaborate the physical and optical journey. Alternative scenographic routes culminate at a curved conference room within a double-height forum best described as a cult space.[2] The roof of the room is curved for the purpose of optical reflection: its convex surface reflects the clerestory light below; its concavity holds a reflecting pool above. In shape it suggests the moon, that disc of reflected light, or the related horns of a bull, replete with mythological content from India and Greece.

front stair

Le Corbusier's description of the building stresses the importance of view: "The situation of the building in a garden dominating the river furnishes a picturesque spectacle of cloth dyers washing and drying their cotton materials on the sand bed in the company of herons, cows, buffalo, and donkeys half immersed in water to keep cool. Such a panorama was an invitation . . . to frame views from each floor of the building. . . ."[3] The building facade is a screen to frame views within which a series of door frames are nested. The smallest red door is suspended within the largest frame which extends the height of the building. These nested doors raise the visual center high within the composition where it provides a lens-like view to the river. In this raised view across a largely empty room to the landscape, the building recalls the similarly empty vision machine of Palladio's Villa Rotunda elevated on its hillside and the Taj Mahal.

The primary scene, textiles spread out across the nature and daily life of India, is important to understanding the architecture. An attention to material detail uncommon in Le Corbusier's work complements the spareness. The patterning of the formwork, the placement of joints, the varying profiles of the screens and structure are all calculated with a precision that makes a palpable impact. The

LOCALE

Ahmedabad has been a textile center from its founding over a thousand years ago until recently when outdated tooling, competing markets and the redirection of capital lead to a steady decline. Ahmedabad's most recent golden age at mid-century saw the wealth of the industrial elite transform the city into a cultural and educational center. The millowners collectively became the patrons first of Le Corbuiser, and then of a member of his atelier Balkrishna Doshi, who in turn helped bring Louis Kahn to Ahmedabad.

You can see all of Le Corbusier's work in Ahmedabad in a single day. The Villa Shodhan is fairly close to the Millowners' Association in Ellisbridge. Continuing south along the river from the Millowners' by rickshaw or foot you reach the museum. The Villa Sarabhai is a twenty-minute cab ride north and across the river to Shahibag.

There are many other important sites of modern architecture, including Kahn's India Institute of Management, Charles Correa's Gandhi

Ashram and a dozen works by Doshi, including Tagore Theater, The Museum of Indology, a gallery at the School of Art and Architecture and his studio Sangath. Both the School and Sangath can provide information.

While waves of modernization and growth have erased most layers of the city's past downtown, the pol market by the railroad station is intact and incredible. There are also a variety of remarkable individual sites including step wells and the Jama Masjid. A complete tour takes about three days.

river elevation

great slash of a control joint between the floor edge and the brise-soleil is inhabitable. The tapering of the front brise-soleil fins is sharp enough to cut. Through the finishes and detailing of every element, the building has a synthetic completeness Le Corbusier often spoke of but did not always achieve. It is both designed and furnished through its architecture. Its surfaces become like the textiles produced by the millowners that clothe the Indian home. Le Corbusier's description of the Delhi Morak stone facing on the brick side walls as "a modulor tapestry"[4] makes explicit this fundamental connection between wall and textile, which he appreciated from the theories of Gottfried Semper.[5] The Indian textile as cladding, as an inhibitor of dust but conductor of breeze perhaps inspired him to drape his architecture in brise-soleil in a unique way, allowing it to extend to the ground in front of the pilotis.

1. Peter Serenyi, "Timeless but of its Time: Le Corbusier in India," in Brooks, *Le Corbusier.*
2. Sunand Prasad, "Le Corbusier in India," in Raeburn and Wilson, *Architect of the Century*, 302.
3. Le Corbusier, *Oeuvre Complète* 6: 144.
4. Ibid.
5. See entry Villa Fallet.

ground floor plan

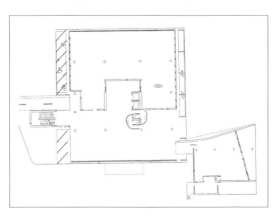

Two alternative strategies for dwelling appear as early as 1923 in *Vers une architecture*, described by Le Corbusier as the "masculine" cube of the Citrohan, and the "feminine" series of Monol vaults. The two houses in Ahmedabad illustrate this coupling:[6] a cubic house originally designed for the bachelor Hutheesing and vaults for Smt Manorama Sarabhai, a widow, and her son Anand.

In the exquisite setting of the lush Sarabhai compound, Le Corbuiser could fulfill a potential character of the Maison Monol, elsewhere circumscribed by demands of western climate and culture. In the environs of Paris, there is an an antecedent of Sarabhai, Maison de weekend (1935), and a contemporaneous relation, the Maisons Jaoul (1952). Both make use of parallel vaults combined on the interior to create rooms wider than a single bay. At Jaoul as at Sarabhai, the vaults are Catalan style with a permanent shuttering of red clay tile. Deep edge beams allow for long spans and large openings in the brick walls below. The Indian house carries this promise of openness furthest: laterally it joins together a long series of vaults (where at Jaoul each house combines

Le Corbusier, Balkrishna Doshi, Jean-Louis Veret

ADDRESS
Shahibag
Ahmedabad, India

ACCESS
Private residence accessible by appointment only. Contact the Vastu-Shilpa Foundation at Sangath or the School of Architecture of the College of Ahmedabad.

DIRECTIONS
Shahibag is north of the center city, on the east side of the river near the railway underbridge.

LOCALE
The house is on the Sarabhai compound in Shahibag. The Museum of Textiles is adjacent and shares the same exquisite setting (open 10:30-2:30 and 2:30–4:30 except Wednesdays).

interior vault

only two); lengthwise it extends them into the garden (where at Jaoul the facades define courtyards). On ground level, each vault is a channeled continuation of the patio and garden beyond. There are few doors per se, just pivoted wall panels set three meters back from the edge of each vault to define a mediating verandah. The roof is a garden too, whose landscaping includes a small pavilion. The concrete fascia is the only separation between garden above and below.

The permeable quality of the house does not vitiate the sense of interior. The vaults are long and the guard rooms, kitchens and bathrooms are episodically buried along them. The two-story wing for Smt Sarabhai's accommodation has a monumental scale that distances its upper apartment from the garden and affords privacy. Smt Sarabhai requested that the vaults not be exposed on the exterior because of their industrial look. As a result, Le Corbusier added the deep concrete fascias. The house appears trabeated from the exterior and vaulted from within, in keeping with the veiled interior life of the traditional Indian home and the role of the woman in it.

This fluidity with nature made for climactic sense as well as Edenic metaphor. The roof garden and the mass of the masonry cool the rooms. Unlike the brise-soleils of Chandigarh which radiate heat back into the building, the open vaults allow the cooled air to circulate. The house is oriented according to the prevalent wind direction (north-east/south-west), but its openness allows for the seasonal shift in the breeze. As in all of Le Corbusier's architecture for India, the house is equipped with sculptural scoops, spouts, gutters and a monumental slide that celebrate monsoon water while disposing of it. In this case, the source of inspiration was not just princely monuments such as Jantar Mantar, but the favorite story book of Anand Sarabhai, *Fatapoufs and Thinifers* by André Maurois, in which the citizens of Thinifer sleep in hydraulic extension beds resembling the Sarabhai water slide that shoot them into

garden view

the bathtub every morning.[7] Even with this most successful confrontation with an extreme climate, the Sarabhais needed to accentuate the shade by letting the garden run free to an extent the Frenchified architect would have preferred to edit.[8]

As the anecdotes suggest, the patronage of the owners shaped the house, an unusual occurrence for Le Corbusier whose client relations were often contentious. The Sarabhais belonged to the millowners of Ahmedabad, a princely class in its combination of intellect, wealth, and patronage who brought Le Corbusier to the city. Manorama Sarabhai was the sister of the mayor. Like the other millowners, they are Jains, who value nature in its pure state and try to limit man's interference in it. Jainism asserts an eternal universe, without a specific godhead, composed of life principles and non-living elements that are manifested as infinite matter and four material substances: space (*akasa*), time (*kala*), motion (*dharma-dravya*) and rest (*adharma-dravya*). The happy coincidence of these substances with the Giedionesque language of "space, time and architecture"[9] suggests an understanding of this house not as a retreat from the modern to the atavistic but the achievement of a different "modern" space. Here the modern is permeable rather than transparent, allowing for an interiority that offers physical and psychic comfort. The clients shared in the creation of this modernity, providing the garden retreat as the site, a program that was a way of life, and subsequent ways of inhabiting the architecture over time: the furnishings, the al fresco dining, the paths worn from verandah to garden. The result is a house that exudes a certain grace.

6. Serenyi makes this point in "Timeless but of its Time," in Brooks, *Le Corbusier*, 172.

7. Prasad, "Le Corbusier in India," Raeburn and Wilson, *Architect of the Century*, 52

8. Conversation with Anand Sarabhai, March 1998.

9. Sigfried Giedion, *Space, Time and Architecture*.

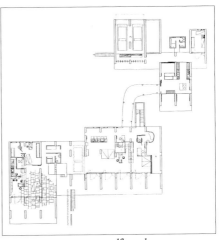

groundfloor plan

Le Corbusier, Balkrishna Doshi,
Jean-Louis Veret

ADDRESS
Kharawala Road
Ahmedabad

ACCESS
Private residence; not visitable.

DIRECTIONS
The house is off the east side
of Kharawala Road just beyond
its intersection with Kirariwala
Road. It is located behind the
hospital. Because the drives
are long and unmarked, it is
not uncommon to explore quite
a few before finding it.

LOCALE
The house is in the affluent
residential district of Ellisbridge not far from the grounds
of the college. It is about a
mile from the Millowners'
Building.

front view

rear view

In the *Oeuvre Complète* it is described as "Villa
Savoye placed in a tropical setting"; in the office it
was called the Arabian Nights. While the cultural
conditions and the quest that had produced the
Parisian villas of the twenties had vanished, this different place with different captains of industry
allowed Le Corbusier to forge an equivalent of his
earlier "Virgilian dream."[10] Le Corbusier designed
several versions of this ideal villa for several clients,
all of whom were millowners. The mayor of Ahmedabad, Chinubhai Chimanbhai and his cousin, Surot-
tam Hutheesing, both commissioned houses in the
winter of 1951. Despite the different programs (the
mayor having a family of four, Hutheesing being a
bachelor) the plans for the houses were stikingly
similar. For reasons of spatial extravagence and
related costs, neither house was built; although
Chimanbhai went so far as to build the foundation.

Hutheesing sold his plans to Shyamubhai Shodhan, who like Chimanbhai had a family of four. Shodan built the house as designed on a different site with the general supervision of Le Corbusier's office.[11]

Le Corbusier's work in Ahmedabad was his first in India, and he developed many material and geometric formulas for the Indian climate here. A rigorous procedure of dividing the cubes into quadrants and then shifting them into a matrix of open and closed spaces produced multi-directional shade and ventilation, at least in principle. (In reverse, one can refold the plans and sections of main house and servants' wing to a single "original" square). In terms of Corbusian precedents, the house owes as much to the interlocking section, tray-like floors, and parasol roof of the Villa Baizeau, which had been designed for the *Sirroco* of Tunisia, as to the cubic geometry and ramp of Savoye. Le Corbusier summed up rhetorically, "What have I given to Shodhan? . . . I have given him: shade in the summer, sun in the winter, air circulating and cool in all seasons. . . . He leaves his house on the first terrace, in the shade, sheltered. In constantly moving air. He climbs to the roof, he sleeps there. Everywhere he or his guests are sheltered, captivated, enchanted."[12]

The climate of enchantment which replaces the Arcadian dream of Villa Savoye takes its inspiration from Mogul miniatures[13] and forts with their imposing walls and seraglio within. It is as if Shodhan's blank monumental cubes and delicate sleeping porches collapse the fortress and the pavilions of the seraglio onto a single building. The slippage between the upper and lower cubes at the front allows a glance into the deep space and privacies of the house. Like the fort/palace, Shodhan is an internalized landscape of terraces and multi-level gardens slightly removed from its gritty urban context.

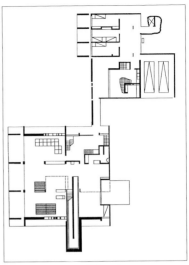

ground floor plan

10. Le Corbusier described Villa Savoye in terms of a Virgilian dream, *Precisions*, 139.
11. Prasad, "Le Corbusier in India," in Raeburn and Wilson, *Architect of the Century*, 304-5.
12. Ibid.; also Le Corbusier, *Sketchbooks* III: 451.
13. Balkrishna Doshi, *Le Corbusier and Lou Kahn: The Acrobat and the Yogi of Architecture*, 5–6.

THE MUSEUM OF THE CITY (SANSKAR KENDRA)
FORMERLY N.C. MEHTA MUSEUM OF MINIATURES
1952–1958

Le Corbusier, Jean-Louis Veret

ADDRESS
Bhagtacharya Road
Sanskar Kendra, Paldi
Ahmedabad, Gujarat

ACCESS
The museum is now The Museum of the City of Ahmedabad. The office of Balkrishna Doshi was in charge of the renovation and installation of permanent exhibits. There is a small Kite Museum installed in a ground floor gallery open 9-11 and 4-7 except Mondays, and a guard on duty during those times who can show you around the building.

DIRECTIONS
The museum is located off of Bhagtacharya Road just west of Sarder Bridge.

LOCALE
The museum is located in the neighborhood of Paldi, about 3 km southwest of the town center, along the river, in a plaza with the Tagore Hall. Nearby is the National Institute of Design of Gautam and Gira Sarabhai, architects who were instrumental in bringing Le Corbusier to Ahmedabad and in the commission of the Sarabhai villa.

The Museum of Unlimited Growth

In his book of 1925, *L'Art décoratif d'aujour d'hui*, Le Corbusier wrote, "Let us imagine a true museum, one that contains everything, one that could present a complete picture after the passage of time. . . . In order to flesh out our idea, let us put together a museum of our own day with objects of our own day; to begin: a plain jacket, a bowler hat, a shoe. . . Clearly this museum does not yet exist."[14] In his critique, Le Corbusier upheld the status of the museum as a "sacred entity," but, extending the encyclopedic tradition of the French Enlightenment, he shifted its role away from the selective interpretation of historical winners toward inclusive catalog. He observed the changes of the machine age: the new kinds of ethnographic facts, the new ways of gathering them, and the new assessment of their value by a consumer-based culture. He wrote, "We are in an entirely new situation. Everything is known."[15]

Le Corbusier proposed the form of this new museum in unbuilt projects: first as a three-dimensional spiral ziggurat for the World Museum of the Mundaneum (1929); and then as a squared and flat spiral on pilotis for the Museum of Modern Art for Paris (1931) and the generic, Museum of Unlimited Growth (*Museé a croissance illimité*) (1939). The spiral interested him from his early studies in La Chaux-de-Fonds as a pattern found in nature that manifests growth according to an increasing series of proportions related to the golden mean. It is a coherent and dynamic system generated from a single center.

In the last decade of his life, Le Corbusier designed three similar buildings based on the ideas of the true museum and the model Museum of Unlimited Growth: the first in Ahmedabad, the next in Tokyo and the last in Chandigarh. None is actually "unlimited"; and Le Corbusier's ideas of history, information and growth remain diagrammatic. They are squared spirals in plan lifted over a field of pilotis. Standard bays of linear galleries wrap around a square court. Conceptually, this wrapping could continue as the collection grew. Skylights illuminate the interior galleries independent of the facades. The museums are "buildings without facade, entered from below, in other words from inside."[16] To mitigate the labyrinthine effect, a "swastika" pattern of passages leads from the central court to the building perimeter. Each passage ends in a monumental puncture in the wall and an exit stair. This pinwheel circulation is a trace of dynamic spin and implicit growth on the largely static exterior of the box.

As blinded, self-referential form with an abstract relation to the ground, the museums are siteless as well as unlimited. Le Corbusier speculated, "it is built in a field of potatoes or beets. If the site is magnificent all the better. If it is ugly, it doesn't matter."[17] Raised but proportionally squat, it intentionally occupies its plot in a neutral fashion, without the classical detachment of Villa Savoye to which it bears comparison.

The Museum at Ahmedabad

The Cultural Center of Ahmedabad began with some commitment to the ideas underlying Le Corbusier's

14. Le Corbusier, *The Decorative Art of Today*, 16
15. Ibid., 22.
16. Le Corbusier, *Oeuvre Complète* 4: 16.
17. Stanislaus von Moos, *Elements of a Synthesis*, 100 and Le Corbusier, *Creation is a Patient Search*, 101.

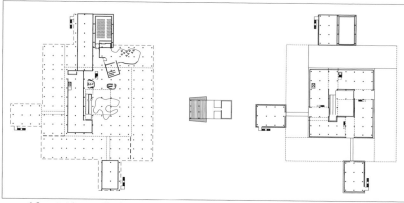

ground floor (with unrealized gallery branches, left) and first floor plans (right)

idea of an unlimited museum. The mayor, Chinubhai Chimanbhai commissioned the building as part of an extensive cultural and educational project that Le Corbusier repeatedly envisioned and never built. The original, unexecuted plan showed gallery branches as the device for unlimited growth, spinning out from the main block at the ends of the pinwheel circulation. Their intended programs of anthropology, archaeology, and natural history would have defined the complete ethnography of the true museum.

The built museum adheres to the generic model in outline, including its indifferent siting as regards the Sabaramati River. In telling contrast to the Millowners' Building, the museum stands in the middle of a small green plaza aloof from both street and river and inattentive to the potential views from the elevation of its embankment. The entrance level offers instead an alternative landscape of shady pilotis, a central court open to the sky, and organically shaped reflecting pools that wind among the columns.

The museum does show traces of its cultural, if not geographic, site. The exterior is of local brick. It was a concrete column in Achyut Kanvinde's ATIRA building in Ahmedabad that convinced Le Corbusier to use *béton brut* here and throughout his work in India.[18] The parasol roof lifted above the walls resonates with the open pavilions of the Indian palace. The lighting from the courtyard windows and beneath the parasol is primitive compared with the clerestories of Tokyo, but it leaves the roof free for an elaborate terrace garden. Inspired by Mogul miniatures and their resonance with Indian contemporary life, Le Corbusier envisioned many activities taking place in the evening on the terrace. The forty-five open tanks of water were to cool the air and galleries below, and hold flowering plants grown to enormous size with the help of special fertilizer obtained from the Institute Pasteur.[19] The continuous trough at the top of the pilotis was to hold vines that would climb the brick facades. In fact, as Le Corbusier must have observed, compared to their European counterparts, the Indian varietals of dahlias, zinnias and water lilies grow unaided to almost lascivious size. "Unlimited growth" was to be the fact of nature.

18. Doshi, *The Acrobat and Yogi*, 5.
19. William Curtis, *Ideas and Forms*, 203 and Prasad, "Le Corbusier in India," in Raeburn and Wilson, *Architect of the Century*, 300.

courtyard

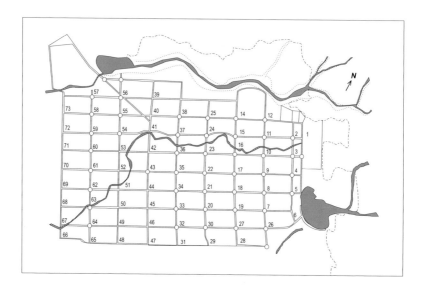

ADDRESS
Delhi 260 km, Manali 313 km,
Simla 113 km

ACCESS
See individual buildings.
http://chandigarh.nic.in.

DIRECTIONS
Leaving from New Delhi station, an express train arrives in
Chandigarh before noon and
returns to Delhi in the evening.
There is also an express at mid-
day. The train station is a cab
ride away from the city center.
Buses of all different categories
including luxury lines leave
from the Interstate Bus terminal in Delhi and arrive in central Chandigarh. Express lines
take from 3 to 5 hours. There
are also flights from Delhi several times a week.

The Founding of Chandigarh:
The Mayer Plan and the Le Corbusier Plan

The treaty that granted India her nationhood in 1947 also ceded the western part of Punjab, including the capital city of Lahore, to Pakistan. After considering several existing cities, Prime Minister Nehru and the Delhi government decided that the Punjab should have a new capitol. P. L. Varma, chief engineer of the Punjab, and P. N. Thapar, State Administrator, led the search first for a site and then for its planners. "Chandigarh" means protective fortress of Chandi, the war goddess, a reference to a temple just north of the city and to the aggressive optimism of the new nation.

The lack of Indian designers produced under colonial rule led officials to entrust the design for the city to the American team of Albert Mayer, a planner with experience in Bombay, his associates Julian Whittlesey, Milton Glass, and Clarence Stein, and the Polish-born Matthew Nowicki, an architect who had participated in the design of the United Nations Headquarters. They had generated preliminary plans for the city and even some of its buildings when, with their contractual terms still under negotiation, Nowicki died in an airplane crash. In search of architects willing to work for rupees, reside in India, and mentor a first generation of national designers, Varma approached Maxwell Fry and Jane Drew, who together convinced Le Corbusier to overcome his initial hesitancy and accept the position as Architect Adviser with the proviso that Pierre Jeanneret join him. For the duration of his involvement in Chandigarh, Le Corbusier traveled there twice a year, first to clarify its planning principles and then to design its Capitol Complex. The other team members were entrusted with the design of the city proper and its housing. Drew and Fry remained in India for three years. Jeanneret became attached to the culture and

LOCALE
Chandigarh lies on a slightly sloping (1 degree) plane at the foot of the Himalayas before the Simla hills. It is a sprawling city, possible but time-consuming to negotiate on foot. Le Corbusier and others recommend bicycle, but rickshaw is also available.

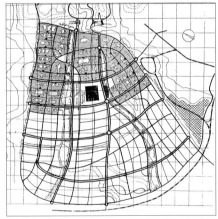

Mayer plan

remained until 1965 as Chief Architect and Planner.

The plan developed by Le Corbusier and his team within six weeks of arriving in India (some accounts claim four days) rhetorically distanced itself from Mayer, although it shared key principles with the Mayer plan in the manner that The Athens Charter shares precepts of the Garden City movement. Le Corbusier and his team kept the geographic layout, and the structure of sectors connected through a network of routes. They further systematized the Mayer plan so that the greenways and bazaar streets continue between sectors as part of an elaborate classification of circulation called the "seven ways" (*sept*

Mayer's plan was a zoned city of a governmental head, a softened grid of residential superblocks, a business district toward the center, and a small industrial zone isolated at the eastern edge. Two axial routes bordered by linear parks connected the zones. Groups of three neighborhood blocks functioned as self-sufficient urban villages and were connected to the city through a hierarchical network of transportation. Each unit had a central greensward dotted with schools and local public facilities, and a bazaar street for artisans and business. Mayer's plan derived many aspects from the Anglo tradition of the Garden City.

20. Norma Evenson, *Chandigarh*, remains the classic source.

21. Ravi Kalia, *Chandigarh in Search of an Identity*, 110. See also Dominique Picard, "A Few Notes on Chandigarh," in Rewal, Véret, and Sharma, *Architecture in India*, 99.

22. Pierre Riboulet, "Concerning the Composition of the Capitol," Rewal et al., *Architecture in India*, 91. Riboulet suggests that the plan is a particularly female body related to Le Corbusier's paintings of the same era.

23. Le Corbusier, *The Athens Charter*. The Athens Charter sets out the canon of modern urbanism as it was collaboratively formulated by CIAM in 1933 and published by Le Corbusier a decade later. It classifies life and zones according to Four Functions of habitation, work, leisure and circulation, that are supported by greenery, light and air.

24. *The Edict of Chandigarh*

25. Ibid.

26. Sehdev Gupta, "Chandigarh! Sociological Issues and Urban Development in India," *AD* 44/6: 365.

27. Nehru in Stanislaus von Moos, "The Politics of the Open Hand" in Walden, *The Open Hand*, 418.

28. Nehru in Norma Evenson, *Le Corbusier: The Machine and the Grand Design*, 98.

29. Nehru in Kalia, *Chandigarh in Search*, 105.

voies). The more picturesque aspects of the Mayer plan were repressed within the dominant orthogonality of the grid, except for a slight bend along the transverse axes to avoid the glare of sunset, and a single linear park, the Leisure Valley, running along the existing stream bed.[20] They compressed the sprawling dimensions of Mayer's total plan and actually reduced the total length and number of roads while expanding the size of the individual sector three-fold and increasing the density overall.[21] The capitol was shifted and consolidated on a higher site to the northwest above an artificial lake. The stamp of Le Corbusier defined the capitol as a monumental head attached to the body of the plan through the spine of the Jan Marg, with great axial arteries leading to the stomach of the commercial center and the limbs of the university and industry, the entirety fed by the lungs of the greenways and protected in its integrity by a periphery of landscape.[22]

The Intention of the Plan

The formal statement of the city's intention, *The Edict of Chandigarh*, limited its scope to concerns of CIAM, echoing the tenets of the Athens Charter[23]: "the physical ideas of human scale, the physical attributes of the residential sectors, the seven ways of circulation, zoning, landscape, and truthfulness of materials."[24] Chandigarh corresponds also to the first of Le Corbusier's *Trois Etablissements Humains* (1945), the radio-concentric city of exchanges, which was to complement the other two linear industrial and agrarian establishments.

According to the Edict, Chandigarh was to be first "a city offering all amenities to the poorest of the poor of its citizens to lead a dignified life" and second "a Government city with a precise function and consequently a precise quality of inhabitants."[25] Perhaps the hope was that, as a city of administration and culture, Chandigarh would define a bourgeois population exempt from the poverty of Indian commercial cities. The plan, as Mayer's before it, inscribed this precise quality of inhabitants through the grading of sectors into three economic classes distinguished by housing density. Despite Fry's claim that Chandigarh was not a social experiment,[26] the implications of grouping population by income rather than the usual determinants of kinship, caste, and religion, were immense. Existing social barriers tumbled but were replaced with a new hierarchy. For Fry, the democracy of the plan extended to the care given to the design of each class of habitation and the (unfulfilled) intention to house everyone.

In a sense, Nehru shared CIAM's avoidance of political contingency and indigenous culture in his belief that "the most essential and revolutionary factor in modern life is not a particular ideology, but technological advance."[27] His mandate for Chandigarh followed accordingly: "Let this be a new town symbolic of the freedom of India, unfettered by the traditions of the past, an expression of the nation's faith in the future."[28] He expected the city to forego established patterns and to forge a "new custom," while he credited the architect with revealing to him the virtue of folk architecture and "Indian conditions in all scales of development."[29] Le Corbusier documented his appreciation of Indian palaces and cows in his sketch books and on his architecture, but the synesthesia of the Indian marketplace and the multi-layered Mogul/Hindu culture filtered through the immediacy of a teeming population are missing. In their place is a garden city, with the scent of a British cantonement or neighborhood of Tony Garnier's *Cité Industrielle* and of Le Corbusier's own Pessac.

View of Secretariat from Leisure Valley

Sector 1: The Capitol Complex

The Capitol stands outside of the body of Chandigarh as the legible mark of the city's reason for being. Le Corbusier and his clients concurred that the aspirations of the new democratic state and its mundane workings should coexist on an elevated and symbolically charged plane. On an area of approximately 400 x 800 meters on high ground—oriented off true north according to the view and prevailing winds, and shielded from the city by low mounds—the three state buildings of parliamentary Assembly, High Court, and Secretariat are composed according to shifted axes and slipped symmetries across the large distances of the landscaped park. The Assembly and the High Court, the independent receptacles of democratic India's legislature and justice, mark the ends of a west-east axis of approximately 455 meters. The Secretariat for the administrative offices is the slipped western edge of the complex. At a third position at the northern end of the landscaped extension of the Jan Marg, Le Corbusier proposed a Governor's residence which Nehru rejected as anti-democratic. Le Corbusier designed in its stead a rather prescient Museum of Knowledge dedicated to information technology, but this too has not been built; and the full effect of the plan remains impossible to gauge.[30] The buildings are set among a series of gardens, courts, reflecting pools, and monuments called "instruments of progress and civilization," some of which have been realized: the Tower of Shadow and Pit of Reflection, the Geometrical Hill, the Monument to the Open Hand and Depth of Consideration. In order to assure the clarity of conversation among these events whose locations are determined to the smallest Modulor unit, the vehicular approaches are sunken five meters below the plaza, and the waste soil is formed into the landscape mounds which figure prominently in the approach to the site.

For Le Corbusier, this was the last and single realization of a series of governmental palaces including the League of Nations and the Palace of the Soviets. He drew on similar exercises of monumental planning and expression of authority in all forms: the Baroque axis from the Louvre to the Place d'Étoile, the runways of the Rome airport,[31] and Lutyen's New Delhi. If the Governor's Palace at Chandigarh had been built, both the analogy with the Raj and ironic (or liberating) slipping of its axes would have been all the clearer. The wedding of building, open space, and landscape in Indian palatial architecture also made an impact. The shifted centerings and diagonal views of Fatehpur Sikri and

30. For the 50th anniversary of Chandigarh, under the direction of Charles Correa, a full scale, fabric model of the facade of the second scheme for the Palace was temporarily erected on its intended site. As one might expect, the building mitigates the sense of distance, adds to the formal interplay among the buildings, creates glancing as well as axial viewpoints, and recalibrates the scale and brutality of the complex through the relative delicacy of its form.
31. Sunand Prasad, "Capitol," Raeburn and Wilson, *Architect of the Century.*
32. Le Corbusier, *Modulor* 2: 214-15.
33. Ibid.

the reflective water gardens of Pinjore seem particularly relevant to the design of the Capitol Complex. In Nehru, Le Corbusier found a sympathy with his own oddly combined authoritarian posture and democratic imperatives, cosmological identifications, and love of spatial allegory. The client gave Le Corbusier an exultant freedom to set his own dimensions and to collapse the sacred and profane.

To place the buildings of the Capitol Complex, Le Corbusier had white and black masts marking the corners of the volumes moved across the site as he watched. As he described it, "The problem was no longer one of reasoning but of sensation. It was a matter of occupying a plain. The geometrical event was, in truth, a sculpture of the intellect."[32] The landscape has no optical middle ground, only distance, which Le Corbusier, purveyor of the yardstick Modulor, proudly called an inexpressible space (*espace indiscible*) "impossible to dimension."[33]

In occupying the plain of the capital, Le Corbusier created several distinguishable landscapes. The primary landscape is the "embattled" relation of the three major buildings to each other and the Himalayas, across a loosely tended meadow that mitigates the distances, although the extremes of climate can make the crossing a chore. The buildings' roofs are landscapes with horizons that connect them to the hills. Because of their significantly smaller scale, the plaza monuments constitute a secondary order of internally related spaces. There is a sunken landscape of rear parking lots and courts in which the bustling daily life takes place and from which the front plinth of the complex appears an empty stage. The approach to this backyard is a landscape of low hills and winding roads, filled at appointed hours by streams of officials,bureaucrats,and plaintiffs. The sunken landscape has related episodes within the front plaza in the Pits of Consideration and Reflection, and in the astonishing gap like an

site of the Assembly

View of the Jan Marg

ironic "haha" between the Assembly and Courthouse. The axial drive of the Jan Marg passes through this deep gully toward the distant Himalayas so that in the absence of the Governor's palace, the entirety disappears; early sitings of the building tops appear as mirages on their own horizons.

The Architecture of the Capitol Complex

Out of his repository of form and the visual stimulation of India, Le Corbusier developed a language that synthetically monumentalizes democracy and climate. Some elements such as the parasol roof and brise-soleil have antecedents in his tropical architecture. Others were developed specifically for India, such as the great curved gutters for monsoon rain and the three-part window of brise-soleil, fixed glass with concrete mullions (*ondulatoire*), and movable shutter (*aérateur*) with mosquito screen. Conceived to mitigate the extremes of weather, these devices had attendant failures, radiating extreme heat and circulating untempered air throughout the building.[34]

The material of this language is concrete, called brutalist or *béton brut*. The finish, while rough, has precisely executed formwork. In its adaptation to the plenitude of labor and the absence of industrial production, the concrete also took on handicrafted aspects; cast in its surfaces are bas-relief symbols related to the climate, the cosmos, and culture. The brutishness comes from the impression of the building as monolithic hulk, sculpted from a homogeneous material into a carcass that is simultaneously skeleton and skin. Some of the detailing reinforces this expression, like the absence of window frames other than a small metal gasket or stop. The complete tectonic reality of the buildings is actually more complex, making use of layers of materials,[35] as in the roof of the General Assembly, which is a sandwich of plywood, insulation, and aluminum sheating supported by steel trusses. The Palace of Justice makes use of gunite and cement plaster finishes over the concrete.

34. Charles Correa, "The View from Benares," in Brooks, *Le Corbusier*.
35. Edward Ford, *The Details of Modern Architecture* 2: 195-99.

Circulation

Multilayered circulation systems designed to separate pedestrian from vehicular traffic were a truism of modern city planning. Le Corbusier first developed the seven ways, or 7v (*sept voies*) for Bogota, Columbia and then applied them here.[36]

While all of the original distinctions in circulation are intact, they are not always discerned and can seem gratuitous as one shifts from artery to path to street at will. The edges of the ways are softened by landscaped and bermed shoulders in the case of the major thoroughfares, and by an intimate relation to the housing in the case of the smaller routes. The overall impression is not of a system but of a landscape traversed by pathways that gathers vegetative intensity as it approaches the Capitol.[37]

The Residential Sectors

Le Corbusier described the residential sector as the "container of family life" and fulfillment of all immediate needs of a twenty-four-hour day. Each sector was to include schools, community facilities, places of worship and shopping. Its Modulor and "golden" perimeter of 800 x 1200 meters represents the limits a pedestrian is willing to walk, ten minutes in any direction, and bears some relation to the Spanish *cuadra*. There were 47 sectors planned, 30 to be completed in the first phase, beginning with Sector 22. While the general form and program of all residential sectors is constant, they differ according to three proscribed densities, from 25 to 100 people per acre or 5,000 to 20,000 people per sector, and concomitant economic class. The highest government workers are housed individually on the largest plots in the least dense sectors closest to the Capitol Complex.

The problems of designing the housing of Chandigarh were tantamount to the problems of urbanization. The village courtyard house, its agrarian based culture, extended family structure, and local caste distinctions all seemed incompatible with the urban plan, its densities, and its assumed standards of hygiene and order.[38] Drew, Fry and Jeanneret developed thirteen categories of dwelling

36. All the circulation of Chandigarh is designed and named according to the ways. Addresses are given by sector number and way. They ways are:

v1 *the inter-city thoroughfare*, the national highways from Delhi (21) and Simla (22).

v2 *the arterial way*, or the Jan Marg

v3 the *vehicular grid* bounding the residential sectors, which is the primary grid with traffic circles at the intersections.

v4 *the shopping streets* within the sector, which shift slightly between sectors so as not to establish a competing axis with the v3.

v5 *the residential street* within the sector, referring to the loop road toward the interior.

v6 the way to the dwelling, which is unpaved.

v7 *the garden path*, allowing children to go to school without crossing a street.

v8 *the bicycle routes* were later formulated as Chandigarh came to life and the rickshaw and bicycle predominated over the automobile.

37. Picard, "A Few Notes," in Rewal et al., *Architecture in India*, 100.

Sector 22 housing

according to government rank, and determined guidelines for government and private development akin to a detailed zoning code.[39] By and large, the guidelines define terrace row houses of between two and three stories, some of which are organized around garden mews or courts. Perhaps most radically, they eliminate the private accommodation of cows, as one superintendent's wife recognized from the absence of rear court walls.[40] The architects also questioned Indian social customs in ways not required by plan, eliminating the purdah verandah and passages for the sweepers. Le Corbusier who did not design the housing, reportedly felt it placed questions of "convenience and subsistence" above those of "economy, sociology and ethics."[41]

Within the strictures of the zoning, the formal characteristics of the housing vary according to the many architects. The original housing stock tends to be most intact in the denser sectors, while many of the affluent private houses have undergone sequential renovations directed if not designed by the head of the household. The dwellings actually designed by the foreign team are limited in number but they constitute a body of work worthy of its own study.[42] Over the 15 years he lived in Chandigarh, Jeanneret developed a clear voice in retort to Le Corbusier's ironically tinged question, "What is the meaning of Indian style in the world today when you accept machines, trousers and democracy."[43] It was Jeanneret who studied and documented "the impact of local construction techniques and climate on construction methods," concluding that oven-baked brick should be the material of choice and that, after years trying to replace human labor with machines, the effort should be "to give the work to the greatest number of men."[44] His furniture combining the at-hand materials of bamboo, rope and piping with the found objects of baskets, mats and steel bowls was perhaps the freest expression of his creative

38. Gupta in AD 44/6: 365.
39. Hartmutt Schmetzer, "Chandigarh Twenty Years Later," AD 44/6:
40. Gupta, AD 44/6: 363.
41. Le Corbusier in conversation with Doshi, The Acrobat and the Yogi of Architecture.
42. Kiran Joshi, Documenting Chandigarh: The Indian Architecture of Jeanneret, Fry and Drew.
43. Mukraj Anand, "Conversation with Le Corbusier," in von Moos, Elements of a Synthesis.
44. Pierre Jeanneret, "The Impact of Local Climate and Techniques on Construction Methods," L'Architecture d'Aujourdhui, 1962 also Hélène Cauquil, "Pierre Jeanneret in India," Rewal et al., Architecture in India, 105.

encounter with India.

Although the majority of the government housing was built for lower-income groups, early on the team recognized that the poorest class of inhabitants was left out. In response, they set a fourteenth category of standards for minimum dwelling: two rooms, a verandah/kitchen, and a courtyard equipped with water, waste, and electricity. Jane Drew designed clusters of these dwellings around open squares and narrow streets in the manner of an Indian village, but few were built.[45] The unhoused population appeared immediately, as they were the laborers and the accompanying micro-culture of hawkers who built Chandigarh.

Sector 16 housing

The unaccounted for labor colonies and their culture of markets and traders authored another plan, or anti-plan, characterized by different rules of appearance and also by a fluid and shifting location. This nomadic village was the creation of the planners in that, after initially failing to house the squatters, they subsequently required the continuous displacement of the indigenous mud villages as they occurred in the excess of open space. Despite a program of "repatriation" including lease and land grants, links to infrastructure, and continued construction of replacement housing, squatter colonies remain.

Madhu Sarin's research traces the failure of the city to house its inhabitants in part to the structuring of property value and its transfer.[46] She finds CIAM doctrine at least complicit in the situation in its assertion that "city planning is a way of *making money*," in the words of Le Corbusier.[47] The combined pressures of unexpected demand and the government's withdrawal from house construction in the late 1960s exacerbated the situation.[48] Since 1980, residential construction has occurred primarily in the surrounding region because the plan of Chandigarh proper is largely complete; and there has been an attempt to integrate social classes in the form of cluster housing around an internal court.

45. With Balkrishna Doshi, Le Corbusier also drew a house for the peon, *Oeuvre Complète* 5: 159-7.
46. The history of these settlements as well as the larger socio-political history of Chandigarh is best documented by Madhu Sarin, *Urban Planning in the Third World: The Chandigarh Experience*. See also Madhu Sarin, "Chandigarh as a Place to Live," in Walden, *The Open Hand*, 375.
47. Le Corbusier, *Precisions*, 179 and *Radiant City*, 71.
48. The government as sole property owner developed land to a high level of infrastructure and amenity and then sold off the property. Because government houses were subsidized, the private sector renter, as last in the chain of exchanges, inherited the costs of development and couldn't afford much. In response to uncontrolled land speculation in the 1970s, the government began to lease property for 99 years rather than selling it outright and established a Housing Board to develop owner-occupied housing. In the 1980s, construction cost and population pressure led to housing design of increased density, namely four-story flats in lieu of the original terraced housing. Since 1980, residential construction has occurred primarily in the surrounding region where there has been an attempt to integrate social classes in the form of cluster housing around an internal court. See Sarin, *Urban Planning*, 108-20 and O.P. Mehta, "Social Housing: The Boomerang of Success" *Chandigarh: Forty Years after Le Corbusier*.

Sector 17 main piazza

Sector 17 courtyard

Commercial Development: Sector 17

The commercial and geographical center of town, Sector 17 is called a *chowk* after the Indian crossroads marketplace even though its scale and uniformity are at odds with the traditional *chowk*'s dense intermingling of functions and narrow passages. Edging the seven-hundred-meter square main piazza are four-story office buildings devoted to commercial enterprise at ground level. The continuous arcades of seventeen-foot bays and second-story verandahs recall the imperial architecture of Connaught Place in Delhi. As typical of Chandigarh, the formal plaza is astonishingly empty for India, while the parking courts are lively with traffic, cows and men lolling on the grassy side yards. The pilotis are festooned with images of Coke bottles despite the town prohibition against the Indian custom of sign painting every available surface. Although the original plan organized commerce in three-story shopping strips, the natural tendency has been more anarchic. Trades group together; small scale and unplanned operations spring up in the housing; a mobile economy of hawkers and peddlers thrives. Several Indian style market places are housed in tents on the greenswards beyond Sector 17. Under pressures of regional growth, two shopping centers have been built in Sectors 34 and 43.

Nature and Culture:
Leisure Valley, Rose Garden, Rock Garden

The Leisure Valley was to be a verdant setting for culture, recreation, and the synchronic nourishment of body and soul, with art schools, museums, and entertainment venues. Moreover, Chandigarh itself was to be a park. Included in the landscaping plans were complex orchestrations of trees and plants that would sequentially bloom throughout the year.[49] The decision not to dam the Ghaggar River as a water source for Chandigarh in combination with population pressure has created water shortages that make the filled reflecting pools and irrigated fairways seasonal events; but in springtime the city is truly a garden replete with bougainvillea.Two delineated gardens achieve delirious lushness consistently, the huge Rose Garden of the original plan and the heretical Rock Garden of construction rubbish begun by Nek Chand in 1965 and continued as a collective work.

The Growth of Chandigarh

If Chandigarh has not fulfilled its utopian promise, it has exceeded the expectations for its growth to an "ultimate" population of 500,000. Today there are 600,000 in the city proper and more in the addenda invented by Indian planners to accommodate the regional growth. These populations overflow the proscribed densities of the residential sectors and the Capitol Complex itself, forcing modifications in its architecture. The projected population for the region is one million in the year 2000.[50]

Considering his gradual disillusionment with the industrialized elite of the West and the increasing primitivism of his own work, it is oddly appropriate that Le Corbusier's only realized urban thinking occurred in the context of the cultural and technological dilemmas of the emerging Indian state. Despite his attraction to this India, he distanced himself from authorship of the city just as the Capitol Complex is separated from the sectors. One can speculate on his ironic frustration at this end of his life, watching the construction of a city linked to his vision of an urban landscape without his housing type, l'Unité d'habitation.[51] This absence simultaneously condemned his beloved Unité to failure for lack of ever achieving its proper setting, and his only city to compromise for lack of proper typology. Nevertheless,Chandigarh bears the lyrical stamp of his imagination.

The Rock Garden is a fantasy of people and animals built of construction rubbish, set amidst hills, waterfalls, bridges and paths within the forbidden site of the Capitol sector.

49. Le Corbusier, *Oeuvre Complète*: 6, 108-13.

50. Initially, much of the population pressure came from the division of the Punjab along ethnic lines into Hindu and Sikh districts in 1966 and the designation of Chandigarh as the Union Territory, an administrative center for three bureaucracies—Haryana, Delhi and Punjab. Although Chandigarh was officially awarded to Punjab in 1975, Haryana continues to use it as a capital. Both governments stake out development in the immediate region, even within the intended greenbelt, but rely on the infrastructure and amenities of the original city. Kalia, *Chandigarh in Search*, 142.

51. Manfredo Tafuri so speculates in "Machine et Memorie," in Brooks, *Le Corbusier*, 212.

PALACE OF JUSTICE (HIGH COURT)

1951–1955; Archive addition, 1963

Le Corbusier, Balkrishna Doshi

ADDRESS
The Capitol, Chandigarh
Sector 1

ACCESS
The buildings are accessible by tour during working hours. Closed weekends and holidays.

DIRECTIONS
See Chandigarh main entry.

LOCALE
See Chandigarh main entry.

The plan of the Court carries a set of intentions regarding the exercise of democracy. In lieu of an internal system of circulation based on a hierarchy of users and security, "the organism is built of a series of autonomous elements, joined together by a single, all-pervading function—the administration of justice—which is made visible through the dynamic, continuous movement of people rather than by any outstanding single element of distribution."[52] The courtrooms to one side and the High Court to the other open directly to the plaza. The portico between them is not an entrance to the courtrooms but the way to the ramp at the rear of the building where much of the activity takes place. Behind the courts at plaza level are waiting rooms similar in dimension to the front esplanade; above the courts are offices along open-air corridors. The daily entry for the total population of the building, excepting the judges, is a long winding affair which begins east of the Capitol and arrives at a lower, rear parking court lined with *wallas* for legal supplies. The great unifying element is the vaulted canopy opening onto the plaza, like a proscenium behind which all the stage mechanics take place.

As in all of the buildings of the Capitol, the architecture fuses the demands of society, politics and climate at a mytho-poetic if not functional level. The canopy is simultaneously the (collapsed) basilica of Constantine, a Mogul audience hall, a parasol for shade, and an umbrella for monsoon rain.[53] The visceral associations of the vault were important enough to the architect that he had arches suspended in plaster cement from the underside of the concrete post-and-beam structure. The space between the canopy and the chamber roofs was intended for the circulation of air. The wall is a 1.4-meter-deep screen of brise-soleil patterned like the inverse of staggered brick,[54] and arched like a monumental fragment of a cornice to shade the glass and divert the rain. Le Corbusier saw the concrete of Chandigarh not as an imported cure-all technology but as a building material of both indigenous collective effort and solar resistance. The *Oeuvre Complète* photographs show men and women with baskets of cement balanced on their heads climbing up the ramp, which served first as the working scaffold.[55] That the disenfranchised laborers lived in illegal settlements and the courtroom tapestries were woven to Modulor dimensions by prisoners in Kashmir remained an unuttered irony. Cultural synthesis was achieved at the level of symbol in the sun, the moon, the trees, lightning, the meander, scales of justice, and the seal of state emblazoned on the carpets.

The chiaroscuro effect of light and shadow, and the feeling of suspension within the great space of the vault prevail over any litany of flaws. Still, the totalizing utopianism of this building can be measured in the ironies of its production and the alterations required by its use. The judges resist the public car park to the rear, park their cars on the

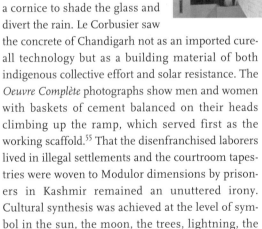

View of ramp

52. Vittorio Pardo, *Le Corbusier*, 32.
53. William Curtis, "The Ancient in the Modern," in Rewal et al., *Architecture in India*, 84.
54. Curtis, *Ideas and Forms*, 194.
55. Le Corbusier, *Oeuvre Complète* 6: 81. The ramp depicted is that of the Secretariat.

esplanade and reserve the front entrance for their own use. A low porch has been added to the front because the original screens do not cast adequate shadow or shed water. During the monsoon season, rain penetrates deep into the building and the ramp. Early on, the archive facilities situated above the courtrooms were found inadequate for the ever-increasing number of records so that Le Corbusier designed an understated brick addition recalling Louis Kahn's work in Ahmedabad,[56] with a cellular arrangement to allow for further expansion. The judges dislike the tapestries, which they find frivolous. The political realignments of the region into distinct Punjab and Haryana states have expanded the population of the building to the extent that the space between the canopy and the courthouses is used for storage. Social unrest has filled the esplanade with a landscape of wire fences and armed guards.

56. Louis Kahn, Indian Institute of Management 1962-74 and also the hostels at the Capitol of Bangladesh (1962-83).

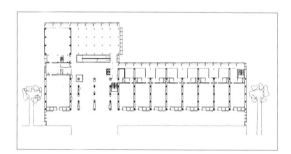

ground floor plan

PALACE OF MINISTRIES (THE SECRETARIAT)

1951–1958

Le Corbusier

ADDRESS
The Capitol, Chandigarh

ACCESS
Visible from the exterior. Visitors are sometimes allowed to the roof during workday hours.

DIRECTIONS
See Chandigarh main entry.

LOCALE
See Chandigarh main entry.

57. Le Corbusier, *Modulor* 2: 221. The quotation reads 280 meters but as built the building approximates 245 meters. The height is about 42 meters. "3.66 + .43" expresses the module as the sum of two modulor units.
58. Correa, "View from Benares," Brooks, *Le Corbusier*, 197.
59. Paul Rudolph in Pardo, *Le Corbusier*, 12.

The most defining characteristic of the Secretariat is its size. Le Corbusier first proposed a tower of comparable height in the mode of the Algiers office project (1942), but when he met resistance from officials and could not obtain local concrete of sufficient bearing capacity, he turned it on its side, in essence, as a horizontal slab . Designed as 250 meters long and 35 meters high, it was meant to accomodate more than 3,000. Its frame has Modulor measurements conceived in porticos 3.66 + .43 meters apart. The 63 porticos are supported by 252 pillars rising from the basement.[57] These porticos form a continuous screen of brise-soleil in front of the six structurally distinct blocks of offices. The impression of size is bound to the nature of a wall that is at once edge and object. As Charles Correa describes, "The building as facade: a thesis straight out of the Beaux -Arts, one that seemingly turned the fundamental tenets of the Modern Movement upside down."[58]

The building functions systematically in a Western way, as expected of modern form. The wall membrane is a three-part machine for mediating climate: the brise-soleil for shade, the floor-to-ceiling glazing for light, called *ondulatoires*, and the twenty-centimeter-wide ventilating shutters of metal with fixed copper mosquito screens, called *aérateurs*. Under the unexpected pressure of housing the administrations of both the Punjab and Haryana states, the depth of the brise-soleil and related balconies have been taken over for the offices. A central corridor running the length of the slab on each of the eight floors is the spine of circulation and services. Above the corridor's lower ceiling are the water lines. The two antipodal towers hold the ramps, which were originally to be the only vertical circulation as well as the path for construction. Ultimately, a series of elevators and stairs were built off the lobbies along the corridor. At the center, opposite the entrance to the Assembly, all of these consistent elements are interrupted by the suites for the higher officials and ministry chambers. Here the offices and brise-soleil are doubled in height. The section is marked also by symbolic inserts in the shape of a bull's horn or sky scoop.

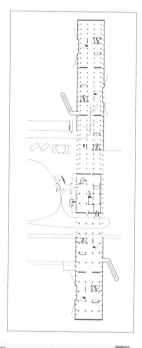

This systematic reading of the building gives way before the site of the Capitol Complex. The quotidian approach to the building is from one end, moving along the length and arriving a level below the Capitol plaza at a forecourt/parking lot. From the Capitol plaza, the top of the building sets a horizon that keeps the Himalayas at bay, while the pilotis slip beneath the plinth, creating an ambiguous baseline. In Paul Rudolph's words, "in every way it opposes the mountains; the angled stair way, the ramp on the roof. . . all these angles are obviously and carefully conceived to oppose the receding angles of the land masses."[59] From the ceremonial approach along the Jan Marg, the Secretariat is the first building to appear, but obliquely. It functions like a drawn perspectival line, moving as an extension of the eye. Its fluctuating presence belies its own size and the population that size represents.

ground floor plan (top); and detail of facade (bottom)

PALACE OF ASSEMBLY
1951–1962, inaugurated April 15, 1964

The Palace of Assembly invites comparison with antecedent projects such as The Palace of the Soviets and the Centrosoyus in which "architecture is circulation"[60] and circulation is the exhibit of culture. In plan, a u-shaped block of offices and a front portico define the square perimeter of a hypostyle concourse within which stand the hyperbolic volume of the General Assembly (Lower Chamber) and the cube of the Governor's Council (Upper Chamber). At the present time, the Punjab government is no longer bicameral and the Harayana state uses the upper chamber. Le Corbusier described the concourse as a forum, "a great space for favorable encounters among law givers."[61] The slender columns, clerestory lighting, and darkened ceiling lend an expansive, fluid quality to the space and passage through it. In pointed reversal of neoclassical planning where centralized domes predominate, the Lower Chamber is an eccentric, freed figure that "invites circumnabulation like a stupa."[62] This sense of "free plan" is deceptive, however, in that the circulation rigidly divides parliament members, visitors, and the press, with the most splendid procession

Le Corbusier

ADDRESS
The Capitol, Chandigarh

ACCESS
By official permission only. Ask at the School of Architecture.

DIRECTIONS
See Chandigarh main entry.

LOCALE
See Chandigarh main entry.

60. Le Corbusier, *Precisions*, 47.
61. Le Corbusier, *Oeuvre Complète* 6: 94.
62. Colin Rowe, *The Mathematics of the Ideal Villa*. Rowe observes the relation to Schinkel's Altes Museum in particular.
63. Le Corbusier, *Oeuvre Complète* 6:
64. Le Corbusier in Evenson, *Chandigarh*.

beginning at the plaza reserved for government officials. The working population has its own approach from the Jan Marg, its own axis centered on the rear facade, and its own arrival at a sunken side court edged with porticos, stairs, and a bridge to the Secretariat.

The sculptural forms of the building are tools in the authority of the Assembly, with imagery highly charged to suggest the coincidence of earthly and cosmic law. The hyperbolic cone of thin-shell concrete, strengthened by its own curvature, recalls the nuclear cooling towers of Ahmedabad, instruments of India's modernity. The top of the cone equipped with machinery for emitting light recalls Jantar Mantar, instruments of eighteenth-century astronomy. The original, unexecuted design included a mobile device for a solar festival dedicated to the first Indian ruler, Ashoka: on the opening of parliament, a light from the oculus would strike a column next to the speaker's rostrum. From the distance, this cone with its curved horn floats above the multiple horizons of the mountains, the artificial hills, the line of the Secretariat, and the Assembly portico. By virtue of its circular form, it appears a stationary point as one moves through the landscape, a seat of optical power.

The imagery of the great enameled door elaborates the themes of architectural form. Most simply described, the exterior panels depict cosmic birth, the big and small arcs of the sun, and the sine curve of the daily solar cycle above a populated landscape with a meander; the interior panels include Modulor spirals of pine cones and shells, a primal maternal scene, and the head of a bull associated with the Minotaur and vernal rebirth. Donated by the French government under the prodding of Le Corbusier for the inauguration of the Assembly, the doors still offi-

main floor plan

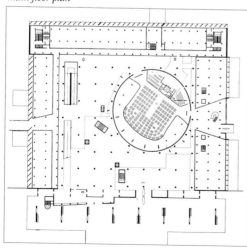

cially open only on the yearly commencement of parliament. As in the cult of the French sun king, solar symbolism takes on an overt political role.

A programmatic emphasis on shade and rain complements the solar narrative. Le Corbusier described the entire concourse as a "cathedral of shade."[63] Its depth, indirect lighting and blackened ceiling cast it in perpetual and dreamy dimness. The portico is a monumental parasol again loaded with images of power such as the horns of a bull and the wing of a plane. The roof has two gutters the size of canals that Le Corbusier likened to the two rivers which border Chandigarh. They direct monsoon rainwater to elaborate scuppers and basins, and finally to the pools around the building. In the manner of traditional Indian palatial architecture, the filled pools reflect the building in an illusory deep space across the horizon of the basin edge. The pools of the Assembly "square the building"[64] in the words of Le Corbusier, meaning that together building and reflection define a cube, until the image-granting sun evaporates the water.

front of assembly

THE MONUMENT OF THE OPEN HAND
THE DEPTH OF CONSIDERATION

1954; executed 1986

Le Corbusier

ADDRESS
The Capitol Complex
Chandigarh

ACCESS
Visible and accessible from the
Jan Marg

DIRECTIONS
See Chandigarh main entry.

LOCALE
Le Corbusier designed an
alternate version of the Open
Hand with viewing platform,
balustrade, and museum for
the top of the Bakhra Dam in
1958. The dam itself has been
built but without the Hand. Its
spectacular engineering and
landscape have made it a
tourist attraction.

Le Corbusier said to Nehru, "Since 1948, I have been obsessed by the symbol of the Open Hand. I would like to place it at the end of the Capitol, in front of the Himalayas."[65] This obsession took many forms and the hand many positions: thumb tense with hand outstretched, palm relaxed and horizontal, hand of the Modulor man, as a cockleshell, as tree, as dove or the crow "corbu," as auto-portrait.[66] The version at Chandigarh might be described as vertical and masculine, suggesting a bird.

As Le Corbusier wrested the hand "from the subconscious to the material and power of the symbol"[67] he generated a variety of accompanying texts. In his *Poème à l'angle droit*, section F.3 reads as a general statement of intention:

> It is open since all is present available
> sizable
> Open to receive
> Open also that each may come there to take[68]

He came to see The Open Hand as the inevitable symbol of the new India "where the second era of the machinist civilization has begun: the era of harmony."[69] He also expressed privately a more ambivalent attitude. The providential and apocalyptic are recurrent themes of The Open Hand. In a sketchbook it appears above the inscription, "the end of the world. . . deliverance."[70] Simultaneous with his design of Chandigarh, Le Corbusier read and notated Georges Bataille's *Cursed Gift*, which interprets giving in terms of the tribal potlatch as an act of rivalry for the acquisition of rank, demonstrating an economy of exhibition and sacrifice rather than utility. Le Corbusier's marginal note suggests that he conflated his own experience with potlatch culture. He fumed, "From one camp, Corbu has been accepted by assholes, from the other he is king. The unselfish practice of painting is an unflagging sacrifice, a gift of time. . . . One day, before or after my death, they will say thank you."[71]

By the end of his life, the hand was still unrealized and insuring its completion became a compulsion for Le Corbusier. To Malraux he wrote: "This open hand, a sign of peace and reconciliation, must rise at Chandigarh. . . to bear witness to harmony. . . God and the devil, the forces present."[72]

The accepted design of 1954 for The Open Hand raises it 25 meters over a Depth of Consideration. From the sunken roadway at the center of the plaza and from the Depth, one sees only the hand against the sky as it turns on ball bearings like a weathervane. The Depth is an intimately scaled public space, 40 meters square and 5 meters deep, conceived as a place of public debate with certain democratic if not Greek features. Along its perimeter are two oppositional sets of stepped seating and a speaker's rostrum set at the same level as the seats. Given the current state of political contingencies that keeps the Depth silent and empty for security reasons, the execution of the hand in somber, weathered steel rather than in the originally intended orange, white, and green enamel seems somehow appropriate. The absence of the Governor's Palace leaves The Open Hand unintentionally isolated, appearing as a huge vessel[73] but a small monument.

65. Jean-Petit, *Le Corbusier Lui-même*, 105.
66. Mary Sekler, "Ruskin, The Tree and The Open Hand," in Walden, *The Open Hand*, 74. Mary Sekler finds reference to "the hand" in Le Corbusier's work as early as 1936 where he speaks with Ruskinian undertones of "branches born down each spring with a new open hand." An image of the hand also appears in drawings of 1943 accompanied by five female nudes.
67. Le Corbusier, *The Last Testament of Père Corbu*, 97.
68. Le Corbusier, *Poème à l'angledroit*, s-67.
69. Le Corbusier to Nehru, in Sekler, "Ruskin," Walden, *The Open Hand*, 83.
70. Le Corbusier, *Sketchbook III*: FLC 916, also Le Corbusier, *Oeuvre Complète* 7: 203.
71. Inscribed in Le Corbusier's copy of the *Cursed Gift*.. Phillipe Duboy "Bataille," Lucan, *Le Corbusier: Une Encyclopédie*, 67 and Nadir Lahiji, "The Gift of the Open Hand: Le Corbusier Reading George Bataille's Le Part Maudit," *JAE* 50/1: 50–56.
72. Le Corbusier, *The Last Testament of Père Corbu*, 97.
73 Le Corbusier refers to the hand as a vessel, *Oeuvre Complète*7:109.

THE TOWER OF SHADOWS
THE GEOMETRICAL HILL
THE MONUMENT TO THE MARTYR
1957, 1968

Le Corbusier

ADDRESS
The Capitol, Chandigarh
Sector 1
ACCESS
Open to the plaza of the Capitol
DIRECTIONS
see Chandigarh main entry
LOCALE
see Chandigarh main entry

The Tower is an instrument that registers the path of the sun through shadow. As such, it belongs as much to the tradition of Indian royal observatories like Jantar Mantar as to Le Corbusier's own research regarding solar angles which he concretized in the brise-soleil. Facing the ordinate points, 45 degrees off of the Capitol Complex axes, each side and level corresponds to calculated angles of incidence. Besides being an instrument, it is also a pavilion with an interior, so that shadows are inversely cast inside and out. A ramp leads down into a pit from which rises the Geometrical Hill.

Currently covered with loosely tended grass, the Geometrical Hill is both more and less than geometrical. It is strikingly solid, a lump and stoppage within the continuous space of the plaza. Models and drawings show its surface inscribed with a large sine curve which was Le Corbusier's symbol of the twenty-four-hour solar cycle. Its opacity contrasts with the permeability of the Tower and also with the views granted from along the other inclines, which are ramps.

The Monument to the Martyr (executed without its figural sculptures and sense of martyrdom) is pure ramp with a summit designed "for viewing the entire Capitol from above."[74] The entire capitol refers not to the buildings so much as to the three-dimensional aspect of the plaza itself. The pits and declivities vanish at ground level, but they appear as sunken volumes from the summit, composed in relation to the horizon. The figure missing from the base of the ramp was intended to lay on a bed gazing at the sky, like the patients Le Corbusier drew in the Venice Hospital, deprived of the immediate scene and looking toward the immanent.

Tower of Shadows

Together the tower, hill, and ramps compose a smaller landscape within the larger space of the plaza. The elements set up immediate foreground relations among themselves and also far-reaching optical power over the distant points. What they avoid is a middle ground, because they are too small to break up the order of the plaza into an intermediate sequence of spaces. Looking from the plaza back toward the Assembly, the Tower of Shadows interrupts only the distant mass of the Secretariat, as Le Corbusier intended.[75] One can imagine the view from the Jan Marg across the missing reflecting pools and gardens toward the completed Governor's Palace.[76] The distant scoop of the Palace would have sat directly on the horizon line at the top of the Geometrical Hill like horns on the humped back of a bull.

fabric mock-up of Governor's Palace

74. Le Corbusier, *Oeuvre Complète* 7:110.
75. Ibid.
76. As part of the 50th anniversary celebration of Chandigargh in January 1999, under the direction of Charles Correa, a fabric mock up of the Governor's Palace was built with the visual effects as described.

Geometrical Hill from Monument to the Martyr

THE YACHT CLUB (LAKE CLUB)

1953-1964

Le Corbusier

ADDRESS
Lake Sukhna,
Sector 1 Chandigarh

ACCESS
Clearly visible from the edge of
the lake.

DIRECTIONS
The club is on the southwest
edge of the lake, less than a
mile east of the Capitol along
Uttar Marg.

LOCALE
The lake is a popular recreation
spot, especially for walks
around the landscaped edge.

P. L. Varma, chief engineer of Punjab and facilitator of the city plan, conceived of damming the Sukhna Cho River to create the huge Sukhna Lake as an amenity to the city, a source of water, and a way to mitigate extremes of local climate. It even keeps down the dust during May and June. Le Corbusier designed the gateway to the landing stages and a memorial stone commemorating the dam's construction. Lining the causeway are river stones rounded by the changing flow of water through the valley.[77]

Le Corbusier did not want either buildings on the lake that would obstruct the view of the mountains, or motor boats that would disturb the silence. Every element was to reinforce the suspended calm and optical depth of this artificial landscape, including the night illumination which he designed to enhance the field of stars and their reflection. When officials pressured him into placing the boat club on the lake, he sunk it three meters below road level and placed a simple concrete colonnade along the shore. The exact site of the building is a small, curved cove off the main expanse of the lake. Framed in views through its colonnade, the club's immediate landscape is intimate in contrast to the landscape of the lake, which has no middle ground other than the single point of a glass watch tower.

The plan of the club has similarities to Le Corbusier's early, purist compositions where curved fragments are disposed within a regular grid. In this case, the concrete colonnade frames a set of brick curtain walls and curved glass screens which, despite their bright yellow mullions, have the flavor of Roman remains. The club and its siting recall any number of ancient porticos along the edge of artificial waters, such as the nymphaeum of Hadrian's Villa and the Sarkej Pavilion[78] near Ahmedabad.

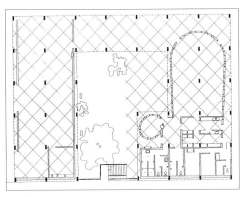

ground floor plan

77. Jacqueline Jeanneret, "Chandigarh," *Parametro* 185: 49 and Le Corbusier, *Creation is a Patient Search*, 277.
78. Curtis, *Ideas and Forms*, 1986.

lake walk

COLLEGE OF ART
1959-1965

Le Corbusier and Aditya Prakash

ADDRESS
Sector 10, Chandigarh

ACCESS
Check with the administrative
office of the school.

DIRECTIONS
The entrance is off the parking
lot side of the Leisure Valley.

LOCALE
The College of Art is located
next to the arts complex of the
Museum and Art Gallery just
above the Rose Garden of the
Leisure Valley.

COLLEGE OF ARCHITECTURE
1959-1965

Le Corbusier and Aditya Prakash

ADDRESS
Sector 12, Chandigarh

ACCESS
Check with the administrative
office of the school.

DIRECTIONS
Take the entrance road off the
Vidya Path into Sector 12 which
also leads to the College of
Engineering.

LOCALE
The College of Architecture is a
good half-hour walk from the
College of Art, adjacent to the
College of Engineering and near
the main campus of Panjab
University. The main university
campus has several major
works by Jeanneret.

The colleges are almost identical in concept, form and terrain. Both have an organization of cells around courtyards which is common to India and also reminiscent of Le Corbusier's youthful project for the art school at La Chaux-de-Fonds (1910) and its source in the Carthusian Monastery at Ema.[79] Le Corbusier considered the cellular fabric the perfect model for a balanced community and used it repeatedly, as in the strictly monastic La Tourette and the Venice Hospital. As intended from the beginning, the schools have added modules of courtyards and studios.In this, they are the only realized example of Le Corbusier's late interest in expandable form and unlimited growth.

School of Art foyer

79. Le Corbusier, *Oeuvre Complète* 8:104.

Recalling Le Corbusier's unbuilt design for his own studio (1929), the rooms are modest masonry structures, ostensibly low to the ground but with dramatic interiors defined by the deep curved concrete roof beams. The side facades of local brick bare figural outlines of the studio clerestory, ventilation slots, and drainspouts. A deep verandah screened by a concrete brise-soleil serves as entrance and corridor on the south face.

Both schools sit in grassy terrain, rotated off the grid to the ordinate points, with studios facing northern light. The College of Art in the Leisure Valley has the more pastoral setting including a slight hill with sunken rooms behind, while the College of Architecture has a more conventional campus context next to the College of Engineering. The primary landscape at both schools is the lawn of the courtyards. These courts are embellished by water basins beneath the sculptural drain spouts. The yards can be seen episodically along the passages from the front entrance to the rear studios. Of all the interior courts of both schools, the sculpture yard of the art school is the most alive and the least pristine, littered with shards of stone and wood and filled with activity like the workshops on the streets of Jaipur.

sculpture courtyard, School of Art

Museum: Le Corbusier and
S. D. Sharma
Gallery: S. D. Sharma according
to the outlines of Le Corbusier.

ADDRESS
Sector 10
Chandigarh

ACCESS
Open daily 10–4:30,
except Mondays.
Tel 91.172.742501.
http://chdmuseum.nic.in.

DIRECTIONS
Take an auto-rickshaw or one of
the bus routes to Sector 10.

LOCALE
The Museum and Gallery, along
with the College of Art, are the
built portion of a educational-
cultural complex adjacent to the
Leisure Valley that was originally
to include other museums and
theaters.

The Museum at Chandigarh adheres to Le Corbusier's model, The Museum of Unlimited Growth, in its spiral arrangement of galleries around a central courtyard extending the height of the building.[80] In lieu of spiral growth which is inhibited here by placing the lecture hall up against the museum, a "rhizome" of subterranean expansion occurs in the biomorphic archives extending from beneath the pilotis toward the organically shaped reflecting pool. All Le Corbusier's museums of this model have a subterranean quality in that they are largely blank enclosures, entered from beneath and lit from above. To be simultaneously raised off the ground on pilotis and yet remote from the light is a paradox within Le Corbusier's language, which usually pairs height and light. The paradox is resolved here on the highest level of the gallery where linear clerestories become occupiable mezzanines so that room and lighting source become one. The passage from the ground to this height and from diffuse to intense light is articulated through several overlaid architectural devices: the internal courtyard and processional ramp which generate the path; the spiral pattern defined by the modulation of the column shape from lozenge to rectangle within the grid; the order of the evenly spaced linear clerestory; the contrasting order of the diagonal fin structure within that clerestory; the strategic painting of walls in strong hues of red, yellow, white, and black; and the swastika plan of mezzanines. Through all this, the visitor can wander distractedly and yet according to the ordained plan.

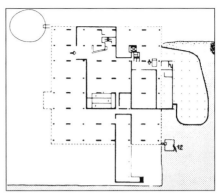

ground floor plan of museum

Not just the museum but the entire complex, including the gallery across the plaza, subscribes to a formulaic cultural center that Le Corbusier used repeatedly. Similar designs exist for Paris (1950), Ahmedabad (1956), Tokyo (1957), Frankfurt (1962), Stockholm (1962), and the constructed Heidi Weber Pavilion (1963). The particulars for this gallery appear only as a double square on a site plan and as a quick elevation sketch in a notebook;[81] yet, through their resemblance to the other projects, their intention is clear. Given the suggestions of metal, membrane, lightness, and assemblage that appear throughout the related images, the posthumous rendering of the gallery at Chandigarh in concrete is startling, as if the building were a homogeneous cast of an original or a replica carved from singular stone as at Fatehpur Sikri. It is an act of rendition that in its purity helps to expose how all of Chandigarh was a simultaneous translation between India and Le Corbusier.

80. See entry for Museum of the City of Ahmedabad for discussion of the model.
81. H. Allen Brooks, ed., *Le Corbusier Archive*, FLC 4833, and Le Corbusier, *Sketchbook* III: FLC 302.

museum

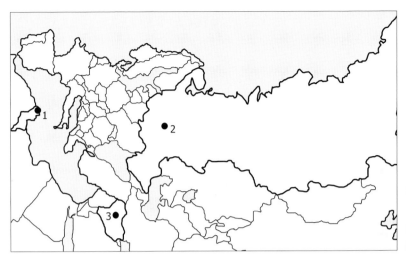

TUNISIA
  1. Villa Baizeau (Bézeult), Carthage

RUSSIA
  2. Centrosoyus, Moscow

IRAQ
  3. Sports Center, Baghdad

JAPAN
  4. National Museum of Western
    Art, Tokyo

Le Corbusier and Pierre
Jeanneret

ADDRESS
Sainte Monique, Carthage

ACCESS
Private residence in poor repair
but not altered.

DIRECTIONS
Carthage is a northeastern suburb of Tunis. Take the TGM
electric train from Place de
l'Afrique station in Tunis, the
La Goulett-La Marsa line.

LOCALE
Located next to the former
Palace grounds of Carthage, in
the suburb of Sainte Monique.

Le Corbusier published two versions of Villa Baizeau
in the first volume of the *Oeuvre Complète*: a first,
preferred scheme and a second one designed and
eventually built according to the client's uncompro-
mising demands. Impressed by the architects' contribution to the Weissenhof Exhibition in Stuttgart,
the Tunisian industrialist Lucien Baizeau approached Le Corbusier's office in Paris to commission a house for his family. He contracted that the
office would provide design and construction documents and an estimate of cost but that his company
would build the house under Tunisian supervision.
In the end, Baizeau rejected the construction methods suggested by Le Corbusier and his contractor
Summer, and instead used his own. Le Corbusier
and Jeanneret received photographs, detailed
descriptions of climate and site, and preliminary
sketches from Baizeau, but they never visited the
site.

From the beginning, the shared goal of client
and architect was to accommodate the sun and the
hot wind of the *Sirocco*.[1] The first scheme addressed
the problem of a tropical architecture through the

complex synthesis of the existing Corbusian canon, the Citrohan and the Dom-ino.[2] It is possible that Baizeau, having seen the Weissenhof exhibition, requested a house of Citrohan type because of its Mediterranean nuance. By overlapping two Citrohan's in section within a larger Dom-ino frame, Le Corbusier created three interlocking, double-height spaces for the circulation of air, and an overarching parasol roof for shade. The architects concurrently explored this logic of arrangement in the Wanner projects in Geneva. Baizeau rejected the scheme because, to his mind, the glass sheathing and single parasol failed to solve the problem of sun and wind, and the orientation of rooms did not sufficiently accommodate the eastern view.

After several attempts to revise the initial scheme, the architects capitulated to Baizeau's increasingly specific requests for a house with terraces on all sides and a more conventional arrangement of single-storied rooms. Working surprisingly closely with a layout the client provided, they developed a version of the Maison Dom-ino concrete frame in which each floor is a continuous tray with turned up edges carrying the free plan of the house. At key points, the walls engage the edge of the tray to define the facades and entry sequence. These trays are simultaneously breezy balconies for the recessed rooms and shade umbrellas for the floors below. Although Le Corbusier projected an ambivalent attitude toward the solution, he also recognized its clarity and included it as the third of his Four Compositions, calling it "very easy."[3] The exposed frame of the villa became his alternative to the northern purist architecture in which the frame is suppressed within a tight-skinned box.

This first building for a tropical setting had distant ramifications in the architects' work. An open building that draws the breeze deep into it, Villa Baizeau prefigures the late tropical architecture designed in Ahmedabad thirty years later. Significantly, both schemes for Baizeau play important roles there. Presented at the time of its construction as a house of machine-age principles for an industrial magnate, Baizeau also began Le Corbusier's search for a response to climate through form.

1. For a detailed history of the project and related correspondence, see Tim Benton, "The Client's Pencil," *Rassegna* 3: 17–24.
2. For an in-depth analysis of the evolution of scheme 1, see Bruno Reichlin, "Solution élégante: L'utile n'est pas beau," in Lucan, *Le Corbusier: Une Encyclopédie*, 372–377.
3. Le Corbusier, *Precisions*, 134–35.

section, first project, 1928

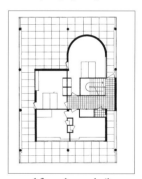

second-floor plan, as built

Le Corbusier and Pierre
Jeanneret with executive
architect Nicolai Kolli

ADDRESS
Miasnitzkaya N35/41 aka
Ulitsa Kirova, 39, Moscow

ACCESS
The building is now Goskom-
stat, the State Statistics Committee. Access with permission.
Tel 095.207.4902,
www.gks.ru/eng.

DIRECTIONS
From Red Square, walk down
Ulitsa Kirova to ring road Bol.
Sadovaia or take the subway.

LOCALE
At the time of design, the Centrosoyus was among other contemporary structures, the
Central Post Office (O. Munts,
the Vesnin Brothers) and the
Gostorg (B. Velikovsky) on the
then Miasnitzkaya Boulevard,
parallel to old Miasnitzkaya

Le Corbusier's involvement with the USSR extends
from his early essays on Soviet politics and culture
published in *l'Esprit Nouveau* through the success of
the Centrosoyus to the rejection of his design for the
Palace of the Soviets (1932) and the subsequent withdrawal of CIAM from its Moscow conference.

A barometer for shifts in Soviet ideology, Le
Corbusier's work was at first suspected of aestheticism by the constructivists, then rejected for its functionalism by the socialist realists, and ultimately
discredited on both counts. Despite this continual
criticism for his unclear socio-political position, during the 1920s, Le Corbusier found a receptive audience for his architecture based on its potentials for
industrialized production. In the conservative milieu
of the 1925 International Exposition of Decorative
Arts in Paris, the pavilion of Konstantin Melnikov
and Le Corbusier's own Pavillon de l'Esprit Nouveau
seemed like-minded critiques of bourgeois capitalist
culture. The Soviets also viewed the houses of the
Weissenhof and Pessac as models of urban revision.[4]

The Centrosoyus commission seemed initially
the key to an extended Soviet relationship and pres-

ence, especially welcomed by Le Corbusier in the economic aftermath of the stock market crash, and in the personal aftermath of his rejection in the League of Nations competition. He was invited first to participate in the competition for the Centrosoyus and then to visit Moscow in October 1928 where, besides consolidating his competition victory, he lectured on architecture and urbanism to great success. As a consequence, the Soviets solicited his design for a power station in Bobriki, his response to a proposed recreational "Green City" outside of Moscow, and his commentary on the future of Moscow itself. This "Response to Moscow,"[5] drafted in Paris during the winter of 1930, became the basis for his utopian Radiant City although not for Soviet planning. This firsthand contact with the Soviet avant-garde also offered much that influenced Le Corbusier: Mosei Ginzburg's Narkomfin project, the concept of a workers' club, N. A. Miliutin's linear cities and an affinity with Sergei Eisenstein in the monumentalization of the everyday.

The Centrosoyus, or Central Union of Consumer Cooperatives, flourished during Lenin's New Economic Policy. Operating with great autonomy, it controlled a major share of the retail economy and initiated projects in finance and cooperative housing. A complex three-phase competition eventually chose Le Corbusier-Jeanneret from entrants who included Max Taut, the Vesnin brothers, Ivan Ilich Leonidov, an OSA team led by Ginzberg and Peter Behrens, and an in-house team. After a protracted period, and under pressure from a group which included the Soviet contestants, the committee eventually retained the French architects for design documents, including interiors, with limited site supervision. Throughout the remainder of the project, including development in the Paris office, the Soviet assistant Nikolai Kolli aided and insured the work for the Soviets. Work halted, however, in July of 1931 with the advent of the first Five-Year Plan and its shifted priorities. Despite accusations regarding the building's extravagance from factions as far afield as Hans Meyer, construction resumed in 1934, but under increasing opposition from the advocates for socialist realism.

Street, as a radial link between the downtown and the rail way stations. Today you may also find no. 8/2 and no. 15 by Kuznetsov, and no. 24 by F. O. Shekhtel. The Narkomfin housing of Mosei Ginzburg is at 25 B. Metro Krasnopresnenskaia-Barikadnaia.

4. The authoritative history of Le Corbusier's involvement is Jean-Louis Cohen, Le Corbusier and the Mystique of the USSR.
5. Le Corbusier, The Radiant City, 182–83.

Le Corbusier describes the moment of his conversion to a sympathetic understanding of the Bolshevik mind. In a definition anticipatory of the Koolhaasian, he learned that: "Bolshoi means big. Bolshoi means: everything as big as possible, the biggest theory, the biggest projects. Maximum..."[6]The bigness of the Centrosoyus begins with the imagining of the "spectral Moscow crowd"[7] who were to inhabit this building. The project brief was for a vast office complex to accommodate 2,500, with a recreational worker's club, restaurant and auditorium. Le Corbusier describes the "obligatory classification of this crowd entering and exiting at the same time; the need for a kind of forum at such hours for people whose overshoes and furs will be covered with snow. . . . Architecture is circulation."[8] He proposed "to set up such an architecture that knows two moments: the first a period of disorderly flux on a horizontal ground plane, vast as a lake, the second a period of stable, immobile work. . . (in) the offices where everyone is in his place and controllable."[9] The second moment is figured in the rectilinear office slabs raised on pilotis. The first is figured in the ground-level field of columns with extensive foyers and coatrooms, punctuated by helical ramps leading to the offices and the auditorium.

It is by circulation through the Centrosoyus that the building "reveals itself entirely" to the moving eye and body. The envelope of glass and stone was another form of lucid circulation, a kind of bio-mechanical skin. Le Corbusier designed a two-part experimental system to control the internal environment of the slabs. The *mur neutralisant* (neutralizing wall) had a wide, hermetically sealed center cavity for the circulation of temperature-controlled, forced air. The cavity surfaces were either thick, pink tuffa stone from the Arctic region, chosen for its insulating capacity or continuous

Ground floor plan

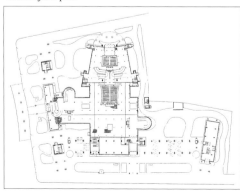

double-glazing for the transmission of maximum daylight. In the interior spaces, dispersed locations called *aération ponctuelle* provided "exact respiration," a form of mechanical ventilation.[10] The clients feared the cost of the mechanical system, especially in the face of growing financial crisis. The various manufacturers and engineers consulted—Gustave Lyon, St. Gobain glass, The American Blower Company—questioned the system as extravagant and potentially noisy and smelly. In the end, heat was provided by perimeter radiators, cooling by window roller blinds.[11]

According to the principle of bigness, the idea of circulation through the building extends to the city itself.[12] Borrowed from the arcadian League of Nations project, the building's formal strategy of separate elements composed through the grading of axes allowed for a perceived expansion of the site into the urban fabric. In design development, the Centrosoyus plan changed from an internally focused courtyard to slabs on pilotis which align with the boulevards but expose the figure of auditorium to the street. Object, urbanism and landscape simultaneously, the building was, according to its author, "three prisms of stone and glass planes, disposed to create specific impressions, here a vertical cliff wall, there a welcoming basin."[13] In his "Response to Moscow," Le Corbusier imagined a classless city on pilotis above a continuous garden, like a next-sized iteration of a Centrosoyus.

The constructed building is a fair reflection of Le Corbusier's exterior design intentions; the major modifications were to the internal systems, details and finishes, especially polychromy. The issue of color was observed during visits to Moscow by Josep Lluís Sert and Charlotte Perriand, but Le Corbusier did not have the authority to correct it and was not invited to the site during the construction process.[14] In the end, the huge slabs took their place as impressive objects within the reality of the Soviet State; the columnar forum with its warped landscape of ramps kept its hold on the architect's imagination.

6. Le Corbusier, *Precisions*, 47.
7. Ibid.
8. Ibid, 49.
9. Le Corbusier, *Oeuvre Complète* 1: 210.
10. Cohen, *Mystique*, 82, 88–98. Gustave Lyon patented *áeration ponctuelle*, while Le Cobusier-Jeanneret held the patent on the *mur neutralisant*.
11. Tim Benton, "The Era of Great Projects," in Raeburn and Wilson, *Le Corbusier: Architect of the Century*, 166-68.
12. For the urbanism of the project, see Alan Colquhoun, "Modernity and the Classical Tradition," 121–61 and Kenneth Frampton, "Le Corbusier's Designs for the League of Nations, Centrosoyus and Palace of the Soviets," in Brooks, *Le Corbusier Archive*, 57–70.
13. Le Corbusier, *Precisions*, 59–60.
14. Cohen, *Mystique*, 96–101.

Le Corbusier and Georges
Présenté

ADDRESS
Baghdad, Iraq

LOCALE
The gymnasium is across from
the Baghdad Stadium designed
by F.K.D. Amaral (1967) on the
east side of the Tigris River.

The original plans for an athletic complex in Baghdad featured a huge stadium for 100,000 spectators, a gymnasium for 3,500, playing fields for 3,000, and a pool for 5,000. Le Corbusier considered the program the spiritual kin to his own unbuilt project for a National Center of Collective Festivals for 100,000 (1937) planned for Paris as a kind of syndicalist rallying grounds and descended from the vast public dreams of the French revolutionary architect Etienne-Louis Boullée.[15] The Iraqis, he concluded, were prepared to realize his work of twenty years before. To bring the power of spectacle up to date, Le Corbusier added to the Iraqi program a building for electronic displays of sound and light similar to his Phillips Pavilion (1952).

The only part of the project executed and the only part completely designed at the time of Le Corbusier's death in 1965 is the gymnasium. In 1973, the Iraqi government charged Présenté, Le Corbusier's original contact with Baghdad and his project engineer, with the execution of the gym on a site across the river from the original site planned by Le Corbusier.

The gymnasium relates to Le Corbusier's late interest in contemporary spectacle. Framed on three sides by stands of seating, the fourth wall is a 32 x 12 meter steel door that slides open along a free-standing concrete frame so that the interior can open directly and completely onto the adjacent playing field and the stadium seating. When closed, the exterior frame stands empty, like a minor proscenium; the interior space is a dim shed naturally illuminated only along the edge of the exposed steel trusses. The closed gymnasium relates specifically to a type of theater Le Corbusier named *boîtes à miracles*, miracle boxes, in reference to the spectacle revealed within a simple black box.[16] Here as in many of his late works, a theatrical concern with darkness and with the intense contrast between dark and light replaced Le Corbusier's earlier enthusiasm for abundant light.

rear view

In contrast to the relative simplicity of the shed, the circulation is an elaborate system of ramps. The wide curve of "the grand ramp" arrives at the mezzanine level where it divides in two, each branch leading to a secondary flight of seating. A third ramp, directionally opposite to the first and coiled tightly around a pier continues to the top level. The ramp and the spiral originate in Mesopotamian architecture and so have a special relevance to a building in Baghdad,[17] as Le Corbusier acknowledged in his earlier ramped ziggurat for the Mundaneum (1929). In his public work, exposed, biomorphic circulation systems are often the glorified objectification of the movement of the crowd. As he wrote regarding the stadium for Paris, through circulation "even 100,000 spectators participate in the games, where everything has self-control, style and enthusiasm."[18]

15. Le Corbusier, converstion with Louise Bourgeois and Robert Goldwater.
16. Suzanne Taj-Eldin, "Baghdad: Box of Miracles," *Architectural Review* 181/1079: 78-83.
17. Ibid.
18. Le Corbusier, *Oeuvre Complète* 3: 90.

NATIONAL MUSEUM OF WESTERN ART

1959

Le Corbusier with Maekawa Kunio and Sakakura Junzo. 1979 addition by Maekawa Kunio.

ADDRESS
7-7 Ueno Koen, Taito-ku, Ueno, Tokyo

ACCESS
Tues.–Sun. 9:30–5, except Fri. 9:30–8. Closed Mon. and Dec. 29–Jan. 1. Free admission 2nd/ 4th Sat. each month. For holiday hours, visitor info., tel 03. 3828.5131. www.nmwa.go.jp.

DIRECTIONS
Ueno is in the northeastern section of central Tokyo. By metro it is within 30 min. of most of the metropolitan area. Easiest access is by the Yamanote or JNR lines to the Ueno stop. Hibiya and Ginza subway lines also have a Ueno stop with an exit directly to the park.

The National Museum is one of three museums built by Le Corbusier according to the outlines of his Museum for Unlimited Growth.[19] The building in Tokyo adheres to the basic organization of a "squared spiral" gallery on pilotis described in the model. An upper level of galleries wraps around the central court and penetrates it with balconies at several points. A secondary system of glass balconies within the galleries is also an elaborate clerestory. Superimposed on this layered spiral is a pinwheel or "swastika" pattern of circulation along linear paths leading to the exit stairs. The asymetrically placed stairs are the only evidence of the spiral on the intentionally faceless exterior and the only feature at an intermediate scale. At the smallest scale, Le Corbusier used a sheathing of green pebbles set in concrete panels, common to the local architecture of the period.

Le Corbusier described the content as well as the form of the exhibition of culture for his Museum for Unlimited Growth. Responding to the unlimited amounts of information available in a machine age, he proposed that the true museum would contain everything and would expand constantly to incorporate the artifacts of history as it occurred. The museum in Tokyo defined "everything" to be an account of modern culture through the history of Western painting. The collection originally belonged to M. Matsuka, a Japanese living in Paris at the time of World War II. Having confiscated the art during the war, the French government agreed to return it to Japan on the condition that it be placed in a museum that, in Le Corbusier's words "would acquaint the Japanese with the past, present, and future of Western art in a scientific manner, beginning with Impressionism."[20] As the cradle of the new machinist civilization, Impressionism was to occupy the center of the spiral in the Hall of Nineteenth Century. Le Corbusier planned large photo murals for its walls that would demonstrate the communicative and fact-finding power of the camera. The murals were not executed, however, and the unlikely scheme for unlimited growth unfulfilled. The quality of the building is the result of the high quality of Japanese craftsmanship which Le Corbusier fundamentally tended to resist[21] as well as of more traditional Corbusian elements such as the ramps ascending to a skylit court and a stair extending into nature.

LOCALE
Founded as one of Japan's first public gardens soon after the Meiji Restoration of 1878, Ueno Park contains Le Corbusier's museum and also a zoo famous for its panda, Shinobazu Pond, and the Tokyo Municipal Museum. The Municipal Museum and the nearby Tokyo Festival Hall are both the work of Maekawa who worked in Le Corbusier's Paris studio before returning to Japan.

19. See entry for N. C Mehta Museum in Ahmedabad.
20. Le Corbusier, *Oeuvre Complète* 7: 182.
21. Peter Blake notes Le Corbusier found the Japanese work overly refined. In conversation, May 1999.

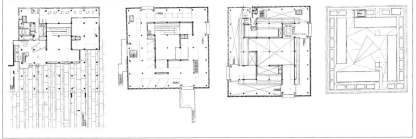

floorplans 1–4

Glossary of Corbusian terms
Selected Bibliography
Maps

GLOSSARY OF CORBUSIAN TERMS

aedicule: framed opening, originally supporting an entablature and pediment.

aérateur: Wall opening for ventilation with fixed mosquito netting and an operable door. One part of a three-part system developed by Le Corbusier to replace the traditional window, the other two parts being a *brise-soleil* for shade and *ondulatoire* for light.

Athens Charter: Developed by CIAM (1933) but published by Le Corbusier (1943), a document of urbanism according to the principle of zoned use.

béton brut: Exposed concrete left with the imprint of the form work, usually deliberately.

bloc à redents: Linear block of apartments with setbacks from Le Corbusier's Contemporary City (1922). The blocks have collective services and recreation.

brise-soleil: Sun-break made of concrete, either as a nonstructural gridded screen or a system of balconies. Eventually integrated as part of Le Corbusier's three-part system of window. The other two parts are the *ondulatoire* for light and the *aérateur* for ventilation.

Catalan vault: Brick vault without true formwork, developed in the Catalonian region.

CIAM: (Congrès Internationaux d'Architecture Moderne or International Congress of Modern Architecture) An international group of architects and critics who met periodically to define architecture's relation to problems of the day such as housing, and who functioned as a kind of spearhead for the cause of modern architecture in general. Le Corbusier, Karl Moser, Sigfried Giedion, and Walter Gropius were the senior founding members in 1928.

dry assembly: The assembly of prefabricated parts on a construction site without mortar.

entablature: Horizontal members supported by columns. Major constituent parts are the architrave, cornice, and frieze.

fascia: A plain horizontal surface. Originally the overlapping planes of an architrave.

Fibonacci series: The unending sequence 1, 1, 2, 3, 5, 8,. . ., where each term equals the sum of its two predecessors.

Five Points of Modern Architecture: Le Corbusier's formulation of architectural principles derived from the potentials of the concrete frame. They are the pilotis beneath the house, the roof garden on top, the free plan inside the house, the free facades outside, and *fenêtre à longeur* or strip windows.

Four Compositions: Le Corbusier's categories of spatial organization derived in part from the Five Points and Maison Domino. Each Composition refers to one of his house designs of the 1920s.

free facade (or plan): In both cases, the wall is free of structural constraints and supports no weight other than its own.

Garden City: Based on the belief in the healthful condition of living in nature, Ebenezer Howard (1898) proposed a planned city in which housing, industry, and garden are interspersed and growth is controlled.

golden section (also called golden mean): A ratio between two portions of a line or between the two dimensions of a rectangle, in which the lesser of the two is to the greater as the greater is to the sum of both. A : B = B : A + B. It is approximately equal to .616.

immeuble-villa (villa apartment): A perimeter apartment block from Le Corbusier's Contemporary City in which each dwelling is a *maisonnette*, a two story apartment with adjoining garden related to his Maison Citrohan. The block has a shared garden court and collective housekeeping services and facilities.

lamella: A vertical fin used as a sun-break on a building facade.

linear city: A city organized along continuous linear infrastructure of roads, rails, and services. Described by Arturo Soria y Mata in the nineteenth century and Miliutin in the

1920s, it became central to Le Corbusier's thinking by the 1930s.

loggia: Roofed porch, gallery, or balcony arcaded on one or more sides.

Maison Citrohan: One of Le Corbusier's prototypical dwellings intended for mass production. There are several versions of this house, some with pilotis. All of them are free-standing, rectangular (double square) boxes with large industrial sash windows at the front and primarily blank side walls. The plan is organized around a double-height salon with sleeping balcony.

Maison Dom-ino: Le Corbusier's formulation of the reinforced concrete frame, characterized by its smooth slabs without expressed beams, straight columns without capitals, and cantilevered edges. Bay widths are square or golden sections.

Maison Monol: One of Le Corbusier's prototypical dwellings intended for mass production. It is a vaulted linear volume of concrete that can stand independently or as a part of a series of attached units.

Modulor: Le Corbusier's system of proportion and measure based on the golden section as it applies to the human figure. First applied in his post- World War II work.

mur neutralisant (neutralizing wall): An exterior wall system with a continuous central plenum for the circulation of temperature-controlled air, such that the building skin can adjust to climate and neutralize the difference between inside and outside.

objet-type: Anonymous object evolved through mass production to a perfected standard.

ondulatoire: Fixed glazing with mullions spaced according to Modulor, mathematical, or musical harmonies. One part of a three-part system developed by Le Corbusier to replace the traditional window in his late architecture. The other parts are *brise-soleil* for shade and *aérateur* for ventilation.

pan de verre: Le Corbusier's version of the glass curtain wall.

piloti(s): Le Corbusier's term for ground-level columns that support a building raised above them. The extension of piles above the ground for the purpose of supporting a raised building so that the ground level is left open.

post and lintel: Construction system of vertical posts spanned by horizontal lintels.

Purism: Artistic movement defined in 1916 in reaction to Cubism, with the intent of restoring the integrity of the object to still-life painting. In mature form, its spatial structure resembled that of Synthetic Cubism. Generalized as a cultural aesthetic, it called for the evolution and refinement of type objects to a perfected standard.

respiration exacte: (exact respiration) Part of a larger system of air-conditioning or *aération ponctuelle* developed with Gustave Lyon in relation to the large buildings of the late 1920s. Treated and purified air circulates through the building without intake from the outside. Le Corbusier's patented form of exact respiration is the air circulation within the *mur neutralisant*.

Taylorization: The scientific study and management of industrial production in order to increase efficiency; named after F. W. Taylor, an American engineer who was its exponent.

Trois Etablissements Humains: The three human establishments of the radiant city or radio-concentric city of exchanges, the linear-industrial city, and the radiant collective farm. Together they formed a total ecology in the postwar thinking of Le Corbusier.

trabeation: Post and lintel construction.

tracés régulateurs (regulating lines): Le Corbusier's first proportioning system of angled lines based on quadrature and the properties of the golden section.

Unité d'habitation: Le Corbuiser's postwar apartment housing type and proposal for a fundamental social unit. A cage structure of duplex apartments is raised above the ground on pilotis. Apartments and commercial facilities are arranged along corridors called interior streets and open onto balconies that double as brise-soleils.

Ville Contemporaine: Contemporary City for Three Million Inhabitants, Le Corbusiers' first city plan on a virgin site, exhibited in 1922. It has a center of office towers in a park surrounded by residential and cultural districts. Industrial zones stand beyond a green belt with accompanying residential garden communities.

Ville Radieuse: Radiant City, Le Corbusier's second ideal city plan, first proposed in 1930 as his "Response to Moscow" and then in the compendium text *The Radiant City*. As a diagram, it has parallel bands zoned for business, residences, recreation, and industry arranged along a central linear circulation spine. In the text and projects for specific places, its plan takes on many forms, some concentrated, others dispersed, that are flexible in nature but fragmentary in scope.

SELECTED BIBLIOGRAPHY

BOOKS

Agrest, Diana, Patricia Conway, and Leslie Kanes Weisman, eds. *The Sex of Architecture*. New York: Harry N. Abrams, 1996.

Bacon, Mardges. *Le Corbusier in America: Travels in the Land of the Timid*. Cambridge: MIT Press, 2001.

Baker, Geoffrey. *The Creative Search*. New York: Van Nostrand Reinhold Co. Ltd., 1996.

Banham, Reyner. *Theory and Design in the First Machine Age*. London: The Architectural Press, 1960.

Benevolo, Leonardo. *History of Modern Architecture*, vol. 2. Translated by H. J. Landry. Cambridge: MIT Press, 1971.

Benton, Tim. *The Villas of Le Corbusier 1920–1930*. Paris, 1984. Reprint, New Haven and London: Yale University Press, 1987.

Blake, Peter. *The Master Builders*. New York: W. W. Norton & Company, Inc., 1963.

———. *No Place Like Utopia*. New York: Alfred Knopf, 1993.

Blau, Eve and Nancy Troy, eds. *Architecture and Cubism*. Cambridge: MIT Press and Canadian Centre for Architecture, 2001.

Bois, Yves-Alain and Bruno Reichlin, eds. *De Stijl et l'architecture en France*. Brussels: Mardaga, 1985.

Boudon, Philippe. *Lived-in Architecture: Le Corbusier's Pessac Revisited*. Cambridge: MIT Press, 1979.

Brooks, H. Allen. *Le Corbusier's Formative Years*. Chicago: University Press of Chicago, 1997.

Brooks, H. Allen, ed. *Le Corbusier*. Princeton: Princeton University Press, 1987; also published as *Le Corbusier: The Garland Essays*. New York: Garland, 1987.

Chiambretto, Bruno. *Le Corbusier à Cap-Martin*. Marseille: Editions Paranthèses, 1987.

Cohen, Jean-Louis. *Le Corbusier and the Mystique of the USSR*. Princeton: Princeton University Press, 1992.

Colomina, Beatriz. *Privacy and Publicity: Modern Architecture as Mass Media*. Cambridge: MIT Press, 1994.

Colquhoun, Alan. *Essays in Architectural Criticism: Modern Architecture and Historical Change*. Cambridge: MIT Press, 1981.

Coombs, Robert. *Mystical Themes in Le Corbusier's Architecture in the Chapel Notre Dame du Haut at Ronchamp*. Lewistown, NY: Edwin Mellen Press, 2000.

Curtis, William J. R. *Le Corbusier: Ideas and Forms*. New York: Rizzoli, 1986.

Doshi, Balkrishna. *Le Corbusier and Louis Kahn: The Acrobat and the Yogi of Architecture*. Ahmedabad, India: Vastu Shilpa, 1992.

Dudley, George. *A Workshop for Peace: Designing the United Nations Headquarters*. Cambridge: MIT Press and The Architectural History Foundation, 1994.

Eardley, Anthony, Kenneth Frampton, and Silvia Kolbowski, eds. *IAUS 14: Le Corbusier's Firminy Church*. New York: The Institute for Architecture and Urban Studies and Rizzoli, 1981.

Etlin, Richard. *Frank Lloyd Wright and Le Corbusier: The Romantic Legacy*. New York: Manchester University Press, 1994.

Evans, Robin. *The Projective Cast*. Cambridge: MIT Press, 1995.

Evenson, Norma. *Chandigarh*. Berkeley: University of California Press, 1966.

————. *The Machine and the Grand Design*. New York: George Braziller, 1969.

Ferro, Segio, et al. *Le Corbusier: Le Couvent de La Tourette*. Marseille: Editions Parenthèse, 1987.

Fishman, Robert. *Urban Utopias in the Twentieth Century: Ebenezer Howard, Frank Lloyd Wright and Le Corbusier*. Cambridge: MIT Press, 1982.

Ford, Edward. *The Details of Modern Architecture,* vol. 1. Cambridge: MIT Press, 1990.

————. *The Details of Modern Architecture*, vol. 2. Cambridge: MIT Press, 1996.

Frampton, Kenneth. *Le Corbusier*. London: Thames and Hudson, 2001.

————. *Le Corbusier: Architect of the Twentieth Century*. New York: Harry N. Abrams, 2002.

————. *Modern Architecture: A Critical History*. London: Thames and Hudson, 1985.

————. *Studies in Tectonic Culture*. Cambridge: MIT Press, 1995.

Giedion, Sigfried. *Space, Time and Architecture*. 1941. Reprint, Cambridge: Harvard University Press, 1967.

Goldberger, Paul. *The City Observed, New York: A Guide to the Architecture of Manhattan*. New York: Vintage Books, 1979.

Goodwin, Philip. *Brazil Builds*. New York: Museum of Modern Art, 1943.

Gresleri, Giuliano. *L'Esprit Nouveau*. Milan: Electa, 1979.

Harris, Elizabeth D. *Le Corbusier: Riscos Brasileiros*. Sao Paulo: Nobel, 1987.

Hegel, George Wilhelm Friedrich. *On the Arts*. Edited and translated by Henry Paolucci. New York: Frederick Ungar Publishing Co., 1979.

Hitchcock, Henry-Russell and Philip Johnson. *The International Style: Architecture Since 1922*. 1932. Reprint, New York: W. W. Norton & Company, Inc., 1966.

Jencks, Charles. *Le Corbusier and the Continual Revolution in Architecture*. New York: Monacelli Press, 2000.

————. *Le Corbusier and the Tragic View of Architecture*. Cambridge: Harvard University Press, 1973.

Jenger, Jean. *Le Corbusier-Choix de Lettres*. Basel: Birkhäuser Verlag and F.L.C., 2001.

Jenkins, David. *Unité d'habitation Marseilles*. London: Phaidon Press, 1993.

Joshi, Kiran. *Documenting Chandigarh: The Architecture of Pierre Jeanneret, Edwin Maxwell Fry and Jane Drew*, vol. 1. Ahmedabad, India: Mapin Publishing, 1999.

Kalia, Ravi. *Chandigarh in Search of an Identity*. Carbondale: Southern Illinois University Press, 1987.

Kirsch, Karin. *The Weissenhofsiedlung Experimental Housing*. New York: Rizzoli, 1989.

Koolhaas, Rem. *Delirious New York*. London: Thames and Hudson, 1978.

————. *SMLXL*. London: Monacelli Press, 1996.

Krustup, Mogens, ed. *Le Corbusier Painter and Architect*. Aalborg, Denmark: Nordjyllands Kunstmuseum, 1995.

Lapunzina, Alejandro. *Maison Curutchet*. New York: Princeton Architectural Press, 1997.

Le Corbusier. *L'Art Décoratif d'Aujourd'hui*. Paris: Éditions Crès, 1925. Translated by James Dynnett as *The Decorative Art of Today* (Cambridge: MIT Press, 1986).

———. *Album La Roche*. New York: Monacelli, 1997.

———. *Almanach d'Architecture Moderne*. Paris: Éditions Crès, 1926. Reprint, Paris: Fondation Le Corbusier and Altimira, 1998.

———. *Charles-Édouard Jeanneret. Étude du mouvement d'art décoratif en Allemagne*. 1911. Reprint La Chaux-de-Fonds: L'Age d'Homme and F.L.C.-Spadem, 1994.

———. *The City of Tomorrow and its Planning*. Translated by Frederick Etchells. Cambridge: MIT Press, 1971. Originally published as *Urbanisme* (Paris: Éditions Crès, 1925).

———. *La Construction des Villes*. La Chaux-de-Fonds: L'Age d'Homme and F.L.C.-Spadem, 1992.

———. *Creation is a Patient Search* Translated by James Palmes, New York: Praeger, 1960.

———. *The Final Testament of Père Corbu*. Translated by Ivan Zaknic. New Haven: Yale University Press, 1997. Originally published as *Mise au Point* (Paris: Editions Forces Vives, 1965).

———. *Journey to the East*. Translated by Ivan Zaknic. Cambridge: MIT Press, 1987.

———. *The Le Corbusier Archive*, vols. 1–32. Edited by H. Allen Brooks. New York: Garland and F.L.C., 1984.

———. *Le Corbusier Architecte, Artiste CD*. Paris: Infinitum and F.L.C., 1996.

———. *Le Corbusier Sketchbooks*, vols. 1–4. Cambridge: MIT Press, The Architectural Foundation, and F.L.C., 1981.

———. *Manière de Penser l'Urbanisme*. Paris: Editions de l'Architecture d'Aujourd'hui, 1946.

———. *Modulor 1 & 2*. Basel: Birkhäuser Verlag and F.L.C., 2000.

———. *My Work*. Translated by James Palmes. London: Architectural Press, 1960.

———. *New World of Space*. New York: Reynal & Hitchcock, 1948.

———. *Poème de l'Angle Droit*. Paris: Tériade, 1955.

———. *Precisions on The Present State of Architecture and City Planning*. Translated by Edith Schreier Aujame. Cambridge: MIT Press, 1991. Originally published as *Précisions sur un état present de l'architecture et de l'urbanisme* (Paris: Vincent, Freal, 1930).

———. *The Radiant City*. London: Faber & Faber, 1964. Originally published as *La Ville Radieuse* (Boulogne-sur-Seine: Editions de l'Architecture d'Aujourd'hui, 1933).

———. *Ronchamp*. Translated by Jacqueline Cullen. New York: Praeger, 1960.

———. *Talks with Students*. New York: Princeton Architectural Press, 2000.

———. *Textes et Dessins pour Ronchamp*. 1965. Reprint, Basel, Switzerland: Association de N. D. du Haut Ronchamp, 1982.

———. *Towards a New Architecture*. Translated by Frederick Etchells. New York: Dover Publications, 1986. Originally published as *Vers une Architecture* (Paris: Vincent Fréal, 1923).

———. *Les Trois Etablissements Humains*. Paris: Denoël, 1945.

———. *Une Maison un Palais*. Paris: Editions Crès, 1928. Reprint, Paris: Fondation Le Corbusier and Altimira, 1998.

———. *Une Petite Maison*. Zurich: Éditions d'Architecture Artemis, 1981.

Le Corbusier and CIAM. *The Athens Charter*. Translated by Anthony Eardley. New York: Grossman Publishers, 1973. Originally published as *La Charte d'Athènes* (Paris: Plon, 1943).

Le Corbusier and Pierre Jeanneret. *Zwei Wohnhäuser*. Stuttgart: Akadem. Verlag, 1927. Reprint, Stuttgart: Karl Krämer Verlag, 1977.

Le Corbusier, Pierre Jeanneret, et al. *Oeuvre Complète*, vols. 1–8. Edited by Willy Boesiger. Zurich: Les Editions d'Architecture, Artemis, 1977.

Lucan, Jacques, ed. *Le Corbusier, Une Encyclopédie*. Paris: Centre Pompidou, 1987.

Lyon, Dominique, et al. *Le Corbusier Alive*. Paris: Vilo International, 2000.

Markus, George. *Le Corbusier: Inside The Machine for Living*. New York: Monacelli, 2000.

Moore, Richard. *Le Corbusier: Myth and Meta Architecture*. Atlanta: Georgia State University, 1977.

Mumford, Eric. *The CIAM Discourse on Urbanism, 1928–1960*. Cambridge: MIT Press, 2002.

Ozenfant, Amédée and Le Corbusier. *La Peinture Moderne*. Paris: Editions Crès, 1912.

Pardo, Vittorio Franchetti. *Le Corbusier*. New York: Grosset and Dunlap, 1971.

Pagnamento, Silvio and Bruno Reichlin, eds. *Le Corbusier: La ricerca paziente*. Lugano: 1980.

Palazzolo, Carlo and Riccardo Vio, eds. *In the Footsteps of Le Corbusier*. New York: Rizzoli, 1991.

Pauly, Danièle. *Ronchamp Lecture d'une architecture*. Strasbourg and Paris: APPU, 1980.

———. *The Chapel at Ronchamp*. Basel: Birkhäuser Verlag and F.L.C., 1997.

Pawley, Martin. *Le Corbusier*. New York: George Braziller, 1970.

Perriand, Charlotte. *Une vie de Création*. Paris: Editions Odile Jacob, 1998.

Petit, Jean, ed. *Le Corbusier lui-même*. Geneva: Rousseau, 1970.

———. *Le Livre de Ronchamp*. Paris: Les Cahiers Forces Vives, 1961.

Pommer, Richard and Christian F. Otto. *Weissenhof 1927 and the Modern Movement in Architecture*. Chicago: University of Chicago Press, 1991.

Prakash, Vikramaditya. *Chandigarh's Le Corbusier: The Struggle for Modernity in Postcolonial India*. Seattle: University of Washington Press, 2002.

Prelorenzo, Claude, ed. *La Conservation de l'Oeuvre Construite de Le Corbusier*. Paris: F.L.C., 1990.

———. *Le Corbusier, Écritures*. Paris: F.L.C., 1990.

———. *Le Corbusier et La Couleur*. Paris: F.L.C., 1990.

———. *Le Corbusier et La Nature*. Paris: F.L.C., 1990.

———. *Le Corbusier, La Ville, L'Urbanisme*. Paris: F.L.C., 1990.

Raeburn, Michael and Victoria Wilson, eds. *Le Corbusier: Architect of the Century*. London: Arts Council of Great Britain and Balding + Mansel, 1987.

Ragot, Gilles and Mathilde Dion. *Le Corbusier en France: Realisations et Projects*. Paris: Electa Moniteur, 1987.

Rewal, Raj et al., eds. *Architecture in India*. Paris: Electa Moniteur, 1985.

Risselada, Max, ed. *Raumplan versus Plan Libre*. New York: Rizzoli, 1987.

Rowe, Colin. *The Architecture of Good Intentions: Towards a Possible Retrospect*. London: Academy Editions, 1994.

Rowe, Colin and Fred Koetter. *Collage City*. Cambridge: MIT Press, 1986.

Rowe, Colin and Robert Slutzky. *The Mathematics of the Ideal Villa and Other Essays*. Cambridge: MIT Press, 1982.

Rüegg, Arthur, ed. *Polychromie Architecturale: Le Corbusier's Color Keyboards from 1931 and 1959*. Basel: Birkhäuser Verlag and F.L.C., 1997.

Ruskin, John. *The Seven Lamps of Architecture*. New York: Dover, 1989.

Russell, Frank, ed. *Art Nouveau Architecture*. New York: Arch Cape Press, 1986.

Sagar, Jagdish, ed. *Celebrating Chandigarh*. Chandigarh: Chandigarh Perspectives, 2001.

Samuel, Flora. *Le Corbusier: Architect and Feminist*. London: Academy, 2004.

Sarin, Madhu. *Urban Planning in the Third World*. London: Manseil, 1982.

Sarkis, Hashim et al., eds. *Case: Le Corbusier's Venice Hospital and the Mat Building Revival*. Munich: Prestel Publishing, 2002.

Sbriglio, Jacques, et al. *L'Unité d'Habitation de Marseille*. Marseille: Éditions Paranthèse, 1987.

Sbriglio, Jacques. *Apartment Block 24 N. C. and Le Corbusier's Home*. Basel: Birkhäuser Verlag and F.L.C., 1996.

———. *Villas La Roche-Jeanneret*. Basel: Birkhäuser Verlag and F.L.C., 1996.

———. *La Villa Savoye*. Basel: Birkhäuser Verlag and F.L.C., 1999.

Scully, Vincent. *Modern Architecture*. New York: George Braziller, 1986.

Sekler, Edouard and William Curtis. *Le Corbusier at Work: The Genesis of the Carpenter Center for the Visual Arts.* Cambridge: Harvard University Press, 1978.

Sherwood, Roger. *Modern Housing Prototypes.* Cambridge: Harvard University Press, 1978.

Serenyi, Peter, ed. *Le Corbusier in Perspective.* Englewood Cliffs: Prentice Hall, 1975.

Tafuri, Manfredo. *Theories and History of Architecture.* New York: Harper and Row, 1980.

Tafuri, Manfredo and Francesco Dal Co. *Modern Architecture.* New York: Harry N. Abrams, 1979.

Taylor, Brian Brace. *Le Corbusier et Pessac.* Paris: F.L.C., 1972.

————. *Le Corbusier: The City of Refuge Paris 1929/33.* Chicago: University of Chicago Press, 1987.

Troy, Nancy. *Modernism and the Decorative Arts in France.* New Haven: Yale University Press, 1991.

Tumer, Paul Venable. *The Education of Le Corbusier.* New York: Garland, 1977.

Tzonis, Alexander. *Le Corbusier: The Poetics of Machine and Metaphor.* New York: Universe, 2002.

Vogt, Adolf M. *Le Corbusier, the Noble Savage: Toward an Archaeology of Modernism.* Cambridge: MIT Press, 1998.

von Moos, Stanislaus. *Le Corbusier: Elements of a Synthesis.* Cambridge: MIT Press, 1982.

von Moos, Stanislaus and Arthur Rüegg. *Le Corbusier before Le Corbusier.* New Haven: Yale, University Press, 2002.

Walden, Russell, ed. *The Open Hand, Essays on Le Corbusier.* Cambridge: MIT Press, 1977.

Wigley, Mark. *White Walls, Designer Dresses: The Fashioning of Modern Architecture.* Cambridge: MIT Press, 1995.

Zaknic, Ivan. *Le Corbusier-Pavillon Suisse: The Biography of a Building.* Basel: Birkhäuser Verlag, 2004.

JOURNALS DEVOTED TO LE CORBUSIER

(Individual articles from these journals are notated fully in the citation at the entry.)

ANQ: Chandigarh 40 Years After Le Corbusier (1989).
Architectural Design 34: 6 (June 1964).
Architectural Design 44: 6 (June 1974).
Architectural Review 3 (November 1955)
Architectural Review 181 (January 1987).
Assemblage 4 (1988).
Assemblage 27 (October1987).
Casabella 531/2 (January 1987).
Domus 687 (October 1987).
Oppositions 15/16: "Le Corbusier 1905–1933."
Oppositions 19/20: "Le Corbusier 1933–1960."
Parametro 49–50 (Sept.–Oct. 1976).
Parametro 185 (July–August 1991).
Rassegna 3: "I Clienti di Le Corbusier" (1980).

INDIVIDUAL ARTICLES

Acerboni, Francesca. "Le Corbusier: Maison Guiette." *Arbitare* 339 (April 1995).

Adam, Peter. "Eileen Gray and Le Corbusier." *9H: On Rigor* (1989).

"Casa Atelier Ozenfant." *Domus* 687 (July–August 1987): 39–42.

Carl, Peter. "Le Corbusier's Penthouse in Paris, 24 Rue Nungesser-et-Coli." *Daidalos* 28 (June 1998): 65–75.

Çelik, Zeypnep. "Le Corbusier, Orientalism, Colonialism." *Assemblage* 17 (April 1992).

Constant, Caroline. "E.1027, The Non-Heroic Modernism of Eileen Gray." *JSAH* 53 (September 1994).

Doshi, Balkrishna. "The Unfolding of the Architect." *Global Architecture* 32 (1974).

Etlin, Richard. "Le Corbusier, Choisy, and French Hellenism: The Search for a New Architecture." *The Art Bulletin* 59: 2 (June 1987).

Frampton, Kenneth. "The City of Dialectic." *Architectural Design* (October 1969).

Gans, Deborah. "Cave, Hut, Tent: Structural Arche types in the Work of Le Corbusier." *TSAR* 11 (1992).

————. "The Architecture of Balanchine." *Choreography and Dance* 3 (1993).

————. "Le Corbusier Drawings at Princeton." *Oculus* 63: 9 (May–June 2001).

————. "Still Life After All: The Paintings of Le Corbusier." *Architectural Design* 73: 3 (June 2003).

Gorlin, Alex. "The Ghost in the Machine: Surrealism in the Work of Le Corbusier." *Perspecta* 20 (1984).

Greseli, Giuliano and Silvio Cassara. "What can we learn from the rebuilt Pavillon de L'Esprit Nouveau?" *A+U* 170 (September 1980).

Hellman, Geoffrey. "From Within to Without." *New Yorker* (April 26, 1947).

Jeanneret, Pierre. "The Impact of Local Climate and Techniques on Construction Methods." *L'Architecture d'Aujourd'hui* (1962).

Lahiji, Nadir. "The Gift of the Open Hand: Le Corbusier Reading George Bataille's Le Part Maudite." *Journal of Architectural Education* 50: 1 (1996).

Lange, Alexandra. "White Collar Corbusier: From Casier to the cite d'affaires." *Grey Room* 9 (Fall 2002).

Lipstadt, Hélène and Harvey Mendelsohn. "Philosophy, History, Autobiography. Manfredo Tafuri and the Unsurpassed Lesson of Le Corbusier." *Assemblage* 22 (1994).

Lowman, Joyce. "Corb as Structural Rationalist." *Architectural Review* 160: 956 (1976).

Maarani, Grant and Herman Spiegel." Site Visits: An Engineer Reads Le Corbusier's Villas." *Perspecta* 31 (2000).

Moriyama, M. "The Theory of Body Culture of Pierre Winter in the period of l'Esprit Nouveau." *Journal of Architecture and Planning* 585 (2004).

McLeod, Mary. "Architecture or Revolution: Taylorism, Technocracy and Social Change." *Architectural Journal* (Summer 1983).

————. "Architecture Stripped: Le Corbusier and Fashion." *Domus* 771 (May 1995).

Naegele, Daniel. "Savoye Space: The Sensation of the Object." *Harvard Design Magazine* 15 (Fall 2001).

Oubrerie, Jose. "Architecture before Geometry: The Primacy of the Imagination." *Assemblage* 39 (August 1999).

Pendleton-Jullian, Ann. "The Collage of Poetics." *Design Book Review* 14 (Spring 1988).

————. "Unknown Le Corbusier." Parametro 156 (May 1987).

Reichlin, Bruno. "Une petite maison on Lake Leman: The Perret-Le Corbusier Controversy." *Lotus* 60 (1988).

————. "La Villa de Mandrot à le Pradet." *Domus* 87–94.

Rüegg, Arthur. "On Color Restoration of the Villa Savoye." *Architecture and Urbanism* 3 (March 2000).

Sarkis, Hashim. "Constants in Motion: Le Corbusier's 'Rule of Motion' at the Carpenter Center." *Perspecta* 33 (2002).

Vidler, Anthony. "The Idea of Unity and Le Corbusier's Urban Form." *Architect's Year Book* 15 (1968).

von Moos, Stanislaus. "Le Corbusier, the Monument and the Metropolis." *Columbia Documents of Architecture and Theory* 3 (1993).

PARIS

1. Villa Planeix
2. Annexe du Palais du Peuple
3. Asile Flottant
4. Cité de Refuge

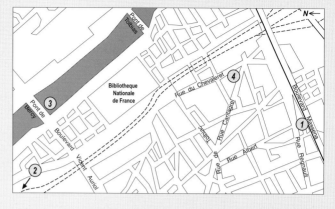

PARIS

5. Atelier Ozenfant
6. Pavillon Suisse
7. Pavillon du Brésil

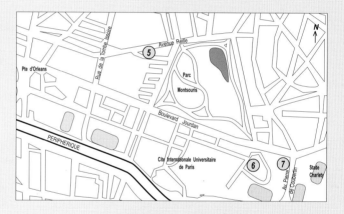

PARIS

8. Villas La Roche-Jeanneret
9. Immeuble et Appartement de Le Corbusier

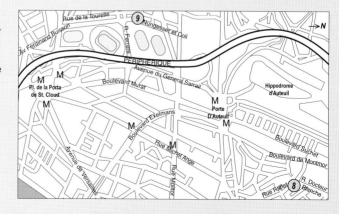

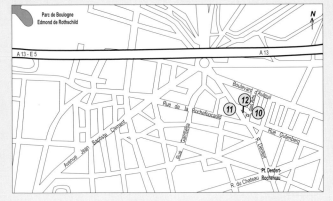

BOULOGNE

10. Villas
    Lipchitz-
    Miestchaninoff
11. Villa Cook
12. Villa Ternisien

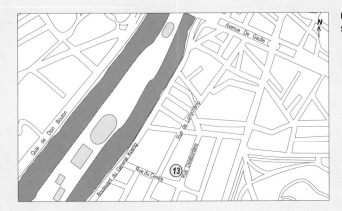

NEUILLY-SUR-
SEINE

13. Maisons Jaoul

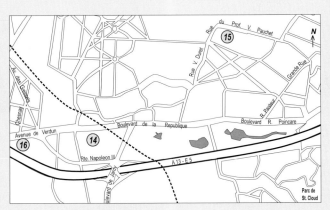

VAUCRESSON/LA
CELLE-ST-CLOUD

14. Villa Besnus
15. Villa Stein
16. La Petite
    Maison de
    Weekend

POISSY
17. Villa Savoye

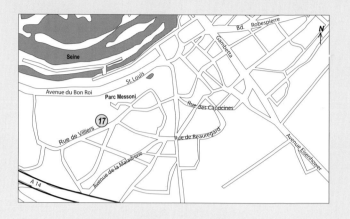

BRIEY-EN-FORÊT
1. Unité d'habitation

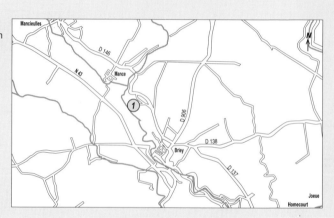

ST DIÉ
2. Usine Duval

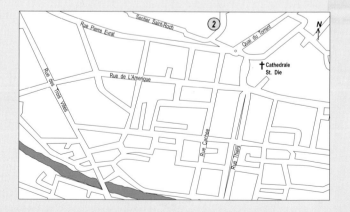

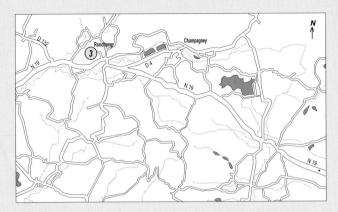

RONCHAMP

3. Chapelle Nôtre-
   Dame-du-Haut

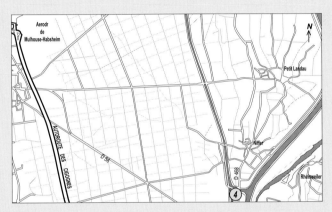

KEMBS-NIFFER

4. Écluse

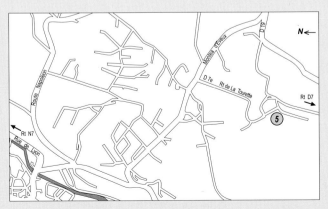

L'ARBRESLE

5. Couvent Sainte-
   Marie-de-la
   Tourette

FIRMINY
6. Firminy-Vert

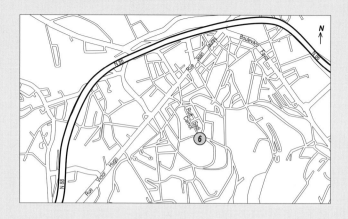

MARSEILLE
7. Unité d'habitation

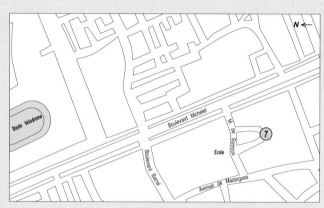

VAR
(LA STE-BAUME)
8. Ateliers La
   Sainte-Baume

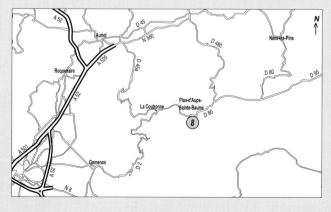

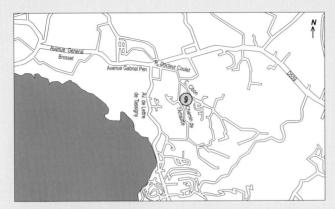

LE PRADET
9. Villa de Mandrot

**ROQUEBRUNE-
CAP-MARTIN**
10. Le Petit
    Cabanon
11. Grave of Le
    Corbusier

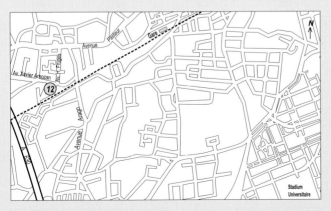

PESSAC
12. Quartier
    Moderne
    Frugès

LA PALMYRE-LES MATHES

13. Villa le Sextant

REZÉ-LES-NANTES

14. Unité d'habitation

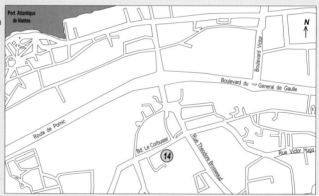

LA CHAUX-DE-FONDS

1. Villa Fallet
2. Villa Stotzer
3. Villa Jacquemet
4. Villa Jeanneret
5. Cinéma La Scala
6. Villa Schwob

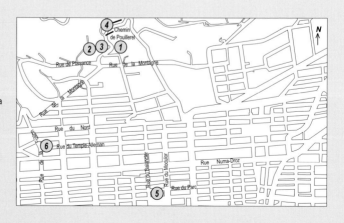

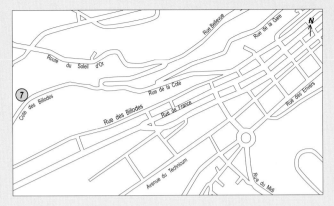

LE LOCLE
7. Villa Favre-Jacot

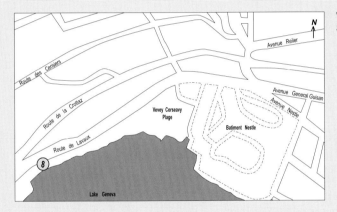

VEVEY
8. La Petite Maison

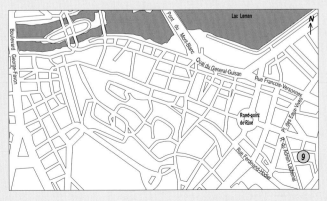

GENEVA
9. Immeuble Clarté

ZÜRICH
10. Centre Le
Corbusier
(Heidi Weber
House, La
Maison de
L'Homme)

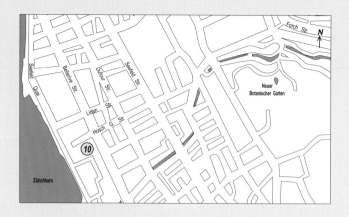

ANTWERP
1. Maison Guiette

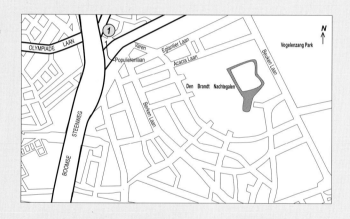

STUTTGART
2. Houses of the
Weissenhof

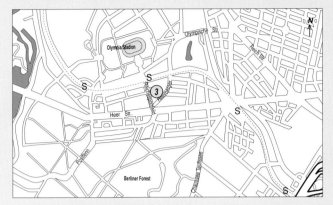

BERLIN
3. Unité
   d'habitation

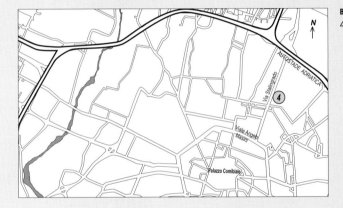

BOLOGNA
4. Pavillon de
   L'Esprit Nouveau

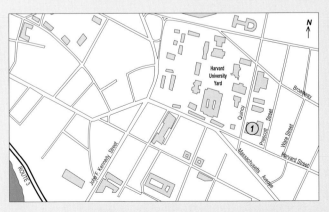

CAMBRIDGE
1. Carpenter Center
   for the Visual
   Arts

NEW YORK
2. United Nations
Headquarters

RIO DE JANEIRO
3. Brazilian
Ministry of
Education and
Public Health
(Palácio Gustavo
Capanema)

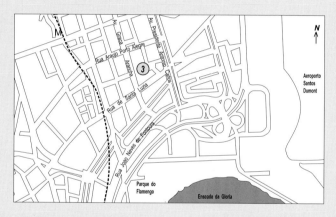

LA PLATA
4. Maison
Curutchet

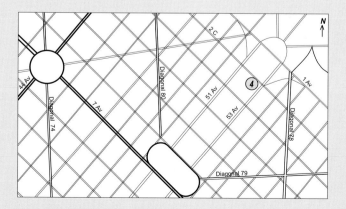

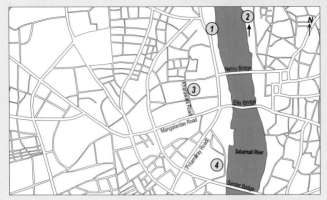

AHMEDEBAD
1. Millowner's Association Building
2. Villa Sarabhai
3. Villa Shodhan
4. Museum of the City

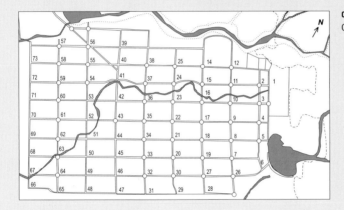

CHANDIGARH
City plan

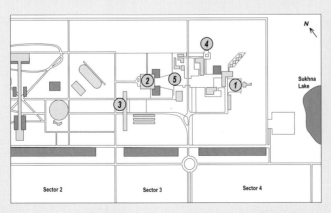

CHANDIGARH SECTOR 1
1. Palace of Justice
2. Palace of Assembly
3. Secretariat
4. Open Hand/ Depth of Consideration
5. Tower of Shadows/ Geometrical Hill/ Monument to the Martyr

CHANDIGARH
SECTOR 10

6. College of Art
7. Museum
8. Art Gallery

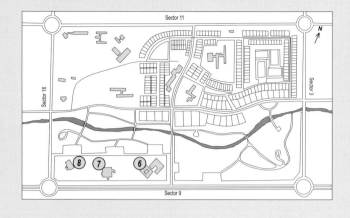

CHANDIGARH
SECTOR 12

9. College of
   Architecture

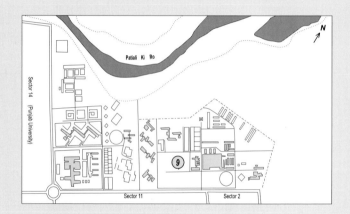

CHANDIGARH
SECTOR 17

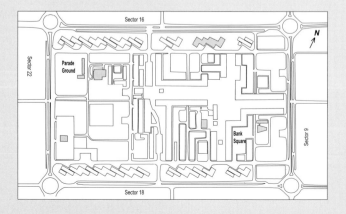

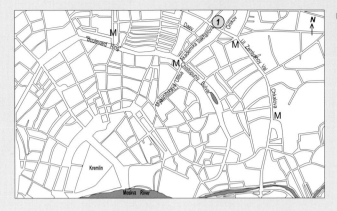

MOSCOW
1. Centrosoyus

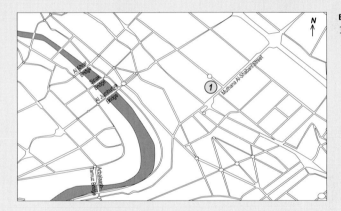

BAGHDAD
1. Sports Center

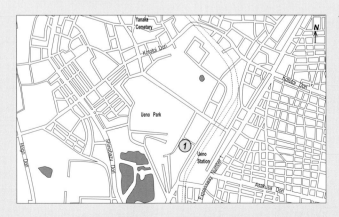

TOKYO
1. National
   Museum of
   Western Art

Deborah Gans is an architect trained at Harvard and Princeton. She has taught at the Institute for Architecture and Urban Studies, Yale, and Columbia and is presently an associate professor in architecture at Pratt Institute where she has also served as department chair. Her publications include the *Bridging the Gap: Rethinking the Relationship of Architect and Engineer*, which was honored by the International Book Awards of the AIA and The Organic Approach.